The Common European Asylum System
Background, Current State of Affairs, Future Direction

The Common European Asylum System

Background, Current State of Affairs, Future Direction

Olga Ferguson Sidorenko

T·M·C·Asser Press
The Hague

Published by T.M.C.ASSER PRESS,
P.O. Box 16163, 2500 BD The Hague, The Netherlands
www.asserpress.nl

T.M.C.ASSER PRESS English language books are distributed exclusively by:

Cambridge University Press, The Edinburgh Building, Shaftesbury Road,
Cambridge CB2 2RU, UK,
or
for customers in the USA, Canada and Mexico:
Cambridge University Press,
100 Brook Hill Drive, West Nyack, NY 10994-2133, USA

www.cambridge.org

ISBN 90-6704-236-6
ISBN 978-90-6704-236-9

PREFACE

The recurring cycles of violence and systemic human rights violations in many parts of the world are generating more and more intractable displacement situations. In the rapidly changing situation in the field of asylum in Europe in recent years, many governments have not only introduced complex changes in their laws and procedures, but have also become increasingly involved in international co-operation and the harmonization aspects of their refugee and asylum policies. The process of multilateral dialogue and finding the most complex solutions, when it concerns asylum issues, is very much alive.

Human rights issues, notably those pertaining to the right to asylum, are an integral part of ensuring the rule of law in a democratic society. It is the issue of asylum and migration that challenges Europe in a very evolutionary manner. It covers human beings in need, in need of freedom, security and justice.

This book contains a study which deals with the Common European Asylum System and its complex evolution, in particular from the mid-1980s until 2005, and an overview of the continual development of EU Legislation on Asylum in the EU context, in parallel with the evolution of the asylum policy and legislation of Slovakia as a new EU Member State. The content also addresses some of the most difficult issues confronting asylum systems in the EU Member States today with a special focus also on the Slovak Republic as one of the EU 'newcomers'.

This publication, to my mind, also as a former UNHCR Legal Officer having dealt with refugees for more than a decade, is the first of its kind as it includes an overview of the evolution of the Slovak asylum system from its very beginning (in the 1990s), starting with the establishment of the independent Slovak Republic taken together and in parallel with building and developing the Common European Asylum System in the framework of the EU, up to the present time in 2005. The author also outlines a vision of the future concerning EU Asylum Policy.

With that in mind, this book will be useful to all those who are involved in dealing with asylum matters, including those who study asylum and refugee issues at university level, but also to practitioners, Parliamentarians, NGOs, and those who are generally interested in EU and European Asylum Law and policy. At the same time, I strongly recommend that this book should be read and widely used.

I hope that this publication will serve as a reference for further discussions and studies in the context of the EU, and it can also be useful as a reference work in the further EU enlargement and the development of the asylum system.

Ján Šikuta
Judge
European Court of Human Rights
Strasbourg, France

TABLE OF CONTENTS

List of Abbreviations XI

Introduction 1

Chapter 1 Towards a Common European Asylum System 7
1.1 Introduction 7
1.2 Geneva Convention (1951) 8
1.3 Internal market: Freedom of movement 10
1.4 Schengen Agreement (1985) and Schengen Implementation Convention (1990) 12
1.5 Dublin Convention (1990) 15
1.6 Treaty of Maastricht (1992) 19
1.7 Treaty of Amsterdam (1997) 20
1.7.1 Area of Freedom, Security and Justice 21
1.7.2 Title IV TEC 24
1.7.3 Protocols 25
1.7.3.1 Asylum for nationals of Member States 25
1.7.3.2 The position of the United Kingdom, Ireland and Denmark 26
1.8 Tampere Conclusions (1999) 28
1.9 Treaty of Nice (2001) 32
1.10 Institutional Aspects 32
1.10.1 Decision making 33
1.10.1.1 Council 33
1.10.1.2 Commission 35
1.10.1.3 European Parliament 36
1.10.2 European Council 37
1.10.3 Court of Justice 37
1.11 Conclusions 38

Chapter 2 EU Legislation on Asylum 41
2.1 Introduction 41
2.2 Responsible Member State 42
2.2.1 Evaluation of the Dublin Convention 43
2.2.2 New hierarchy of criteria 49
2.2.3 Evaluation of the 'Dublin II' Regulation 51
2.2.4 Eurodac 57
2.3 Reception 58
2.4 Qualification 63
2.4.1 Assessment of applications 66
2.4.2 Refugee 70
2.4.3 Subsidiary protection 75
2.4.4 Content of International Protection 77
2.5 Procedures 79

2.5.1 General provisions. . . . 81
2.5.2 Basic principles and guarantees 82
2.5.3 Procedures at first instance 88
2.5.4 Procedures for the withdrawal of refugee status 103
2.5.5 Appeal procedures. . . . 105
2.6 Temporary protection and burden sharing. . . . 108
2.6.1 Temporary protection 112
2.6.2 Solidarity between Member States (burden sharing). . . . 115
2.6.2.1 European Refugee Fund 115
2.7 Other Directives 118
2.7.1 Family reunification 119
2.7.2 Long-term residents. . . . 121
2.8 Conclusions. . . . 123

Chapter 3 The Perspective of a new Member State: Slovakia 125
3.1 Introduction. . . . 125
3.2 EU-Slovakia relations before joining the EU 126
3.3 The challenges of harmonisation. . . . 128
3.4 Evolution of the Slovak Asylum Legislation 130
3.4.1 The beginnings of the Slovak asylum law. . . . 131
3.4.2 Amendment to the 283/1995 Refugee Law. . . . 135
3.4.3 Asylum Law 480/2002 136
3.4.3.1 Procedural aspects. . . . 140
3.4.3.2 Review of decisions 141
3.4.4 Two examples of Court decisions 143
3.4.5 Considerations concerning the Slovak Asylum Law. . . . 146
3.4.6 Amendments to the 480/2002 Asylum Law 147
3.5 Assessment by the European Commission 151
3.6 Implementation 154
3.6.1 A fictitious case. . . . 155
3.6.1.1 Entry into the asylum procedure 157
3.6.1.2 Registration at the reception centre 158
3.6.1.3 Procedure leading to a first-instance decision 160
3.6.1.4 First-instance decision. . . . 161
3.6.1.5 Appeal against a first-instance decision 163
3.7 Conclusions. . . . 167

Chapter 4 EU Policy on Asylum 173
4.1 Introduction. . . . 173
4.2 Communications of the Commission 174
4.2.1 'Towards more accessible, equitable and managed asylum systems' . . . 175
4.2.2 'Area of freedom, security and justice: assessment of the Tampere programme and future orientations' 178

4.2.3 'On the managed entry in the EU of persons in need of international protection and the enhancement of the protection capacity of the regions of origin – Improving access to durable solutions' . . . 181
4.2.4 'A more efficient Common European Asylum System: the Single Procedure as the next step' . . . 187
4.2.5 'On Strengthened Practical Cooperation. New Structures, New Approaches: Improving the Quality of Decision Making in the Common European Asylum System' . . . 190
4.3 Activities of the Council and the European Council . . . 192
4.3.1 Evaluation of the Conclusions of Tampere (6 December 2001) . . . 192
4.3.2 Laeken European Council (14–15 December 2001) . . . 194
4.3.2.1 Laeken Declaration on the future of the European Union . . . 195
4.3.3 Seville European Council (21–22 June 2002) . . . 196
4.3.4 Council (5–6 June 2003) . . . 198
4.3.5 Thessaloniki European Council (19–20 June 2003) . . . 199
4.3.6 Brussels European Council (12–13 December 2003) . . . 200
4.3.7 Council (29–30 April 2004) . . . 201
4.3.8 Council (19 July 2004) . . . 202
4.3.9 Brussels European Council (4–5 November 2004) . . . 202
4.4 The Hague Programme . . . 203
4.4.1 Common European Asylum System . . . 204
4.4.2 External dimension of asylum and migration . . . 206
4.4.3 Action Plan . . . 208
4.5 Conclusions . . . 212

Concluding Remarks . . . 215
1. Common European Asylum System . . . 215
2. Implementation in Slovakia . . . 215
3. More effective solutions? . . . 217
4. A complex problem . . . 218
5. A balanced approach . . . 218
6. External dimension . . . 219
7. Internal dimension . . . 220
8. Constitutional Treaty . . . 220
9. The immediate future . . . 222

Selected Bibliography . . . 223

Selected Documents . . . 231

Index . . . 239

LIST OF ABBREVIATIONS

AENEAS	Programme for financial and technical assistance to third countries in the areas of migration and asylum
ARGO	Action Programme for administrative cooperation at EU level in the fields of asylum, visas, immigration and external borders
BO	Branch Office
CETS	Council of Europe Treaty Series
CFSP	common foreign and security policy
CNS	Consultation procedure
COI	Country of Origin Information
CSFR	Czech and Slovak Federal Republic
EC	European Communities
ECHR	European Convention for the Protection of Human Rights and Fundamental Freedoms
ECJ	European Court of Justice
ECRE	European Council on Refugees and Exiles
ECSC	European Coal and Steel Community
EEC	European Economic Community
ERF	European Refugee Fund
EU	European Union
Eurasil	European Union Network for Asylum Practitioners
Euratom	European Atomic Energy Community
Eurodac	European system for identification of asylum seekers and other categories of aliens
IGC	Intergovernmental Conference
ILPA	Immigration Law Practitioners' Association
JHA	justice and home affairs
MEP	Member of the European Parliament
NATO	North Atlantic Treaty Organisation
NGOs	Non-Governmental organisations
OJ	Official Journal
PEPs	Protected Entry Procedures
PHARE	Programme of Community aid to the countries of Central and Eastern Europe
QMV	qualified majority voting
SEA	Single European Act
TCN	third-country national
TEC	Treaty establishing the European Community
TEU	Treaty on European Union
UN	United Nations
UNHCR	United Nations High Commissioner for Refugees

INTRODUCTION

The right to asylum is rooted in the history of mankind (religious right of asylum (sanctuary)) and since the beginning of the modern State it has been rooted in the sovereignty of the State itself (the right of territorial asylum). The State retains the right to grant its protection to certain non-nationals or stateless persons, as a consequence of its territorial sovereignty, once the conditions laid down by the State have been complied with. In principle, it is the sovereign State itself, which decides in which circumstances a person deserves such protection.[1]

Refugee status, on the other hand, is a concept that arose in international law in the 20th century and is defined through international agreements. It protects certain persons, especially when they have had to flee from the countries of their nationality or their habitual residence owing to a well-founded fear of persecution for reasons which concern their race, nationality, membership in a particular social group or their political opinions.[2] Despite the underlying humanitarian principles, there is no doubt that the granting of asylum is intimately connected with politics at all levels.[3] Therefore, the term 'political asylum' is also used.

As far as refugee status is concerned, the treaty instruments are the Convention Relating to the Status of Refugees (further referred to as the 1951 Geneva Convention)[4] and the Protocol Relating to the Status of Refugees (further referred to as the 1967 New York Protocol).[5] Although there are references to asylum in the Preamble to the 1951 Geneva Convention, the granting of asylum (i.e., granting of full and lasting protection) is not dealt with further in the text of this convention or the 1967 New York Protocol.[6]

---

1. On the historical background of asylum see, e.g., Goodwin-Gill, G.: *The Refugee in International Law*, 2nd ed. (Oxford 1996); Prakas, Sinha, S.: *Asylum and International Law* (The Hague 1971); Grahl-Madsen, A.: *The Status of Refugees in International Law* (Leiden 1966).
2. Ibid.
3. Clayton, G.: *Textbook on Immigration and Asylum Law* (Oxford 2004), 348.
4. The Convention Relating to the Status of Refugees (the 1951 Geneva Convention) was adopted in Geneva on 28 July 1951, entry into force 22 April 1954. United Nations, Treaty Series, vol. 189, 137. All EU Member States are States Parties to this Convention.
5. The Protocol Relating to the Status of Refugees (the 1967 New York Protocol) was adopted in New York on 31 January 1967, entry into force 4 October 1967. United Nations, Treaty Series, vol. 606, 267. All EU Member States are States Parties to this Protocol.
6. See the UNHCR Handbook on procedures and criteria for determining refugee status under the 1951 Convention and the 1967 Protocol relating to the Status of Refugees (further referred to as the *UNHCR Handbook*), Geneva, January 1992, par. 25.

The 1951 Geneva Convention was originally drafted to deal with the displacement of people as a result of the Second World War. It restricted the definition of refugees to those whose fear of persecution arose from events occurring in Europe before 1 January 1951. The 1967 New York Protocol removed the time restriction and promoted a gradual removal of the geographical restriction. However, the definition of refugee was not changed.[7]

The 1951 Geneva Convention sets out the internationally agreed definition of who is a refugee and standards for treatment of refugees and is the legal basis for refugee claims. Refugee law is thus still fundamentally a part of international law. Notwithstanding the international origin of refugee law, it must be emphasised that the right to seek and obtain asylum is an institution shared between international and national law. Moreover, regional instruments relating to refugees have also played an important role in the refugee protection. As regards Europe, there are several legal instruments adopted within the Council of Europe,[8] which are directly or indirectly related to asylum, for example the Convention for the Protection of Human Rights and Fundamental Freedoms (ECHR),[9] the European Convention for the Prevention of Torture and Inhuman or Degrading Treatment or Punishment,[10] the European Convention on Extradition[11] and the European Agreement on the Abolition of Visas for Refugees.[12]

In the European context, moreover, the cooperation between the European Union (EU) Member States in the area of immigration and asylum has gradually developed from a bilateral and multilateral cooperation to a cooperation at the EU level. The Treaty of Amsterdam, which further amended the founding Treaties, entered into force on 1 May 1999. A new concept of an area of freedom, security and justice was introduced; and on the basis of this concept a new and important task began for the EU Institutions: to adopt for the first time a complete set of common European legislation on asylum. This ambitious task was to be completed within five years, i.e., before 1 May 2004. On the same day (1 May 2004) the territory of the EU was enlarged by the accession of ten new Member States – Cyprus, the Czech Republic, Estonia, Hungary, Latvia, Lithuania, Malta, Poland, Slovakia and Slovenia. One of the consequences of this enlargement has been the moving eastwards of the external borders of the EU, which brought about a chal-

7. Clayton, G.: *Textbook on Immigration and Asylum Law* (Oxford 2004). The *UNHCR Handbook* states that a person is a *refugee* within the meaning of the 1951 Geneva Convention as soon as he/she fulfils the criteria contained in the definition. This would necessarily occur prior to the time at which his/her refugee status is formally determined. Recognition of his/her refugee status does not therefore make him/her a refugee but declares him/her to be one. He/she does not become a refugee because of recognition, but is recognised because he/she is a refugee. On the definition of the term 'asylum seeker' see chapter 1, 1.4.

8. All EU Member States are member States of the Council of Europe.

9. Council of Europe Treaty Series (CETS) No. 005; entry into force 3 September 1953.

10. CETS No. 126; entry into force 1 February 1989.

11. CETS No. 024; entry into force 18 April 1960.

12. CETS No. 031; entry into force 4 September 1960.

lenging task for the new Member States (most of them situated on the external border of the EU); namely, to provide proper protection of the EU external borders (the security aspect) and at the same time to comply with the obligations of the 1951 Geneva Convention and other relevant human rights instruments (the aspect of respecting and promoting the right to seek asylum).

The primary purpose of this book is to evaluate the current state of affairs of the Common European Asylum System and to point out the direction that this System has been taking. The Tampere Presidency Conclusions, adopted by the Tampere European Council of 15 and 16 October 1999,[13] are a milestone in the development of the Common European Asylum System. They not only reaffirmed the legislative working programme determined by the Treaty of Amsterdam, but also announced a policy programme for the EU in the field of asylum and migration. The Tampere Presidency Conclusions thus constitute a positive point of departure towards achieving fair refugee protection in the EU and its Member States. For that reason they were chosen as a 'measuring instrument' for the evaluation whether the legislation and policy on asylum follow the 'spirit of Tampere'. There is also a secondary goal to be achieved: to provide the reader with an overview of the previous development related to asylum matters at the EU level, which preceded the coming into force of the Treaty of Amsterdam (1999), and also to give a thorough overview of the current EU legislation on asylum. The EU *asylum legislation* analysed in this book comprises the EU secondary legislation (regulations and directives). The European Treaties (Treaties of Maastricht, Amsterdam, Nice and the Treaty establishing the Constitution for Europe) are also discussed, as far as they refer to the subject matter of asylum. Whilst Chapter 1 introduces the topic from a broader perspective, presenting a background of the EU asylum law and policy, Chapter 2 focuses on the developments following the coming into force of the Treaty of Amsterdam. The EU asylum legislation, as adopted according to Article 63(1) and (2) of the Treaty establishing the European Community (TEC), as amended by the Treaties of Amsterdam and Nice, is analysed in order to provide an in depth view of the first stage of the Common European Asylum System and its compliance with the objectives set forth in the Presidency Conclusions of the Tampere European Council.

The *implementation* of EU law consists of several stages. Some of them (e.g., transposition) are also called 'abstract implementation', since they refer to the implementation of European legislation (primary or secondary) into the national legislation of the Member States. Other stages (application, enforcement) represent 'concrete implementation', i.e., application of the already harmonised national legislation in practice and its enforcement by administrative or judicial author-

13. Presidency Conclusions, Tampere European Council, 15 and 16 October 1999, SN 200/99 (further referred to as *Tampere*).

ities.[14] The implementation of the EU asylum legislation in a new Member State is the subject of Chapter 3. The implementation of EU legislation on asylum occurs at the national level. In order to assess that implementation, it is necessary to examine at least one Member State's asylum system. The Slovak Republic (Slovakia) was chosen as an example due to its geographical location (at the EU external border) and the extreme increase of asylum applications lodged in the past few years. It is important to note that since an accurate transposition of EU law into the Slovak national law was one of the conditions for its accession to the EU, 'implementation' is here understood as the application of the legislation in practice and its enforcement by the national authorities.

Though Slovakia is among the smaller Member States, it plays and certainly will play an important role in the future in the Common European Asylum System. For example in the second quarter of 2004, the number of asylum applications in Slovakia increased by 52 percent.[15] On the other hand, in Slovakia where many asylum seekers were Chechens, only two of them out of 1,081 cases examined that year (by 30 September 2004), were granted asylum in the Slovak Republic. It is worth noting that this group has, for good reason, a recognition rate of well over 50 percent in several other EU countries.[16]

The trend of very sudden, high numbers of asylum applications lodged in Slovakia decreased tremendously in the first months of 2005 (January–May).[17] In spite of this, Slovakia still remains an important and interesting case to examine with respect to the developments in its asylum system and the changing asylum trends. Moreover, the current direction of migratory flows, the duration of the aliens' stay in Slovakia before they irregularly cross the Slovak borders and move westwards and the number of deliberate departures from asylum facilities are all facts which indicate that many of these people still only transit through the territory of Slovakia.[18] This tendency is likely to vary in the course of time, especially since Slovakia's membership in the EU might change its character from a transit to a target State.

---

14. On the concept of implementation, see Jans, J.H., Lange, R. de, Prechal, S., Widdershoven, R.J.G.M.: *Inleiding tot het Europees Bestuursrecht*, 2nd ed. (Nijmegen 2002), 32 et seq.; Brink, A. van den: *Regelgeving in Nederland ter implementatie van EU-recht* (Deventer 2004), 8–9.

15. Based on information from the UNHCR branch office (BO), Bratislava, Slovakia.

16. See Lubbers, R.: 'EU should share asylum responsibilities, not shift them', UNHCR Briefing Notes, 5 November 2004.

17. In comparison with the first months of 2004, the number of asylum seekers dropped in the same months of 2005 as follows: January from 982 to 377; February from 751 to 127; March from 801 to 138; April from 1621 to 299; May from 1117 to 217. Source: the Migration Office of the Ministry of Interior, the Slovak Republic; available at: www.minv.sk/mumvsr/STAT/statistika.htm.

18. During the period of establishment of the Slovak Republic (1 January 1993) until 31 December 2003, an overall number of 78,493 illegal migrants were detected while unlawfully crossing or attempting to cross the Slovak border. Source: Assessment of the Asylum System in the Slovak Republic (May 2003–February 2004) – Final Report, 10.

The Tampere Presidency Conclusions announced a policy programme for the EU in the field of asylum and migration. Chapter 4 focuses on other policy instruments related to the Common European Asylum System, which were adopted after Tampere. Selected policy documents (Commission Communications, Justice and Home Affairs Council Conclusions, European Council Presidency Conclusions) are examined in order to assess the continuity of the policy direction set in Tampere. By doing this, one can better perceive the evolution of the Common European Asylum Policy, which led to the adoption of the Hague Programme (a multi-annual policy programme in the field of justice and home affairs) and an Action Plan to translate the Hague Programme into specific action.

The concluding remarks sum up the key issues and provide views and expectations concerning the future direction of the Common European Asylum System. In this context the Treaty establishing a Constitution for Europe (referred to as the EU Constitutional Treaty) is also taken into consideration.[19]

---

19. It should be noted that for the EU Constitutional Treaty (OJ C 310, 16.12.2004) to come into force it has to be ratified by all Member States (Art. IV-447). France voted against the Constitutional Treaty at a referendum on 29 May 2005 as did the Netherlands on 1 June 2005. The UK then announced that plans for a referendum, which was to be held in spring 2006, have been put on hold. This leaves the future of the Constitutional Treaty uncertain. Source: *BBC news*, 17 June 2005.

Chapter 1

TOWARDS A COMMON EUROPEAN ASYLUM SYSTEM

1.1 INTRODUCTION

Refugee status has its origin in international law, and at the universal level it is governed by the 1951 Geneva Convention and the 1967 New York Protocol. The main provisions of these international legal instruments will be described, with the purpose of a better understanding of the background of the EU asylum law and policy.

With regard to the cooperation in Europe, in the first place the concept of the internal market, the free movement of persons and the legal instruments which preceded the current European legislation on asylum have to be referred to in this chapter. In order to recognise the *raison d'être* of the Common European Asylum System, it is imperative to get an insight into the above-mentioned concepts and the following documents:

Both the Schengen Implementation Convention of 1990,[20] namely Articles 28 to 38, and the Dublin Convention, which replaced them,[21] referred to the rules on responsibility for processing applications for asylum and were adopted outside the framework of Community legislation. These conventions for the first time paid particular attention to asylum issues at the European Community level.

The Treaty of Maastricht[22] introduced in Article K.1 the policies on asylum and immigration, among other policies, as 'matters of common interest' to the EU Member States. Although being part of the mostly intergovernmental third pillar, the fact that these policies were considered as matters of common interest, made them a foreword to the supranational cooperation among the Member States, expected to result in a Common European Asylum System, envisaged later on by the Treaty of Amsterdam.

The Treaty of Amsterdam[23] brought about far-reaching innovations crucial to the development of a common European asylum law and policy ('communitarisa-

20. The Convention Implementing the Schengen Agreement of 14 June 1985 between the Governments of the States of the Benelux Economic Union, the Federal Republic of Germany and the French Republic on the gradual abolition of checks at their common borders (OJ L 239, 22.9.2000, 19) was signed on 19 June 1990 and entered into force on 1 September 1993.

21. Convention determining the State responsible for examining applications for asylum lodged in one of the Member States of the EC (Dublin Convention), OJ 254, 19.8.1997, 1.

22. The Treaty of Maastricht (formally, the Treaty on European Union; OJ C 191, 29.07.1992) was signed on 7 February 1992 between the members of the European Community and entered into force on 1 November 1993. It led to the creation of the European Union.

23. The Treaty of Amsterdam was signed on 2 October 1997 and entered into force on 1 May 1999 (OJ C 340, 10.11.1997).

tion', the area of freedom, security and justice). The Action Plan of the Council and the Commission on how best to implement the provisions of the Treaty of Amsterdam on the creation of an area of freedom, security and justice (the 'Vienna Action Plan')[24] defined common priorities and the detailed measures to be taken both in the short term (two years) and in the long term (five years). This Action Plan paved the path for the European Council in Tampere of October 1999.

The Tampere summit focused exclusively on justice and home affairs issues, and set out the basis for EU's objectives of maintaining and developing the Union as an area of freedom, security and justice. Asylum and migration policies were on the top of the agenda. The Treaty of Nice[25] did not introduce any substantial changes in the field of asylum. Nevertheless, it amended the provisions on the decision making in Article 67 TEC by introducing the qualified majority voting (QMV) concept.

The discussion on the afore-mentioned instruments will be followed by an overview of the evolving role, which the European Institutions have played in the adoption of the EU asylum legislation (the right of initiative and the decision making). The role of the European Council and the European Court of Justice (ECJ) in asylum matters will also be described.

1.2 Geneva Convention (1951)

The Tampere European Council agreed to work towards establishing a Common European Asylum System, based on the full and inclusive application of the 1951 Geneva Convention, thus ensuring that nobody is sent back to persecution.[26] Given that the Common European Asylum System is based on the principles introduced by the Geneva Convention; before considering the developments at EU level which gradually led to the introduction of the common asylum law and policy and the Common European Asylum System, main provisions of the 1951 Geneva Convention and the 1967 New York Protocol will be briefly referred to.

The 1951 Geneva Convention contains three types of provisions:

- provisions defining who is and who is not a refugee and who, having been a refugee, has ceased to be one (Chapter I);
- provisions defining the legal status of refugees, their rights and duties in the country of refuge (Chapters II–V); and

24. The so-called 'Vienna Action Plan' was adopted by the Justice and Home Affairs (JHA) Council of 3 December 1998, OJ C 19, 23.01.1999, 1.

25. Treaty of Nice (OJ C 80, 10.3.2001) was signed on 26 February 2001 and entered into force on 1 February 2003.

26. Tampere, par. 13.

- provisions regulating the implementation of the convention (Chapters VI–VII).[27]

As far as the first group of provisions is concerned, according to Article 1A(2), for the purpose of this convention, the term 'refugee' applies to any person who as a result of events occurring before 1 January 1951 and owing to well-founded fear of being persecuted for reasons of race, religion, nationality, membership of a particular social group or political opinion, is outside the country of his nationality and is unable or, owing to such fear, is unwilling to avail himself of the protection of that country; or who, not having a nationality and being outside the country of his former habitual residence as a result of such events, is unable or, owing to such fear, is unwilling to return to it.

According to Article 1B(1) the words 'events occurring before 1 January 1951' in Article 1A should be understood to mean either events occurring in Europe before 1 January 1951 or events occurring in Europe or elsewhere before 1 January 1951. The 1967 New York Protocol removed the time restriction present in Article 1A(2) of the Geneva Convention and the geographical limitation of Article 1B(1)(a).[28]

The *cessation clauses* (Art. 1C(1) to (6) of the Geneva Convention) specify the situations when a refugee ceases to be a refugee. The first four cessation clauses consider changes in the situation of a refugee which he/she creates himself/herself:

1. he/she voluntarily reavails himself/herself of the protection of the country of his/her nationality; or
2. having lost his nationality he/she has voluntarily reacquired it; or
3. he/she has acquired a new nationality, and enjoys the protection of the country of his/her new nationality; or
4. he/she has voluntarily re-established himself/herself in the country which he left or outside which he remained owing to fear of persecution.

The two other cessation clauses are based on the fact that the circumstances in connection with which he/she has been recognised as a refugee do not presently exist, and:

5. he/she can no longer continue to refuse to avail himself/herself of the protection of the country of his/her nationality, unless justified; or
6. in cases of persons who have no nationality, he/she is able to return to the country of his/her former habitual residence.

---

27. On a detailed interpretation of these provisions see the *UNHCR Handbook*.
28. See 1967 New York Protocol, Art. I(2), (3).

The so-called 'exclusion clauses' are contained in Article 1D, E and F of the Geneva Convention. The Geneva Convention does not apply to persons who are already receiving protection or assistance (Art. 1D) from organs or agencies of the United Nations other than the UNHCR; who are not considered to be in need of international protection since they possess in the country of their residence the same rights and obligations as nationals of this country (Art. 1E); to those with respect to whom there are serious reasons for considering that they have committed a crime against peace, a war crime, or a crime against humanity; a serious non-political crime outside the country of refuge prior to their admission to that country as refugees; or they have been guilty of acts contrary to the purposes and principles of the United Nations (Art. 1F). Thus, persons who would otherwise qualify for being refugees according to the definition in Article 1A(2) are excluded from refugee status if they fall under one of the above-mentioned situations.

The second group of provisions includes provisions on the personal status of a refugee, which should be governed by the law of the country of his/her domicile, or by the law of the country of his/her residence if he/she has no domicile (Art. 12). Other provisions deal with refugees' property (Art. 13), access to courts (Art. 16), employment (Arts. 17–19), housing (Art. 21), public education (Art. 22), social security (Art. 24), freedom of movement (Art. 26), identity and travel documents (Arts. 27–28), irregular presence in the country of refuge (Art. 31).

One provision of this group deserves a special attention. The reason is that it represents the core of the refugee protection. The so-called principle of *non-refoulement* (Art. 33(1)) is part of customary international law and is binding on all states,[29] whether or not Contracting States to the 1951 Geneva Convention. Therefore no government should expel or return (*refouler*) a person back to persecution. Exceptions to this principle are laid down in Article 33(2).

The third group of provisions consists of executory and transitory provisions and final clauses (Arts. 35–46).

1.3 Internal market: Freedom of movement

The concept of the internal market has been a framework for further actions concerning the abolition of checks on persons at common EU internal borders (the borders between the EU Member States).[30] During the early years of the European Community, the issue of asylum could not be dealt with at the European level, because the European Economic Community (EEC) did not have competence in this area. The full title of the Treaty of Rome, adopted in 1957, was the 'The

29. See, e.g., UNHCR, *The 1951 Refugee Convention, Questions & Answers* (Geneva 2003), 13.

30. On the internal market see, e.g., Barnard, C., Scott, J.: *The Law of the Single European Market: Unpacking the Premises* (Oxford 2002).

Treaty establishing the European Economic Community'.[31] The title itself already suggests that the central objective of the construction of Europe was to create a European economic market. Economic integration was promoted through the Community and it provided for creating an ever closer union and relations among the Member States.[32] There are no provisions referring to *a person* as a citizen, a third-country national (TCN), an immigrant or an asylum seeker in this Treaty because it was focused only on the economic aspects of the European Community.

In the 1960s, Western Europe enjoyed a period of sustained economic prosperity. In this period provisions on immigration already started to emerge in the European Community framework, however, still only in relation to the migration of workers and their families.[33] Once more the economic element was fundamental.

With the beginning of the economic recession in the early 1970s, the demand for foreign workers decreased. In spite of this fact, foreigners were still interested in finding jobs and staying in Western Europe. Family reunification also remained a significant factor, which allowed immigrants to continue to arrive from outside the EC.

Approaching the mid-1980s, in 1986 the term 'internal market' was introduced in the Single European Act (SEA).[34] At present the TEC thus contains four freedoms, upon which the Community is built: the free movement of goods, persons,

---

31. The Treaty establishing the European Economic Community (EEC) was adopted on 25 March 1957 and entered into force on 1 January 1958.

32. Cf. the Preamble to the EEC Treaty.

33. On migration into the European Union see, e.g., Guild, E.: *European Community Law from a Migrant's Perspective* (Nijmegen 2000); Hailbronner, K.: *Immigration and Asylum Law and Policy of the European Union* (The Hague 2000).

34. The Single European Act was signed on 17 February 1986 in Luxembourg and The Hague and entered into force on 1 July 1987 (OJ) L 169, 29.6.1987). It was the first major revision of the Treaty of Rome. Art. 13 of the SEA stipulated that the following provisions should supplement the EEC Treaty:

'The Community shall adopt measures with the aim of progressively establishing the internal market over a period expiring on 31 December 1992...and without prejudice to the other provisions of this Treaty.

The internal market shall comprise an area without internal frontiers in which the free movement of goods, persons, services and capital is ensured in accordance with the provisions of this Treaty.'

As a consequence of the Treaty renumbering, this provision is currently to be found in Art. 14 TEC. Art. 14 TEC, as well as the wording of the SEA, refers to the 'internal market'. On the other hand Art. 2 TEC refers to a 'common market'. In the context of the Community, SEA introduced the term 'internal market', also known as the 'single market'. This has a broadly similar meaning as the term 'common market' – an economic term to describe an abstract model – but is a term particular to the Community, implying a common market in the precise form laid down by the SEA. In a common market all members are to remove restrictions between themselves on what are known as factors of production (labour, capital, material, etc.). In the European Community this requirement has been translated into 'freedom of movement of goods, persons, services and capital'. Therefore, even though often used as synonymous, there is a difference in scope. The common market, in addition to the four freedoms, also deals with common commercial policy (commercial relations with third countries) and competition policy. On this basis, the term 'common market' is slightly wider than internal market. Further see Steiner, J., Woods, L.: *Textbook on EC Law*, 8th ed. (Oxford 2003), 187; Deards,

services and capital, all of which serve the central purpose, stated in Article 14 TEC as a goal of establishing an area of freedom of movement 'without internal frontiers'. The internal market comprises an area without internal borders, in which the free movement of goods, persons, services and capital is ensured. The right for people to move freely from one Member State to another is therefore one of the distinctive features of the internal market. Although there is no explicit definition of 'person' available in the TEC, the Member States practically limited the interpretation merely to their nationals. Nonetheless, some TCNs, subject to fulfilment of the conditions laid down in the Treaties, the secondary legislation, as well as in the national laws of the Member States, have also been able to enjoy free movement within the EU. These are in principle the TCNs, who are family members of Member States' nationals, and also those TCNs and their family members, who are legally residing in the territory of an EU Member State.[35]

To create a real internal market, as suggested by the SEA, it became necessary to abolish the checks on persons at the common borders between the Member States (*the internal borders of the EU*). Although the idea of creating an internal market was accepted by the Member States and inserted into the TEC, some Member States were reluctant to transfer the competence related to the open-borders-policy to the EEC. One can understand a reserved attitude of the Member States towards this policy. To abolish the checks at the internal borders automatically means their abolishment towards any person, including TCNs. On the other hand, if the elimination of the checks on persons at the internal borders would not take place, the idea behind the notion of the internal market and of the free movement of persons within this territory would not be fulfilled. The free movement of persons would not be really *free* if subject to checks at the internal borders. By approving the abolishment of such checks, there could no longer be a distinction between TCNs and nationals of the Member States.

1.4 Schengen Agreement (1985) and Schengen Implementation Convention (1990)

The Agreement of 14 June 1985 between the Governments of the States of the Benelux Economic Union, the Federal Republic of Germany and the French Republic on the gradual abolition of checks at their common borders (the 'Schengen Agreement')[36] provided for the abolition of checks on persons crossing a land border or those flying or taking a ferry between two Schengen countries. The five

E., Hargreaves, S.: *European Union Law* (Oxford 2001), 5–6; Clayton, G.: *Textbook on Immigration and Asylum Law* (Oxford 2004), 109.

35. See Council Directive 2003/86/EC on the right to family reunification, OJ L 251, 3.10.2003, 12; Council Directive 2003/109/EC concerning the status of third-country nationals who are long-term residents, OJ L 16, 23.1.2004, 44.

36. OJ L 239, 22.9.2000, 13.

original signatory States to the Schengen Agreement decided to create a territory without checks at the internal borders known as the 'Schengen area'. In the Preamble the Contracting Parties proclaimed their awareness of the fact that the ever closer union of the peoples of the Member States of the European Communities (EC) should find its expression in the freedom to cross the internal borders of all Member States and in the free movement of goods and services.

The Convention Implementing the Schengen Agreement (further referred to as the Schengen Implementation Convention) was signed on 19 June 1990 and entered into force on 1 September 1993; however, in practice it took effect on 26 March 1995 for the original Parties to the Schengen Agreement, Spain and Portugal.[37] In the Preamble the Contracting Parties referred to the Schengen Agreement and to the TEC supplemented by the SEA, which provides that the internal market shall comprise an area without internal frontiers. The aim pursued by the Contracting Parties corresponds with that objective. The implementation of that intention required a series of appropriate measures and close cooperation between the Contracting Parties.

For the purposes of the Schengen Implementation Convention the following terms mean, as laid down in Title I, Article 1:

- the *internal borders* mean the common land borders of the contracting parties, their airports for internal flights and their sea ports for regular ferry connections exclusively from or to other ports within the territories of the contracting parties and not calling at any ports outside those territories;
- the *external border* means the contracting parties' land and sea borders and their airports and seaports, provided that they are not internal borders;
- *third state* means any state other than the contracting parties;
- *alien* means any person other than a national of a Member State of the EC;
- *border crossing point* means any crossing point authorised by the competent authorities for crossing external borders;
- *border check* means a check carried out at a border in response exclusively to an intention to cross that border, regardless of any other consideration;
- *application for asylum* means any application submitted in writing, orally or otherwise by an alien at an external border or within the territory of a contracting party with a view to obtaining recognition as a refugee in accordance with the Geneva Convention relating to the Status of Refugees of 28 July 1951, as amended by the New York Protocol of 31 January 1967, and as such obtaining the right of residence;
- *asylum seeker* means any alien who has lodged an application for asylum within the meaning of this convention and in respect of which a final decision has not yet been taken;

37. Since 1995 Italy, Greece, Austria, Denmark, Finland and Sweden have acceded to the Convention.

– *processing applications for asylum* shall mean all the procedures for examining and taking a decision on applications for asylum, including measures taken under a final decision thereon, with the exception of the determination of the contracting party responsible for processing applications for asylum pursuant to this convention.[38]

It is necessary to emphasise that originally the Schengen cooperation between the Contracting Parties took place outside the legal framework of the European Community. As a result, the Community Institutions had no role to play in the framework of this cooperation. The cooperation at that stage was functioning only on an intergovernmental level. All Member States of the European Community became parties to the Schengen Agreement, except for the United Kingdom and Ireland. On the other hand, two non-EU members (Norway and Iceland) have been associated with the implementation, application and development of the Schengen *acquis*.[39] They have fully implemented the Schengen regime since 25 March 2001.[40]

As a consequence of the adoption of the Schengen Agreement and the convention implementing the Schengen Agreement, the checks on persons were gradually abolished on the internal borders between the Contracting Parties.[41] Therefore the free movement of persons within the internal market could be achieved. On the other hand, in order to compensate for the removal of the checks on persons at the internal borders, compensatory measures were established at the *external borders*. Individuals are subject to stricter checks, including passport controls and the duty to submit valid visas, if so required.[42]

---

38. Articles dealing with the movement of persons and the abolition of checks at internal borders are to be found in Title II of the Convention. The Convention further sets measures on police and security, the Schengen Information System, transport and movement of goods, protection of personal data.

39. See OJ L 176, 10.7.1999, 31.

40. It should be noted that on 5 June 2005 the Swiss people approved the Schengen/Dublin association agreement by 54.6% (see OJ L 368, 15.12.2004, 26). On 'Schengen' further see, e.g., Hurwitz, A.: 'The "Schengen" Practice and Case-Law in Belgium', *European Journal of Migration and Law* 2 (2000) 37–48; Staples, H.: 'Adjudicating the Schengen Agreements in the Netherlands', *European Journal of Migration and Law* 2 (2000) 49–83; Wiener, A.: 'Forging Flexibility – The British "No" to Schengen', *European Journal of Migration and Law* 1 (1999) 441–463; Guild, E.: 'Adjudicating Schengen: National Judicial Control in France', *European Journal of Migration and Law* 1 (1999) 419–439; Gless, S. (ed.): *Auslieferungsrecht der Schengen – Vertragsstaaten: neuere Entwicklungen* (Freiburg im Breisgau 2002); Boer, M. den (ed.): *Schengen Still Going Strong: Evaluation and Update* (Maastricht 2000); Boer, M. den (ed.): *Schengen's Final Days?: The Incorporation of Schengen into the New TEU, External Borders and Information Systems* (Maastricht 1998); Boer, M. den (ed.): *The Implementation of Schengen: First the Widening, Now the Deepening* (Maastricht 1997).

41. Schengen Implementation Convention, Art. 2(1). Exceptions are laid down in Art. 2(2).

42. Id., Arts. 3–8.

The subject matter of asylum is particularly interrelated with the crossing of the external borders of the EU. Asylum seekers can apply for asylum at the border crossing points or in the territory of the Member States.[43] The border crossing points are the external land borders, the international airports and seaports of the Member States.

The cooperation in the framework of Schengen encompassed among other rules the rules on responsibility for processing applications for asylum.[44] The Schengen Implementation Convention became operational in 1995; in 1990 the Dublin Convention, replacing the provisions on responsibility for processing asylum applications, was signed. To prevent a possible conflict between the Schengen *acquis* and the Dublin Convention, the Member States agreed that when the Dublin Convention would enter into force, the above-mentioned provisions of the Schengen Implementation Convention would cease to apply.[45]

1.5 Dublin Convention (1990)

The Convention determining the State responsible for examining applications for asylum lodged in one of the Member States of the EC (the Dublin Convention) was signed on 15 June 1990; it entered into force on 1 September 1997 for the twelve original signatories,[46] on 1 October 1997 for Austria and Sweden and on 1 January 1998 for Finland. However, it was not an instrument of Community law within the meaning of the TEC, but a treaty under international law.[47] Ratification by all signatory states was necessary to put it into effect. The general objectives of the Dublin Convention were laid down in the Preamble:

---

43. Cf. the Council Directive on minimum standards on procedures in Member States for granting and withdrawing refugee status (OJ L 326, 13.12.2005, 13), Art. 3.

44. Schengen Implementation Convention, Arts. 28–38.

45. See the Bonn Protocol of 26 April 1994 on the consequences of the entry into force of the Dublin Convention for certain provisions of the Schengen Convention, Trb. [Dutch Treaties Series] 1994, 185. The Bonn Protocol entered into force on 1 August 1997 (Trb. 1997, 237).

46. Belgium, Denmark, France, Germany, Greece, Ireland, Italy, Luxembourg, The Netherlands, Portugal, Spain and the United Kingdom.

47. The Dublin Convention (OJ C 254, 19.8.1997, 1) has been replaced by Council Regulation 343/2003 of 18 February 2003 establishing the criteria and mechanisms for determining the Member State responsible for examining an asylum application lodged in one of the Member States by a third country national. This Regulation is a Community instrument and it is analysed in more detail in chapter 2, 2.2.2, 2.2.3. See also Agreement between the European Community and the Republic of Iceland and the Kingdom of Norway concerning the criteria and mechanisms for establishing the State responsible for examining a request for asylum lodged in a Member State or in Iceland or Norway, OJ L 93, 3.4.2001, 40; and Council Decision of 21 February 2006 on the conclusion of a Protocol to the Agreement between the European Community and the Republic of Iceland and the Kingdom of Norway concerning the criteria and mechanisms for establishing the State responsible for examining a request for asylum lodged in a Member State or in Iceland or Norway, OJ L 57, 28.2.2006, 15.

- To keep with the common humanitarian tradition, to guarantee adequate protection to refugees in accordance with the terms of the Geneva Convention of 28 July 1951, as amended by the New York Protocol of 31 January 1967 relating to the Status of Refugees;
- To ensure that applicants for asylum are not referred successively from one Member State to the other without any of these States acknowledging itself to be competent to examine the application for asylum, i.e., to avoid the cases of the so-called refugees in orbit;
- To take measures to avoid any situations arising, with the result that applicants for asylum are left in doubt for too long as regards the likely outcome of their applications and concerned to provide all applicants for asylum with a guarantee that their applications will be examined by one of the Member States;
- To continue the dialogue with the United Nations High Commissioner for Refugees in order to achieve the above objectives.

The Dublin system had two distinct components with different purposes: the criteria for determining which Member State is responsible for considering an asylum application (Arts. 4 to 8); and the readmission rules which apply when a person, who has previously lodged an asylum claim in one Member State, is subsequently present in a second Member State (Arts. 3(7) and 10).[48] Article 3 was of a major importance to the Dublin Convention. It contained provisions on the Member States' obligation to examine applications for asylum and the order in which the responsibility criteria had to be applied, as well as the provision that the applications had to be examined in accordance with the Member States' national laws and their international obligations. In addition, Article 3 also provided Member States with the option to examine an application for asylum itself, even if the criteria suggested otherwise. It recognised the Member States' right to send an applicant for asylum to a third state in compliance with the national laws and the provisions of the 1951 Geneva Convention.[49]

Articles 4 to 8 set the criteria for determining which State was responsible for considering an asylum application, as follows:

1. The State where a spouse or a child under 18, or in the case of such a child a parent, has been recognised as a refugee within the meaning of the Geneva Convention on refugees (Art. 4);

---

48. Further see Commission staff working paper 'Revisiting the Dublin Convention: developing Community legislation for determining which Member State is responsible for considering an application for asylum submitted in one of the Member States' (further referred to as 'Revisiting the Dublin Convention'), SEC(2000) 522, par. 4.

49. See also Kloth, K.: 'The Dublin Convention on Asylum – An Introduction', in Marinho, C. (ed.): *The Dublin Convention on Asylum: Its Essence, Implementation and Prospects* (Maastricht 2000), 8–10.

2. The State that issued the applicant with a valid residence permit or visa (Art. 5);
3. The State where illegal entry was made from outside the EU save where the application was made after a six months residence in another Member State (Art. 6);
4. The State responsible for controlling the entry across the external frontiers of Member States (Art. 7);
5. In all other cases, the State of first application for asylum, including any previous applications for asylum that have been refused (Art. 8).

The responsibility rules incumbent in Articles 4 to 8 were supplemented by the provisions of two important discretionary rules: Article 3(4), the so-called *sovereignty clause*[50] and Article 9, the *humanitarian clause*.[51] Pursuant to Article 3(4) a Member State could opt in, meaning that it had the right to examine an application for asylum even if it was not in fact responsible. The sovereignty clause was very general and therefore enabled a high degree of flexibility and discretion on the Member States' part.

The process of determining the Member State responsible for examining the application for asylum under the Dublin Convention should start as soon as an application for asylum is first lodged with a Member State. That application must be examined by the State in accordance with its national laws and its international obligations. In order to establish the identity of applicants for asylum and of persons apprehended in connection with the unlawful crossing of the external borders of the Community, the system of computerised data on fingerprints of asylum seekers and other categories of aliens (Eurodac) was established in accordance with the 1990 Dublin Convention; in order to apply it more effectively.[52] Finger-

---

50. Art. 3(4) reads:
'Each Member State shall have the right to examine an application for asylum submitted to it by an alien, even if such examination is not its responsibility under the criteria defined in this Convention, provided that the applicant for asylum agrees thereto.
The Member State responsible under the above criteria is then relieved of its obligations, which are transferred to the Member State which expressed the wish to examine the application. The latter State shall inform the Member State responsible under the said criteria if the application has been referred to it.'

51. Art. 9 reads:
'Any Member State, even when it is not responsible under the criteria laid out in this Convention, may, for humanitarian reasons, based in particular on family or cultural grounds, examine an application for asylum at the request of another Member State, provided that the applicant so desires.
If the Member State thus approached accedes to the request, responsibility for examining the application shall be transferred to it.'

52. Council Regulation 2725/2000, OJ L 316, 15.12.2000, 1; see also Council Regulation (EC) No. 407/2002 of 28 February 2002 laying down certain rules to implement Regulation (EC) No. 2725/2000 concerning the establishment of 'Eurodac' for the comparison of fingerprints for the effective application of the Dublin Convention (OJ L 62, 5.3.2002,1); and Council Decision of 21 February 2006 on the conclusion of the Agreement between the European Community and the Kingdom of

prints constitute an important element in establishing the exact identity of a person.

The main purpose of the provisions of Articles 28–38 of the Schengen Implementation Convention and then the Dublin Convention evidently was to prevent the frequent cases of the so-called 'refugees in orbit' that is, cases when asylum seekers who had lodged an application for refugee status in one Member State and were rejected, subsequently applied in other Member State.[53] There have also been cases when a person applied simultaneously or consecutively in two Member States. Such cases of multiple applications could continue over and over again.[54] The provisions in question were expected to prevent such situations. The purpose of the Dublin Convention was to make only one State responsible for processing the asylum application of a TCN. That application had to be examined by that State in accordance with its national laws and its international obligations.[55] This State also must examine the asylum application, take decisions and, in case the application is rejected, take measures to ensure that the asylum applicant leaves the EU territory.

Even though there were several shortcomings in the functioning of the Dublin Convention, its positive feature is that the Dublin system was based – at least in theory – on the mutual trust in the asylum procedures of the Contracting Parties. In practice, therefore, if an asylum seeker already launched his/her claim in one of the Member States and this was dismissed, the other Member State could at once reject his/her repeated claim. However, the convention itself did not provide any obligation to recognise asylum decisions of the other Contracting Parties. The Dublin Convention applied only when the asylum seeker could not be sent back to a safe country.[56] One thing that was spoken highly of was the solving of the problem of refugees in orbit. Still, an asylum seeker whose application was rejected and was sent back to a third country might circle around third countries. The problem of refugees in orbit was therefore solved with a positive effect only within the European Community. Although the Dublin Convention did not har-

---

Denmark extending to Denmark the provisions of Council Regulation (EC) No. 343/2003 establishing the criteria and mechanisms for determining the Member State responsible for examining an asylum application lodged in one of the Member States by a third-country national and Council Regulation (EC) No. 2725/2000 concerning the establishment of Eurodac for the comparison of fingerprints for the effective application of the Dublin Convention (OJ L 66, 8.3.2006, 37). On Eurodac see further chapter 2, 2.2.4.

53. A term 'asylum seekers in orbit' would be more accurate, however, the term 'refugees in orbit' will be used in this text, due to its common use.

54. On the prevention of asylum applicants from being able to pursue multiple asylum applications (either concurrently or consecutively) see, e.g., 'Revisiting the Dublin Convention' (*supra* 48).

55. Art. 3(2), (3).

56. On the concept of a safe third country, a safe country of asylum and a safe country of origin further see chapter 2, 2.5.3.

monise either substantive or procedural asylum law, it gave an impetus for its harmonisation.[57]

The Dublin Convention is further evaluated in Chapter 2, in order to make a clear link between this legal instrument (adopted outside the framework of the Community law) and its successor, the so-called 'Dublin II' Regulation, adopted on the basis of Article 63(1)(a) TEC.[58]

1.6 Treaty of Maastricht (1992)

The Treaty on European Union, known as the Treaty of Maastricht, was signed on 7 February 1992 and entered into force on 1 November 1993. The Maastricht Treaty changed the name of the European Economic Community to simply 'the European Community'. It also introduced the *pillar structure,* where the EC (the European Community, the European Coal and Steel Community (ECSC)[59] and the Euratom) represent what is known as the first pillar. The second pillar comprises the common foreign and security policy (CFSP) and the third pillar under the Maastricht Treaty consisted of the policies on justice and home affairs (JHA).[60] The concept of the EU in this framework can be understood as an overarching political entity, beyond all the three pillars. The second and third pillars are mainly *intergovernmental* in their nature. Therefore the role of the EU Institutions in these pillars is limited, with the national governments playing the decisive role. The policies belonging to the second and the third pillars have been under the domain of public international law and institutional intergovernmental cooperation within the EU structure. The policies on JHA are very sensitive, one of the

---

57. On the Dublin Convention see, e.g., Marx, R.: 'Adjusting the Dublin Convention: New Approaches to Member State Responsibility for Asylum Applications', *European Journal of Migration and Law* 3 (2001) 7–22; Nicol QC, A., Harrison, S.: 'The Law and Practice in the Application of the Dublin Convention in the United Kingdom', *European Journal of Migration and Law* 1 (1999) 465–481; Marinho, C. (ed.): *The Dublin Convention on Asylum: Its Essence, Implementation and Prospects* (Maastricht 2000); Faria, C. (ed.): *The Dublin Convention on Asylum: Between Reality and Aspirations* (Maastricht 2001); Blake, N.: 'The Dublin Convention and Rights of Asylum Seekers in the European Union', in Guild, E., Harlow, C. (eds.): *Implementing Amsterdam: Immigration and Asylum Rights in EC Law* (Oxford 2001), 95–120.

58. For the evaluation of the Dublin Convention further see chapter 2, 2.2.1.

59. The Treaty establishing the European Coal and Steel Community (ECSC) was signed in Paris on 18 April 1951 by Belgium, Germany, France, Italy, Luxembourg and the Netherlands. It was concluded for a period of fifty years and, having entered into force on 23 July 1952, it expired on 23 July 2002.

60. Since the Treaty of Maastricht entered into force, there has been a structure in the Treaty of the policies on justice and home affairs (JHA). Previously, it used to be only an ad hoc cooperation. Please note that the cooperation in justice and home affairs has been renamed to justice, freedom and security.

reasons being that there is a close link between these policies and the state sovereignty of the Member States.

The third pillar under the Maastricht Treaty set up the framework in which policies on JHA were introduced for the first time. According to Article K.1 of the TEU,[61] for the purposes of achieving the objectives of the Union, in particular the *free movement of persons* and without prejudice to the powers of the European Community, Member States shall regard the following areas as *matters of common interest:*

- asylum policy;
- crossing by persons of the external borders and the exercise of controls thereon;
- immigration policy and policy regarding nationals of third countries;
- combating drug addiction;
- combating fraud on an international scale;
- judicial cooperation in civil matters;
- judicial cooperation in criminal matters;
- customs cooperation; and
- police cooperation for the purposes of preventing and combating terrorism, unlawful drug trafficking and other serious forms of international crime.

Besides the fact that asylum policy was mentioned as the first one on the list, Article K.2 TEU stipulated that the matters referred to in Article K.1 should be dealt with in compliance with the ECHR and the 1951 Geneva Convention. This is an important point, since the Member States were required to take into account the protection aspect of the asylum policy, when dealing with any other policy mentioned above.

1.7 Treaty of Amsterdam (1997)

Institutional issues were among the priorities of the Intergovernmental Conference (IGC) in 1996, which resulted in the signing of the Treaty of Amsterdam. The Treaty of Amsterdam was signed on 2 October 1997 and entered into force on 1 May 1999. The subject matter of asylum, among others, was transferred from the third to the first pillar (the Community pillar) as a result of the process of *communitarisation;* meaning that the policies concerning visas, asylum, immigration and judicial cooperation in civil matters were transferred from the mainly intergovernmental third pillar to the supranational first pillar. In spite of this fact, United Kingdom, Ireland and Denmark opted out from the new Title IV TEC.

61. Please take into consideration that the Articles were renumbered. However, for the sake of clarity the original denomination (under the Maastricht Treaty) will be used in this chapter.

Furthermore, a concept of an area of freedom, security and justice was introduced by the Treaty of Amsterdam. This new concept entails the policies on asylum, immigration and other policies related to free movement of persons, like judicial cooperation in civil and criminal matters, customs cooperation, police cooperation, controls on external borders and external borders management. The introduction of the area of freedom, security and justice is essential for the development of the Common European Asylum System, because it has affirmed that the EU is an area where people in need of international protection can seek refuge.

1.7.1 Area of Freedom, Security and Justice

One of the objectives of the EU is to 'maintain and develop the Union as an area of freedom, security and justice'. The free movement of persons should be assured 'in conjunction with appropriate measures with respect to external border controls, asylum, immigration and the prevention and combating of crime.'[62] According to the first sentence of Article 61 TEC, the aspiration of the measures to be adopted by the Council in order to harmonise the law on immigration and asylum, is to 'establish progressively an area of freedom, security and justice'. Article 61 TEC clearly refers to Article 2 TEU, which sets the objectives of the Union.

There is no explicit definition to be found in the EU and EC Treaties on what is to be understood under the expression 'area of freedom, security and justice'. Therefore a brief consideration on the meaning of 'area', 'freedom', 'security' and 'justice' from an asylum perspective is well justified.

Area

In the context of the EU the borders which delimit the area are obviously the external borders of the Union. In a strict territorial point of view, the 'area' should correspond with the area mentioned in Article 2 TEU and Article 14(2) TEC.[63] However, taking into consideration that the 'area' relates also to the actions undertaken under the second pillar (with the substance of the CFSP),[64] it should be understood in a broader context. The functioning of the 'area' is relevant also for persons who apply for visas or other types of permission concerning admission or residence in the EU Member States at their diplomatic missions abroad, for example. Having regard to what was said before, it seems to be more appropriate to understand the 'area' as jurisdiction.[65]

---

62. Art. 2 TEU.

63. Art. 14(2) TEC reads: 'The internal market shall comprise an area without internal frontiers in which the free movement of goods, persons, services and capital is ensured in accordance with the provisions of this Treaty.'

64. See Art. 11(1) TEU.

65. See Boeles, P.: 'Introduction: Freedom, Security and Justice for all', in Guild, E., Harlow, C. (eds.): *Implementing Amsterdam: Immigration and Asylum Rights in EC Law* (Oxford 2001), 4.

In contrast, concerning asylum, the Asylum Procedures Directive[66] provides that it should apply to all applications for asylum made in the territory, including at the border or in the transit zones of the Member States; but it should not apply in cases of requests for diplomatic or territorial asylum submitted to representations of Member States abroad.[67] This provision obviously limits the scope of the 'area', as described above, for those seeking international protection in the EU Member States.

Freedom

'Freedom' in this context should be interpreted in two ways: as a concept of fundamental rights and freedoms, including protection from any form of discrimination (according to Articles 12 and 13 TEC and Article 6 TEU) and as freedom of movement of persons.[68]

It should be remembered that all EU Member States are parties to the ECHR adopted within the Council of Europe. ECHR provides an indirect protection of refugees and asylum seekers: Article 3 (prohibition of torture and inhuman and degrading treatment), Article 8 (protection of family and private life), Article 13 (the right to an effective appeal), Article 14 (non-discrimination as regards the enjoyment of rights recognised by the ECHR) and Article 4 of the Fourth Additional Protocol which prohibits a massive expulsion of aliens. Neither the EU nor the European Community is a party to the ECHR; nonetheless Article 6(2) TEU states that the Union shall respect fundamental rights, as guaranteed by the ECHR and as they result from the constitutional traditions common to the Member States, as general principles of Community law. The right to asylum and the principle of *non-refoulement* are guaranteed by the Treaty establishing the Constitution for Europe (the Charter of Fundamental Rights of the Union, Articles II-78, II-79) with due respect for the provisions of the 1951 Geneva Convention. Nevertheless the EU Constitutional Treaty is not yet in force.

The Treaty of Amsterdam introduced a new view regarding the *freedom of movement*. The most notable example is Article 61 TEC, which speaks of measures aimed at ensuring the free movement of persons in accordance with Article 14 TEC.[69] Title IV TEC (of which Article 61 is part) deals with the policies on visas, asylum, immigration and other policies related to the free movement of persons, policies obviously related to TCNs. Due to the link made between Articles 14 and 61 TEC, it can be assumed that the freedom of movement within the internal market shall be guaranteed to all persons, therefore also to refugees.

66. OJ L 326, 13.12.2005, 13. See also chapter 2, 2.5.
67. Id., Art. 3(1), (2).
68. *Supra* 65, at 4–6; see also Vienna Action Plan (OJ C 19, 23.01.1999), par. 6–8.
69. *Supra* 63.

Security

Article 61(b) TEC refers to *security* when it mentions the safeguarding of the rights of nationals of third countries, in accordance with the provisions of Article 63 TEC (measures on asylum and immigration policy). It is apparent that this aspect of safety and *security* should apply to persons in need of international protection. On the other hand, by introducing the flanking measures to the external border controls, persons in need of international protection might be deprived of the protection promised in Article 61(b) TEC by coming across obstacles to actually enter the territory of the Member States (the 'area') and apply for asylum (for example when they are not in possession of valid visas, if required).

Moreover, the maintaining of the internal security of Member States may be a reason for excluding a person from refugee status. The 1951 Geneva Convention contains several provisions which allow exempting a refugee from the benefits guaranteed by this convention; if there are reasonable grounds for regarding him/her as a danger to the security of the country.[70] The current EU legislation in the field of asylum also contains provisions to allow for the exclusion of any TCN, who may be perceived as a threat to public security, from the right to international protection, residency or access to certain benefits.[71] Although the security measures carried out by the EU Member States are inevitable, especially bearing in mind the recent terrorist attacks in some Member States; this should not lead to the neglecting of the international law obligations to protect persons in need of international protection. The security policy and the asylum policy should always be well-balanced; otherwise if the internal security aspect prevails over the refugee protection, the international protection obligations, as well as the rights of persons seeking asylum or other form of international protection could be infringed.[72]

Justice

The Treaty of Maastricht introduced the pillar structure where the third pillar covered the cooperation in the field of JHA. In this context, the expressions 'justice' and 'home affairs' indicates the national ministries responsible for the areas at issue.[73] In paragraph 15 of the Vienna Action Plan, the Council and the Commission stated that

70. See 1951 Geneva Convention, Art. 9 (provisional measures), Art. 32(1), Art. 33(2).

71. See, e.g., Temporary Protection Directive, Art. 28(1)(b); see also Commission working document: 'The relationship between safeguarding internal security and complying with international protection obligations and instruments', COM(2001) 743 final.

72. See Commission working document: 'The relationship between safeguarding internal security and complying with international protection obligations and instruments'.

73. *Supra* 65, at 8–9.

> 'the ambition is to give citizens a common sense of justice throughout the Union. Justice must be seen as facilitating the day-to-day life of people and bringing to justice those who threaten the freedom and security of individuals and society. This includes both access to justice and full judicial cooperation among Member States.'

Persons applying for asylum in the Member States should be able to have access to justice in order to protect their rights. Therefore decisions taken on an application for asylum should be subject to an appeal consisting of an examination on both facts and points of law by a court. The applicant should be entitled not to be expelled until a court has ruled on the right to remain, pending the outcome of this appeal; except in a limited number of cases, for example for reasons of national security or public order. A just asylum procedure should counterbalance the injustice suffered by asylum seekers in their countries of origin or previous residence.

'The full benefits of any area of freedom will never be enjoyed unless they are exercised in an area where people can feel safe and secure.'[74] The benefit of the values expressed by the words 'freedom', 'security' and 'justice' shall be guaranteed to everyone within the jurisdiction of any Member State and the EU, whether an EU citizen, an immigrant or an asylum seeker.[75]

1.7.2 **Title IV TEC**

After the entry into force of the Treaty of Amsterdam, the policies related to the free movement of persons, as well as the policies related to judicial cooperation in civil matters, were transferred from the third to the first pillar, the new Title IV TEC (Arts. 61–69). Consequently, the third pillar (Title VI TEU) was reformed and renamed and now includes policies on police and judicial cooperation in criminal matters. The structure of the new Title IV TEC, introduced by the Treaty of Amsterdam, is as follows:

Article 61 is an introductory article that illustrates the kind of measures that must be adopted by the Council in order to establish progressively an area of freedom, security and justice. Articles 62, 63 and 65 comprise the substance, the 'working programme' for the Council concerning the absence of any controls on persons when crossing internal borders, measures on the crossing of external borders of the Member States – checks on persons, rules on visas (Art. 62), measures on asylum and immigration policy (Art. 63) and in the field of judicial cooperation in civil matters having cross-border implication (Art. 65). In general, Article 64 refers to public order and a decision-making procedure carried out by the Council on a proposal from the Commission in an emergency situation, characterised by a sudden inflow of nationals of third countries. The Council may act by qualified majority and adopt measures of a duration not exceeding six months for the bene-

---

74. Vienna Action Plan, par. 9.
75. *Supra* 65, at 8–9; Vienna Action Plan, par. 15–20.

fit of the State or States concerned. Article 66 calls for administrative cooperation between the responsible authorities of the Member States. Articles 67 and 68 regard the role of the European Institutions.[76] Article 69 points out that the application of this Title shall be subject to the provisions of the Protocol on the position of the United Kingdom and Ireland and to the Protocol on the position of Denmark and also without prejudice to the Protocol on the application of certain aspects of Article 14 TEC to the United Kingdom and to Ireland.[77]

1.7.3 **Protocols**

There were several Protocols annexed to the Treaty of Amsterdam. In the context of this chapter Protocol (No. 29) on asylum for nationals of Member States of the EU,[78] Protocol (No. 4) on the position of the United Kingdom and Ireland[79] and Protocol (No. 5) on the position of Denmark[80] will be briefly discussed.

1.7.3.1 *Asylum for nationals of Member States*

The 'Protocol on asylum for nationals of Member States of the EU' (the so-called 'Aznar Protocol', named after the former Spanish Prime Minister), is based on the presumption that the EU Member States must be 'safe countries'. Therefore it assumes that an asylum application lodged by a national of a Member State in other Member State is unfounded. In principle no application for asylum lodged by a citizen of a Member State is taken into consideration in another Member State, unless it is proven reasonable according to the conditions laid down in this Protocol.[81]

The sole Article of the Protocol on asylum for nationals of Member States of the EU states that application for asylum made by a national of a Member State may be taken into consideration or declared admissible for processing by another Member State only if:

---

76. On the institutional aspects see further chapter 1, 1.10.

77. On Title IV TEC (as amended by the Treaty of Amsterdam) see e.g., Steenbergen, J.D.M.: 'All the King's Horses...: Probabilities and Possibilities for the Implementation of the New Title IV EC Treaty', *European Journal of Migration and Law* 1 (1999) 29–60; Marinho, C. (ed.): *Asylum, Immigration and Schengen Post-Amsterdam: A First Assessment* (Maastricht 2001); Hailbronner, K.; Weil, P. (eds.): *Von Schengen nach Amsterdam: auf dem Weg zu einem europäischen Einwanderungs- und* Asylrecht [From Schengen to Amsterdam: Towards a European immigration and asylum legislation] (Köln 1999).

78. Origin: Treaty of Amsterdam; Protocol annexed to the TEC.

79. Origin: Treaty of Amsterdam; Protocol annexed to the Treaty on European Union and to the TEC.

80. Ibid.

81. This initiative has to be seen against the background of a protracted Spanish-Belgian conflict involving asylum claims by Basque separatists in Belgium. Further see Noll, G.: *Negotiating Asylum: the EU acquis, extraterritorial protection and the common market of deflection* (The Hague 2000), 224.

- the Member State of which the applicant is a national takes measures derogating in its territory from its obligations under the ECHR, according to Article 15 of this convention ('derogation in time of emergency');
- the procedure on determining that there is a clear risk of a serious breach of principles of liberty, democracy, respect for human rights and fundamental freedoms and the rule of law[82] has been initiated and until the Council takes a decision in that respect;
- the Council has determined in respect of the Member State of which the applicant is a national, the existence of a serious and persistent breach by that Member State of principles of liberty, democracy, respect for human rights and fundamental freedoms and the rule of law;
- a Member State decides unilaterally as regards the application of a national of another Member State; nonetheless in such case the Council should be immediately informed.

It is interesting to observe that the EU Member States in fact placed their own nationals in a less favourable position than the citizens of third countries, raising claims of discriminatory treatment.[83] One can also see a risk of infringement of the 1951 Geneva Convention (Art. 1), which should apply to 'any person' that fulfils the criteria laid down in the convention. All EU Member States are Parties to the Geneva Convention; however, neither the EU nor the European Community are parties. Therefore the Member States are individually accountable for the observation of its provisions. In case that Article 1 of the Geneva Convention would be infringed, the Member State against which a case would be brought in this respect will be held responsible; even though it acted on the basis of a Protocol annexed to the TEC.

1.7.3.2 *The position of the United Kingdom, Ireland and Denmark*

The United Kingdom, Ireland and Denmark were opposed to the *communitarisation* of JHA policies previously covered by the third pillar, under the Treaty of Maastricht. They have agreed, however, to the ambition of other Member States to achieve a closer cooperation in these areas. The necessary price to pay in order to achieve the communitarisation has been to tolerate the opting-out of these three Member States.[84] In addition to their opt-out, the United Kingdom and Ireland

82. See Art. 6(1), 7(1) TEU.

83. On a separate analysis of the discrimination claim with regard to the 'Aznar Protocol', see Noll, G.: *Negotiating Asylum: The EU acquis, extraterritorial protection and the common market of deflection* (The Hague 2000), chapter 12.3.

84. On the Opt-Out Protocols further see Hailbronner, K.: 'The Treaty of Amsterdam and Migration Law', *European Journal of Migration and Law* 1 (1999) 20.

have also maintained their Common Travel Area,[85] which does not form part of the internal market since the latter 'shall comprise an area without internal frontiers in which the free movement of [...] persons [...] is ensured'.[86] The opt-outs of the United Kingdom, Ireland and Denmark are governed by the Protocol integrating the Schengen *acquis* into the framework of the EU and the Protocols on the position of the said Member States.[87]

The 'Protocol on the Position of the United Kingdom and Ireland' governs the opt-out from the provisions of Title IV EC Treaty by the United Kingdom and Ireland. They do not participate in the adoption of measures under this Title, nor are they bound by any measure or decision based upon this Title. They may, however, participate in the adoption and application of proposed measures under Title IV TEC, if they express their wish to do so within three months after a proposal or initiative has been presented to the Council (Art. 3 of the Protocol). They may also opt in with regards to Community legislation adopted by the other Member States, subject to admission by the Commission (Art. 4 of the Protocol read together with Article 11(3) TEC). Ireland may also renounce its opt-out, pursuant to Article 8 of the Protocol. Irrespective of whether the United Kingdom and Ireland participate in the adoption of Community legislation or opt in after adoption, they may only choose to opt in fully.[88]

The Danish opt-out from both the implementation of Title IV TEC and the Schengen follow-up process is governed by the 'Protocol on the position of Denmark'. In contrast to the situation of the United Kingdom and Ireland, Denmark has only the possibility to inform the other Member State that it no longer wishes to avail itself of all or part of the Protocol. In that case it will be bound to apply in full all measures passed by that time on the basis of Title IV TEC. Denmark may not participate in the adoption of individual measures under Title IV. However, measures building on the Schengen *acquis* are open to a Danish acceptance, notwithstanding the fact that they must be based upon Title IV TEC legal bases.[89] By not being subjected entirely to Title IV TEC, United Kingdom, Ireland and Denmark cannot fully participate in the Community legislation (and policy) on asylum and immigration.

---

85. Under the conditions of the common travel area there are no checks on persons travelling between these two countries. There is no formal agreement between Ireland and the UK regarding the common travel area. Its recognition between Ireland and the UK is in the Treaty of Amsterdam, Art. 2.

86. The Common Travel Area is shielded from the internal market by virtue of the Protocol on the application of certain aspects of Art. 14 TEC to the United Kingdom and to Ireland.

87. All these Protocols originate in the Treaty of Amsterdam and are annexed to the TEU and to the TEC. Further see Hailbronner, K.: *Immigration and Asylum Law and Policy of the European Union* (The Hague 2000), 103.

88. Id., at 103–104.

89. Id., at 104; cf. Thun-Hohenstein, C.: *Der Vertrag von Amsterdam: Die neue Verfassung der EU* (Vienna 1997), 55.

After the intention to establish progressively an area of freedom, security and justice, expressed in the Treaty of Amsterdam, a step further was needed in order to move towards this ambitious goal. Following the Vienna Action Plan of 3 December 1998, the European Council in Tampere took this step forward.

1.8 Tampere Conclusions (1999)

During the Finnish Presidency, the European Council held its meeting in Tampere, on 15 and 16 October 1999. This European Council provided the necessary impetus for the development of the Union and its general political guidelines[90] in the field of asylum. The Tampere European Council was determined to develop the Union as an 'area of freedom, security and justice' by making full use of the possibilities offered by the Treaty of Amsterdam. The European Council at Tampere also proclaimed to place and to maintain this objective at the very top of the EU political agenda.[91] This European Council agreed to work towards establishing a Common European Asylum System, based on the full and inclusive application of the 1951 Geneva Convention, as supplemented by the 1967 New York Protocol, and thus ensuring that nobody is sent back to persecution (the principle of *non-refoulement*).[92]

In the part of the Tampere Presidency Conclusions called 'Towards a Union of Freedom, Security and Justice' the most significant statements regarding the asylum policy are given in paragraphs 2, 3 and 4. In reference to the Treaty of Amsterdam, the free movement of persons throughout the Union must be ensured. This should be enjoyed in conditions of security and justice accessible to all.[93] Freedom should not, however, be regarded as the exclusive safeguard of the Union's own citizens. The Tampere Conclusions further state that 'it would be in contradiction with Europe's traditions to deny such freedom to those whose circumstances lead them justifiably to seek access to our territory'.[94] This therefore requires the Union to develop common policies on asylum and immigration (while taking into account the need for a consistent control of external borders to stop illegal immigration and to combat those who organise it and commit related international crimes). These common policies have to be based on principles which are both clear to the EU citizens and also offer guarantees to those who seek protection or access to the EU.[95]

The aim expressed in the Tampere Conclusions is an open and secure EU, fully committed to the obligations of the 1951 Geneva Convention and other relevant

90. Cf. Art. 4 TEU.
91. *Tampere*, Preamble.
92. Id., par. 13.
93. Id., par. 2.
94. Id., par. 3.
95. Ibid.

human rights instruments, and able to respond to humanitarian needs on the basis of solidarity. Moreover, to ensure the integration of those TCNs who are lawfully resident in the EU, a common approach is required.[96]

Paragraph 10, in spite of its brevity, is important as it acknowledges that asylum and migration are closely related, but still two different issues and therefore they should be dealt with separately. This approach is very important especially because asylum seekers, presuming they are in genuine need of international protection, are not voluntary migrants, and therefore must be subject to different procedures than 'regular' migrants (e.g., economic migrants).

The Tampere Conclusions call for a comprehensive approach to migration (addressing political, human rights and development issues in the countries and regions of origin and transit). This requires combating poverty, improving living conditions and job opportunities, preventing conflicts and consolidating democratic states, as well as ensuring respect for human rights. For this purpose the Union and the Member States are invited to contribute, within their respective competence under the Treaties, to a greater coherence of internal and external policies of the Union. Partnership with third countries is one of the key elements for the success of such policy.[97]

Paragraph 13 could be considered as one of the most essential paragraphs of the Tampere Conclusions, as far as the establishment of a Common European Asylum System is concerned. The European Council reaffirms the importance of an 'absolute respect of the right to seek asylum' and provides that the Common European Asylum System should be based on 'the full and inclusive application of the Geneva Convention, and so ensuring that nobody is sent back to persecution, i.e., maintaining the principle of non-refoulement'.[98] To this end the UNHCR as a guarantor of the 1951 Geneva Convention on Refugees plays an important role as a consulting body.

The Conclusions further enumerate the legislative measures to be adopted, in order to constitute a Common European Asylum System. This System should include, in the short term:

- a clear and workable determination of the State responsible for the examination of an asylum application;
- common standards for a fair and efficient asylum procedure;
- common minimum conditions of reception of asylum seekers; and
- the approximation of rules on the recognition and content of the refugee status.

It should also be completed with measures on subsidiary forms of protection offering an appropriate status to any person in need of such protection.

---

96. Id., par. 4.
97. Id., par. 11, 12.
98. Id., par. 13.

To that end, the Council is urged to adopt, on the basis of the Commission proposals, the necessary decisions according to the timetable set in the Treaty of Amsterdam and the Vienna Action Plan.[99]

Paragraph 15 states that in the longer term, the Community *rules* 'should lead to a common asylum procedure and a uniform status for those who are granted asylum valid throughout the Union'.[100] In paragraph 16 of the Tampere Conclusions, the European Council acknowledged a need for an instrument on temporary protection in cases of a mass influx of refugees and displaced persons. The temporary protection and the subsidiary protection are viewed separately, which should be appreciated, since they are aimed at different situations and therefore also require different regimes.[101] The European Council called for a prompt finalisation of the system for identification of asylum seekers (Eurodac).[102]

Conclusions made in regards to the fair treatment of TCNs legally residing in the territory of the EU Member States call for a more vigorous integration policy.[103] Although not expressly mentioned in the text of the Tampere Conclusions, it is reasonable that refugees whose status has been recognised should also have access to rights comparable to those of EU citizens, as do other legally residing TCNs. Paragraph 18 read together with paragraph 2 should provide for the right to free movement within the Union for recognised refugees.

Regarding the management of migration flows, the European Council stressed the importance of the effective control of the Union's future external borders by specialised trained professionals and called for a closer cooperation and mutual technical assistance between the Member States border control services.[104] Taking into consideration the strong commitment to asylum stated in paragraphs 3, 4 and 13 of the Tampere Conclusions, it could be assumed that the management of migration flows should also include means to allow access to international protection, *vis-à-vis* measures taken at the EU external borders, which might infringe the right to seek asylum. This could mean a reconsideration of visa regimes and other immigration controls from a refugee protection perspective.

The European Council further required assistance to the countries of origin and transit. Such assistance should be developed in order to promote voluntary returns as well as to help the authorities of those countries to strengthen their ability to

99. Id., par. 14.

100. In order to report on the developments made, the European Council called for the Commission to prepare a communication on this matter. See Communication from the Commission to the Council and the European Parliament 'Towards a common asylum procedure and a uniform status, valid throughout the Union, for persons granted asylum', Brussels, 22.11.2000, COM(2000) 755 final.

101. On temporary protection in the EU further see chapter 2, 2.6.1.; on subsidiary protection 2.4.3.

102. *Tampere*, par. 17.

103. Id., par. 18.

104. Id., par. 22–25.

effectively combat trafficking in human beings and to cope with their readmission obligations towards the EU and the Member States.[105] The aim to provide third countries with aid that can help them for example to stop or at least to decrease a crisis, and by doing so prevent a 'refugee generating' atmosphere, is very constructive.

The Treaty of Amsterdam conferred powers on the European Community in the field of readmission, by giving the Community powers to negotiate a common immigration and asylum policy. In the Tampere Presidency Conclusions the European Council invited the Council to conclude such agreements or to include standard clauses in other agreements between the European Community and third countries or groups of countries concerned.[106] The readmission agreements are important for the sending back of persons who are not legally present on the territory of the EU Member States. A careful distinction should be therefore made between illegal immigrants and asylum seekers.

To sum up, the Tampere Presidency Conclusions gave a political impetus to the EU policy in the areas of asylum and migration and set for the first time the concept of a 'Common European Asylum System'. These Conclusions gave also valuable importance to the right to seek asylum by affirming this right and calling for a full and inclusive application of the 1951 Geneva Convention on Refugees. The fact that the measures regarding the protection of asylum seekers were discussed before the measures on border controls and the measures aimed at stemming illegal immigration may indicate the importance given to this problem.

Another positive observation is that the Tampere Conclusions referred to asylum and immigration policies separately, when dealing with them in different paragraphs (on asylum, legal migration and illegal immigration), though taking into account that they are inter-related areas. The Tampere Conclusions affirmed that asylum is an absolute human right, while migration is seen as being conditioned by socio-economic, demographic, judicial and police cooperation factors. On the other hand, the Conclusions did not clarify how to balance the guarantees to offer protection to those in need of it with the measures to restrain illegal immigration. Therefore there is a risk that access to the territory and to the asylum procedure will be undermined if stringent controls are launched without sufficient guarantees responding to the situation of persons seeking protection.[107]

---

105. Id., par. 26.

106. Id., par. 27.

107. Further see the European Council on Refugees and Exiles (ECRE) Tampere Dossier, June 2000, The Tampere Summit Conclusions – UNHCR's Observations, 86.

1.9 Treaty of Nice (2001)

Only one month after the Treaty of Amsterdam entered into force (1 May 1999), the Cologne European Council summit (3–4 June 1999) called for an IGC, in order to resolve the institutional issues left open in Amsterdam and to ensure that the EU Institutions can continue to work efficiently after the Union's enlargement. In accordance with the Amsterdam 'Protocol on the Institutions with the prospect of enlargement of the EU' and the declarations made with regard to it, the IGC was expected to cover the following topics:

- size and composition of the Commission;
- weighting of votes in the Council (reweighting, introduction of a dual majority; and threshold for qualified-majority decision making);
- possible extension of qualified-majority voting in the Council.[108]

The Treaty of Nice was a result of the IGC and as explained above, it was mainly about institutional changes (composition, size, way of appointment and functioning of the Institutions),[109] preparing the EU Institutions to function in an enlarged Union. The Treaty consists of two parts: the first part containing the substantive amendments to the EU and EC Treaties and the second part containing the transitional and final provisions. The Treaty of Nice was signed on 26 February 2001 and entered into force on 1 February 2003. This Treaty did not introduce any substantial changes in the field of asylum. Nevertheless, it amended the provisions on the decision making in Article 67 TEC by adding a new paragraph (5), introducing the QMV concept in the Council and the codecision with the European Parliament. Under the new provisions of Article 67, the Council may, acting by qualified majority, adopt certain measures on asylum, refugees and displaced persons, immigration policy and the rights of nationals of third countries legally resident in a Member State (Art. 63 TEC), provided that it has previously, acting unanimously, adopted Community legislation defining the common rules and basic principles governing these issues. The introduction of QMV therefore remains subject to these conditions and to the prior definition of common principles in this area.[110]

1.10 Institutional Aspects

Before discussing the EU asylum legislation, the evolving role of the EU Institutions (the Council, the Commission and the European Parliament) in the law-

108. Presidency Conclusions, Cologne European Council, 3–4 June 1999, par. 52–53.

109. On the institutional design in the Treaty of Nice further see, e.g., Bradley, K. St. C.: 'Institutional design in the Treaty of Nice', *Common Market Law Review* 38 (2001) 1095–1124.

110. Treaty of Nice, Art. 2(4), 1st indent.

making procedure (the decision-making procedure) in the field of asylum will be briefly explained. The main purpose of this part is to illustrate the process of changes in the decision making and to show how these changes affected the position of each of the above-mentioned Institutions; as well as the importance given to asylum issues by the Community. The role of the Institutions under the Treaties of Maastricht, Amsterdam and Nice, and most recently under the Council Decision of 22 December 2004 will be discussed. The role of the European Council and the competence of the ECJ in asylum matters will also be referred to.

1.10.1 **Decision making**

1.10.1.1 *Council*

The Council exercises a significant role in the legislative process. Before legislative proposals become law, the Council has to agree on them. Different voting requirements in the Council apply to different issues. The system of voting in the Council is based on the weighting of the votes cast; votes from different Member States have different weight.[111] The outcome thus depends on the voting of the members in the Council (i.e., the Member States' ministers). It is common for the composition of meetings of the Council to be arranged by subject matter with different ministers attending from the Member States. One of the configurations is the JHA Council.[112]

The Treaty of Maastricht, namely Article K.1 TEU, introduced for the first time the asylum policy in the European Treaty text as one of the areas, 'matters of common interest'. Regarding the role of the Council in the legislative process, it could on the initiative of any Member State or the Commission adopt *joint positions*,[113] *joint actions*,[114] in so far as the objectives of the Union could be attained

111. See Art. 205(2) TEC, as amended in accordance with the Protocol on the enlargement of the European Union, adopted at Nice.

112. See Craig, P., Búrca, G. de: *EU Law: Texts, Cases and Materials*, 3rd ed. (Oxford 2003), 65. Some activities of the Council, where the policy aspect of asylum matters is considered, will be further discussed in chapter 4. In this respect where there is a reference to 'the Council', the Justice and Home Affairs Council is referred to.

113. The *joint position* was introduced by the Treaty of Maastricht under the heading of cooperation in the fields of justice and home affairs. The Treaty of Amsterdam retains this instrument in the new Title VI TEU (police and judicial cooperation in criminal matters).
The joint position is a legal instrument enabling the Council to define the Union's approach on any specific issue. Member States are required to give full effect, both domestically and in foreign policy, to decisions adopted unanimously in meetings of the Council. See glossary at www.europa.eu.int.

114. *Joint action* was a legal instrument under former Title VI TEU, used between 1993 and 1999. It meant coordinated action by the Member States on behalf of the Union or within the EU framework in cases where, owing to the scale or effects of the envisaged action, the Union's objectives could be attained more effectively by joint action than by the Member States acting individually. It has been abolished by the Treaty of Amsterdam and replaced by 'decisions' and 'framework decisions'.

better, and draw up *conventions*[115] which it shall recommend to the Member States for adoption. The Council could act *unanimously*, except on matters of procedure and in cases where expressly provided for other voting rules.[116]

The Treaty of Amsterdam introduced the 'communitarisation';[117] as a consequence of this, the position of the Community Institutions in the area of asylum was strengthened. During the transitional period of five years following the entry into force of the Treaty of Amsterdam (i.e., until 1 May 2004) the Council acted *unanimously* on a proposal from the Commission or on an initiative of a Member State, after consulting the European Parliament. As from 1 May 2004, the Council has to act on a proposal from the Commission only. Regarding the unanimity requirement, according to the Treaty of Amsterdam, it should stay in place also after the period of five years; although the Council could decide unanimously and after consulting the European Parliament to apply QMV and the codecision procedure.[118] The codecision with the European Parliament, nonetheless, did not apply until the entry into force of the Treaty of Nice.

Although the Treaty of Nice did not bring about any substantial changes in the field of asylum, it amended the provisions on decision making in Article 67 TEC by adding a new paragraph (5). As a result, measures provided for in Article 63(1) and (2)(a)[119] were listed among provisions, which had to be decided upon by a QMV in the Council and by codecision with the European Parliament, instead of the unanimity vote; provided that 'the Council has previously adopted Community legislation defining the common rules and basic principles governing these issues'.[120] The replacing of unanimity voting by QMV proved to be inevitable, taking into account that within the newly enlarged EU of twenty five Member States, it would be very difficult to reach unanimity in the Council. The QMV was established in order to bring more flexibility to the decision-making mechanism in the field of asylum.

By implementing a commitment laid down in the Hague Programme of November 2004, on 22 December 2004 the Council agreed on a Decision (further referred to as the 'Council Decision of 22 December 2004') to change the decision-making procedure to QMV in the Council and codecision with the European

115. See Art. K.3(2) TEU (Maastricht wording).

116. See Art. K.4(3) TEU (Maastricht wording).

117. See chapter 1, 1.7.

118. See Art. 67(2) TEC.

119. These measures include the following areas: criteria and mechanisms for determining which Member State is responsible for considering an application for asylum submitted by a national of a third country in one of the Member States; minimum standards on the reception of asylum seekers; minimum standards with respect to the qualification of nationals of third countries as refugees; minimum standards on procedures in Member States for granting or withdrawing refugee status; minimum standards for giving temporary protection to displaced persons from third countries who cannot return to their country of origin and for persons who otherwise need international protection. The burden-sharing was thus excluded from the QMV.

120. Treaty of Nice, Art. 2(4).

Parliament in all asylum matters. As a consequence, as from 1 January 2005 measures on asylum under Title IV TEC concerning measures on refugees and displaced persons, including burden sharing among Member States, are governed by the procedure set in Article 251 TEC.[121]

Pursuant to Article 68(3) TEC, the Council may request the ECJ to give a ruling on the question of interpretation of Title IV TEC, therefore also the question regarding asylum, or of acts of the Institutions of the Community based on this Title.

1.10.1.2 *Commission*

The European Commission (Commission) plays a unique and significant role in the legislative process through its right of initiative.[122] The evolution of the legislative initiative power of the Commission in the field of asylum will now be examined.

According to the Treaty of Maastricht, the first subparagraph of Article K.3(2) TEU, the Commission shared its legislative initiative power in the area of asylum with the Member States. The Commission could prepare proposals for the new legislative acts in this area and submit them to the Council. This indicates that even before the 'communitarisation' took place, the Commission already played a role in the field of asylum. For that reason alone one could say that the character of the third pillar was not purely intergovernmental.

As already mentioned, the Treaty of Amsterdam provided for two different regimes (one applying during the five-year transitional period and the other one applying after this period). During the transitional period the Commission shared the legislative initiative with the Member States. After the transitional period, which expired on 1 May 2004, it is exclusively the Commission, on whose proposals the Council would act in the area of asylum law. Nevertheless, the Commission shall examine any request made by a Member State.[123] This suggests that the European asylum law became fully a Community matter, as far as the legislative initiative is concerned.

Neither the Treaty of Nice nor the 'Council Decision of 22 December 2004' introduced any changes in reference to the Commission's role in the field of asylum.

121. See Council Decision of 22 December 2004 providing for certain areas covered by Title IV of Part Three of the TEC to be governed by the procedure laid down in Art. 251 of that Treaty, OJ L 396, 31.12.2004, 45. See also Steve Peers, 'A Common European Asylum System by 2010?', EPC Working Paper No. 15: The Hague Programme – Strengthening Freedom, Security and Justice in the EU, February 2005, 37.

122. On the powers of the Commission see, e.g., Craig, P., Búrca, G. de: *EU Law: Texts, Cases and Materials,* 3rd ed. (Oxford 2003), 59–65.

123. Art. 67(1), (2) TEC.

The Commission may also request the ECJ to give a ruling on the question of interpretation of Title IV TEC or of acts of the Institutions of the Community based on this Title.

1.10.1.3 *European Parliament*

The changing position of the European Parliament (the Parliament) in the decision making in the field of asylum is a good example of how the influence of an Institution can increase in the course of time.

According to the Treaty of Maastricht, Article K.6 TEU, the Presidency and the Commission had to regularly inform the European Parliament of discussions in the areas covered by Title VI TEU, and therefore also in asylum matters. The Presidency also had to consult the Parliament on the principal aspects of activities in the areas referred to in Title VI TEU and ensure that the views of the Parliament were duly taken into consideration. The Parliament could ask questions to the Council or make recommendations to it. Each year, it would hold a debate on the progress made in implementation of the areas under Title VI TEU. Taking into account that the Parliament is the only directly elected EU Institution, its position in accordance with the Treaty of Maastricht was very weak, consisting only of the right to be informed and consulted. Likewise, Parliament's opinions did not have a binding character.

During the transitional period of five years, following the entry into force of the Treaty of Amsterdam, the Parliament had to be formally consulted by the Council in the legislative procedure.[124] After the transitional period, the codecision procedure, typical for the Community pillar, could apply to all or parts of the areas covered by the new Title IV TEC. The Council could take such decision acting unanimously after consulting the European Parliament.[125] Nevertheless, such a decision was not taken until the negotiations on the Treaty of Nice.

The Treaty of Nice introduced the codecision procedure for the adoption of measures provided for in Article 63(1) and (2)(a) TEC if the Council has previously adopted Community legislation defining the common rules and basic principles governing these issues.[126] Codecision between the Council and the Parliament was thus introduced for asylum matters (except for burden sharing), meaning that if the Parliament refuses a proposal, the Council cannot approve it on its own. This step considerably improved the position of the Parliament in the field of asylum.

As a consequence of the Council Decision of 22 December 2004, also burden sharing among Member States concerning measures on refugees and displaced

---

124. Art. 67(1) TEC.
125. Art. 67(2) TEC.
126. Art. 67(5) TEC.

persons,[127] which was set aside the codecision procedure by the Treaty of Nice, is now decided by the codecision procedure.

1.10.2 European Council

The brief outline of the evolving role of the EU Institutions in the specific decision-making procedure that applies to asylum matters has illustrated the institutional and procedural aspects of the evolution of asylum legislation at EU level. In this context the role of the European Council has to be briefly referred to, since it is also active in the area of JHA.

The European Council was established at the second Paris Summit on 9–10 December 1974. The establishment of the European Council in fact meant the institutionalisation of the European Summits. The first mention of the European Council within a Treaty came in the SEA; and its position is now set out in Article 4 TEU. Despite the fact that the European Council does not participate in the formal decision-making process, it does make political statements and determines broad policy lines. The conclusions reached by the European Council will provide the framework within which the other Institutions will consider more specific actions.[128] For example the European Council that took place in Tampere in October 1999, agreed on the Conclusions that provided the framework for the Common European Asylum System.[129]

1.10.3 Court of Justice

The ECJ had no jurisdiction on questions regarding asylum under the Treaty of Maastricht. The jurisdiction of the ECJ was effectively excluded from the entire third pillar by the terms of Article L TEU. Member States were only permitted by Article K.3(2)(c) TEU to confer interpretative jurisdiction on the ECJ with respect to conventions, recommended by the Council to the Member States for adoption. This provision did not apply to *joint positions* or *joint actions* adopted under the same Article.[130]

When the Treaty of Amsterdam came into force, the full jurisdiction of the ECJ[131] has been extended to the matters under the new Title IV TEC; save the

127. Art. 63(2)(b) TEC.

128. See Kapteyn, P.J.G., VerLoren van Themaat, P.: *Introduction to the Law of the European Communities*, 3rd ed. (London, The Hague, Boston 1998), 182–186; Craig, P., Búrca, G. de: *EU Law: Text, Cases and Materials*, 3rd ed. (Oxford 2003), 71–75; see also Art. 4 TEU.

129. In chapter 4 other selected European Council Conclusions will be discussed together with other general policy instruments related to the Common European Asylum System.

130. Further see Fennelly, N.: 'The area of "freedom, security and justice" and the European Court of Justice – a personal view', *International and Comparative Law Quarterly* 49 (January 2000) 1–14.

131. See Arts. 226–243 TEC.

preliminary rulings jurisdiction under Article 234 TEC.[132] This 'standard' preliminary rulings jurisdiction is limited by the provisions of Article 68 TEC. Compared to Article 234 TEC, Article 68 TEC limits the preliminary ruling procedure to requests made by the courts or tribunals of the Member States 'against whose decisions there is no judicial remedy under national law' (i.e., supreme or last instance courts).[133] But it is well known that the difficulties of interpretation are raised mainly before the first-instance courts. This implies that the individual has to lodge appeals until the last instance in order to request that a question of interpretation (or validity) be put to the ECJ. This is particularly problematic in cases like asylum, where speedy legal proceedings are crucial. Moreover, the jurisdiction of the ECJ is excluded from measures related to the maintenance of law and order and the safeguarding of internal security (control of persons crossing internal borders).[134]

The Treaty of Nice amended Article 220 TEC by introducing *judicial panels*, which may be attached to the Court of First Instance in order to exercise, 'in certain specific areas', the judicial competence laid down in the TEC. The Treaty of Nice also inserted a new Article 225a to the TEC concerning their creation; nonetheless, the areas have not been specified. Regarding asylum cases, the future will show whether these judicial panels would also be created to hear and determine at first instance specific actions brought in asylum matters. This could speed up the legal proceedings, currently decelerated as a consequence of the application of Article 68 TEC.

1.11 Conclusions

The establishment of the *internal market* has as a consequence the gradual abolishment of the checks on persons at the common internal borders between the

132. Art. 234 TEC provides the Court of Justice with the jurisdiction to give preliminary rulings concerning the interpretation of this Treaty; the validity and interpretation of acts of the Institutions of the Community; and the interpretation of the statuses of bodies established by an act of the Council (when those statuses so provide). If such a question arises before any court or tribunal of a Member State, that court or tribunal *may* request the Court of Justice to give a ruling thereon if it considers that a decision on the question is necessary to enable it to give judgement. However, when any such question is in a case pending before a court or tribunal of a Member State, against whose decisions there is no judicial remedy under national law, that court or tribunal *shall* bring the matter before the Court of Justice.

133. On the Court's lacking jurisdiction to give a preliminary ruling see for example Order of the Court of 10 June 2004, in case *Magali Warbecq v Ryanair Ltd.* (C-555/03).

134. In the final report to the European Convention (CONV 426/02) the Working Group X 'Freedom, Security and Justice' considered that the specific mechanisms foreseen in Arts. 35 TEU (which limit the jurisdiction of the ECJ in giving preliminary rulings in reference to the provisions on police and judicial cooperation in criminal matters) and 68 TEC should be abolished. Accordingly, the general system of jurisdiction of the Court of Justice should be extended to the area of freedom, security and justice, including action by Union bodies in this field.

Member States, achieved by the cooperation within Schengen. The 'opening' of the internal borders inevitably brought about the introduction of common measures on strengthening the external borders of the Union. The main purpose of such measures clearly was, on the one hand, to enable the free movement of persons within the Community and, on the other hand, to prevent illegal immigration.

The internal market is viewed as a major component of a shared area of prosperity and peace.[135] The Treaty of Amsterdam introduced an additional concept, namely the area of freedom, security and justice. The Vienna Action Plan provided for a working programme for the implementation the area of freedom, security and justice. The Tampere European Council gave political importance to asylum matters and reaffirmed the full commitment of the EU to the obligations of the 1951 Geneva Convention by reaffirming the significance that the Union and the Member States attach to the absolute respect of the right to seek asylum.

The *raison d'etre* of the Common European Asylum System can be traced back to the concept of the internal market and the consequences of the Schengen *acquis* implementation. The strengthening of the external borders required a counterweight, as it were, in order to continue carrying out the obligations entailed by the 1951 Geneva Convention at the EU level. The establishment of a Common European Asylum System was the next logical step to take. The introduction of the concept of an area of freedom, security and justice next to the internal market could not be realised without common policies. Immigration and asylum are, for obvious reasons, integral components of policies on security and justice; therefore common policies on asylum and immigration were needed in the EU.

If one looks at the evolution of the role of the EU Institutions in the legislative procedure concerning asylum matters, one can see how the Member States gradually lost their power to propose EU legislation in this area. Although the Commission has to examine any request made by a Member State to submit a proposal to the Council, the Member States' influence on EU asylum legislation has been weakened. Moreover, by replacing the unanimity voting in the Council by the QMV, and the introduction of the codecision procedure with the European Parliament, asylum became clearly a Community matter. Regrettably, the preliminary rulings jurisdiction of the ECJ in Title IV TEC is still limited, in comparison to other areas of the Community pillar.

The following chapter illustrates the EU asylum legislation, as adopted according to the 'time-table' introduced by the Treaty of Amsterdam. The 'working programme' taken from Article 63(1) and (2) TEC will be used to provide an order to the developments of the legislation on asylum at the EU level.

135. *Tampere*, par. 2.

Chapter 2

EU LEGISLATION ON ASYLUM

'The European Council is determined to develop the Union as an area of freedom, security and justice by making full use of the possibilities offered by the Treaty of Amsterdam. The European Council sends a strong political message to reaffirm the importance of this objective and has agreed on a number of policy orientations and priorities which will speedily make this area a reality.'[136]

2.1 Introduction

According to the Tampere Presidency Conclusions, a Common European Asylum System was to include, in the short term, a clear and workable determination of the State responsible for the examination of an asylum application, common standards for a fair and efficient asylum procedure, common minimum conditions of reception of asylum seekers and the approximation of rules on the recognition and content of the refugee status.[137] Having regard to Title IV of the TEC, in particular Article 63(1) and (2) thereof, the Council's task was to adopt, before 1 May 2004, measures on:

- criteria and mechanisms for determining which Member State is responsible for considering an application for asylum submitted by a national of a third country in one of the Member States (Art. 63(1)(a));
- minimum standards on the reception of asylum seekers in Member States (Art. 63(1)(b));
- minimum standards with respect to the qualification of nationals of third countries as refugees (Art. 63(1)(c));
- minimum standards on procedures in Member States for granting or withdrawing refugee status (Art. 63(1)(d));
- minimum standards for giving temporary protection to displaced persons from third countries who cannot return to their country of origin and for persons who otherwise need international protection (Art. 63(2)(a)); and on
- promoting a balance of effort between Member States in receiving and bearing the consequences of receiving refugees and displaced persons (Art. 63(2)(b)).

The asylum legislation adopted pursuant to Title IV TEC will be discussed and evaluated. The main evaluation criteria will be the Tampere Conclusions, requir-

136. *Tampere*, the Preamble.
137. Id., par. 14.

ing the setting up of a Common European Asylum System. The EU legislation on asylum discussed in this chapter consists of the 'Dublin II' Regulation, the Reception Directive, the Qualification Directive, the Asylum Procedures Directive and the Temporary Protection Directive. In addition, two other directives are evaluated here (the Family Reunification Directive and the Directive on long-term residents), taking into consideration their relevance to the position of asylum seekers and refugees.

The legislation will be compared, where appropriate, with the draft legislation (the Commission proposals) or earlier legal instruments. Through this comparison, the direction which the Common European Asylum System is taking will be examined.

2.2 Responsible Member State

'This (Common European Asylum) System should include, in the short term, a clear and workable determination of the State responsible for the examination of an asylum application, ...[138]

The Dublin Convention of 1990 was the first attempt to set a standard in appointing only one Member State responsible for examining an application for asylum lodged in the territory of the EU.[139] As discussed in the previous chapter, this cooperation took place outside the Community legal framework. Although often criticised for its drawbacks, the willingness to co-operate in this area is certainly a positive feature. The implementation of the Dublin Convention stimulated the process of harmonising asylum policies of the Member States. On 18 February 2003, on the basis of Article 63(1)(a) TEC the Council adopted the so-called 'Dublin II' Regulation, replacing the 1990 Dublin Convention.[140]

As mentioned in chapter 1, the Dublin Convention will be further evaluated in this chapter, in order to more clearly illustrate the link between this convention and the 'Dublin II' Regulation. The same set of evaluation criteria will be applied to both instruments, to clarify whether the shortcomings of the 1990 Dublin Convention were improved in the 2003 Community instrument.

---

138. *Tampere*, par. 14.

139. On the Dublin Convention see also chapter 1, 1.5.

140. Council Regulation (EC) 343/2003, OJ L 50, 25.2.2003, 1, establishing the criteria and mechanisms for determining the Member State responsible for examining an asylum application lodged in one of the Member States by a third-country national entered into force on 25 February 2003. It should be noted that on 19 January 2001 the European Community concluded an agreement with the Republic of Iceland and the Kingdom of Norway concerning the criteria and mechanisms for establishing the State responsible for examining a request for asylum lodged in a Member State or in Iceland or Norway (OJ L 93, 3.4.2001, 40); and a Protocol to the above-mentioned Agreement (OJ L 57, 28.2.2006, 15); see *supra* 47.

2.2.1 Evaluation of the Dublin Convention

The Dublin Convention did not lay down any monitoring or evaluation standards. Some of the principles and objectives set by this convention, as well as statistics made by the Member States, will be used as the evaluation criteria for this study. The following objectives were chosen, since they reliably portray the central goals to be achieved by the Dublin Convention and also by the 'Dublin II' Regulation:

- to prevent asylum applicants from being able to pursue multiple asylum applications in different Member States (either concurrently or consecutively);
- to ensure that applicants for asylum are not referred successively from one Member State to the other without any of these States acknowledging itself to be competent to examine the application for asylum, i.e., to avoid the cases of the so-called 'refugees in orbit';
- to take measures to avoid any situations arising where applicants for asylum are left in doubt for too long as regards the likely outcome of their applications;
- to maintain the unity of families and to reunite separated families;
- to ensure a fair distribution of asylum applicants between the Member States, in proportion to each Member State's capacity to receive asylum applicants.

First, the success of the Dublin Convention in *preventing multiple asylum applications* will be examined. The Dublin Convention was generally regarded as an instrument designed to determine the State responsible for examining applications for asylum lodged in one of the Member States. As previously mentioned, in the Dublin Convention one has to distinguish the responsibility criteria and the readmission criteria. The purpose of the readmission criteria clearly was to prevent a person from pursuing multiple asylum applications, either concurrently or consecutively, in different Member States. This was in line with the principle that a case should be dealt with by one State only. In order to assess the proportion of the total number of multiple applications successfully identified and dealt with under the Dublin Convention, Eurodac[141] could make a convincing decisive contribution. In due course, it should provide proof of a previous asylum application in another Member State (although the system will only become fully effective after several years of operation). Even though it is not possible to evaluate the extent to which the Dublin Convention deterred multiple asylum applications in the past, it is reasonable to assume that the introduction of Eurodac will increase the deterrent effect.[142] The readmission rules (between the Member States themselves) proved necessary and Eurodac should make it possible to identify all cases in which they

141. On Eurodac see *supra* 52.

142. During the first year of its activity, Eurodac detected 7% of multiple asylum applications (in 17,287 cases of the total number of asylum applications). Source: Commission Press Room of 5 May 2004 (www.europa.eu.int).

could be applied.[143] From a total of 246,902 asylum applications recorded by Eurodac in the first year of operations, in 17,287 cases the same person already made at least one asylum application (in the same country or in another Member State). In other words, in 7% of cases, national asylum authorities were confronted with a multiple application. The Eurodac Central Unit has registered a high number of multiple hits (i.e., two or more hits). For instance, in 1,632 cases, a third application was registered.[144] There is not much evidence available from the Member States on proving to which extent the Dublin Convention contributed to the prevention of multiple asylum applications. Nonetheless, it is clear that there is a need for a common approach in order to prevent multiple asylum applications.

Second, the achievement of the Dublin Convention in avoiding the cases of so-called 'refugees in orbit' (applicants for asylum referred successively from one State to another, without any of these States acknowledging itself to be competent to examine their application for asylum) will be now examined. Since there is a reference to this problem in the Preamble to the Dublin Convention, a solution of this problem can be considered as one of the convention's fundamental goals. The hierarchy of the responsibility criteria in the Dublin Convention guaranteed that one of the Member States had to accept responsibility to examine an asylum application. This was expected to ensure that the phenomenon of 'refugees in orbit' between the Member States would no longer occur. It was therefore a comprehensive solution only among the EU Member States, however, disregarding the whole scope of the phenomenon (refugee in orbit) occurring further outside the EU borders. In this respect the provision laid down in Article 3(5) of the Dublin Convention should be mentioned, according to which the Member States retain their right to send an asylum applicant to a third country.[145] As regards this provision, another problem could arise in cases where the Member State to which a transfer request was made would apply the safe third country concept whilst the requesting State did not consider this third country safe for the applicant.

The 1992 'Resolution on a harmonised approach to questions concerning host third countries'[146] deals with the relationship between the Dublin Convention and the safe third country concept, however, in practice it did not prevent the above-mentioned problem to arise. The Resolution states that the Member State in which the asylum application has been lodged will examine whether or not the principle

143. 'Revisiting the Dublin Convention' (see supra 48), par. 22.

144. Commission staff working paper 'First Annual Report to the Council and the European Parliament on the activities of the Eurodac Central Unit', SEC(2004) 557, 12 and Annex III.

145. Art. 3(5) reads: 'Any Member State shall retain the right, pursuant to its national laws, to send an applicant for asylum to a third State, in compliance with the provisions of the Geneva Convention, as amended by the New York Protocol.'

146. Resolution of 30 November and 1 December 1992 of the ministers of the Member States of the EC responsible for immigration on a harmonised approach to questions concerning host third countries, SN 4823/92 WGI 1283 AS 147. The term 'host third country' is apparently used as a synonym of 'safe third country'. On the terminology and the 'safe third country' concept see chapter 2, 2.5.3.

of the host third country can be applied. If that State decides to apply the principle, it will start the procedures necessary for sending the asylum applicant to the host third country before considering whether or not to transfer responsibility for examining the application for asylum to another Member State pursuant to the Dublin Convention.[147] A Member State may not refuse responsibility for examining an application for asylum, pursuant to the Dublin Convention, by claiming that the requesting Member State should have returned the applicant to a safe third country. Notwithstanding the above, the Member State responsible for examining the application would retain the right, pursuant to its national laws, to send an applicant for asylum to a host third country.[148] This gave rise to concerns in some Member States about so-called 'chain refoulement', and it is only one of a number of examples which illustrate that if a mechanism for allocating responsibility for asylum applicants is to operate effectively, it must be accompanied by common standards in procedural and substantive areas of asylum law.[149]

Third, the effectiveness of the Dublin Convention in *preventing cases where asylum seekers were left in doubt for too long* regarding the outcome of their applications will be examined. This objective was also mentioned in the Preamble to the Dublin Convention. A workable system of speedy asylum procedures should be a due aim of the whole Common European Asylum System. It does not seem realistic to achieve this aim solely by an instrument concerned with criteria and mechanisms for allocating responsibility for considering asylum applications. The speed of an asylum system further depends on the efficiency of the substantive asylum rules, based on the national laws of the Member States. Although the determination of responsibility for asylum applications between the Member States is only a preliminary step in the whole asylum system, it is necessary that the allocation of responsibility is done quickly.[150] The Dublin Convention has been frequently criticised for operating too slowly in practice. For example the statistics provided by the Member States indicate that the average time for responding to a transfer request frequently exceeded the target of one month set down in Article 4(1) of Decision 1/97.[151] With respect to some Member States the average delay was as much as 90 days, which is the maximum allowed under Article 11(4) of the Dublin Convention, before the State to which the request was made was automatically deemed to have accepted responsibility.[152]

---

147. Id., par. 3 (a).

148. Id., par. 3 (b)–(d). These provisions did not prejudice the application of Art. 3(4) and Art. 9 of the Dublin Convention by the Member State in which the application for asylum was lodged.

149. Commission working paper 'Towards Common Standards on Asylum Procedure', SEC (1999) 271 final, par. 14.

150. 'Revisiting the Dublin Convention', par. 14.

151. Decision 1/97 of 9 September 1997 of the Committee set up by Art. 18 of the Dublin Convention of 15 June 1990 ('Art. 18 Committee') concerning provisions on implementation of the Convention, OJ L 281, 14.10.1997, 1. Decision 1/97 was supplemented by Decision No. 1/98 of 30 June 1998, OJ L 196, 14.7.1998, 49.

152. 'Revisiting the Dublin Convention', par. 15.

Little was done to encourage Member States to make any request to a second Member State to take charge of an applicant under Article 11(1) of the Dublin Convention[153] at the earliest possible moment, or to facilitate this. Moreover, the Dublin Convention itself does not lay down any time limit within which a Member State must reply to a request for information made under Article 15 of the Convention. Decision 1/97 simply instructs the Member State concerned to 'make every effort' to reply to the request if possible immediately and in any case within one month.[154]

It is essential that the system for determining which Member State is responsible for considering an asylum application lodged in one of the Member States operates quickly. This is necessary in order to provide certainty for both asylum applicants and the Member States. Taking into account what has been said in the previous paragraphs, it shows that the legal instrument replacing the Dublin Convention should improve the situation under the Dublin Convention.

The following discussion examines if the Dublin Convention was successful in *maintaining the unity of families* and in the *reunification of separated families*. Article 4 was designed to ensure family reunification and to maintain family unity in cases where the asylum applicant had an immediate family member, recognised as a refugee, and legally residing in one of the Member States. On the other hand, there was no objective criterion ensuring family reunification or maintaining family unity if an asylum applicant had a family member legally residing in one of the Member States who was not a recognised refugee. By limiting family reunification only to cases where the family member was already legally residing in one of the Member States and holding a refugee status, the decisive criterion seems to be the refugee status rather than the family ties.

According to the statistics from the Member States, Article 4 of the Dublin Convention was used very little.[155] This indicates that,

> 'if anything, the family members or refugees residing in the Member States go through the regular channels for bringing families together and that, where this is not the case, there are few (applicants) who have to make out an application for asylum en route in a Member State other than where the refugee resides'.[156]

---

153. Art. 11(1) reads: 'If a Member State with which an application for asylum has been lodged considers that another Member State is responsible for examining the application, it may, as quickly as possible and in any case within the six months following the date on which the application was lodged, call upon the other Member State to take charge of the applicant.
If the request that charge be taken is not made within the six-month time limit, responsibility for examining the application for asylum shall rest with the State in which the application was lodged.'

154. Revisiting the Dublin Convention, par. 16.

155. In two years it has concerned 1 case out of 286 in Portugal; 16 out of 961 in Belgium; 20 out of 295 in the United Kingdom and 64 out of 1464 in the Netherlands. Further see Commission staff working paper 'Evaluation of the Dublin Convention of 13 June 2001', SEC(2001) 756, 5.

156. Commission staff working paper 'Evaluation of the Dublin Convention of 13 June 2001', SEC(2001) 756, 5.

More precise and binding rules on the right to family reunification should be adopted, in order to improve the operation of the Dublin Convention. Having mentioned the necessity of the binding character of the rules on the right to family reunification, reference should be made to Articles 3(4) and 9 of the Dublin Convention.[157] These provisions could be used to maintain family groups and to reunite families in a much wider range of cases, at the discretion of a Member State. This gap in the Dublin Convention created problems in its practical application.[158]

The following paragraphs focus on the Dublin Convention *ensuring a fair distribution of asylum applications* between the Member States, in proportion to each Member State's capacity to receive asylum applicants. The Dublin system did not operate on the basis that each Member State would take responsibility for a fixed proportion of the total numbers of asylum applicants. It was therefore criticised in some quarters on the grounds that it put a too great burden on Member States which have external borders and are particularly exposed to migratory pressures.[159] A well-balanced system of burden sharing among the Member States is an important component of a fair Common European Asylum System. The system of burden sharing consists of two main elements: a financial burden sharing and a physical burden sharing (i.e., distribution of asylum applications within the EU). The financial aspect will be further discussed in relation to the European Refugee Fund (ERF).[160]

The aspect of the physical burden sharing seems to be more problematic than the financial aspect. It concerns a more complex involvement of the authorities of each Member State responsible for examining asylum applications (and also for further care of those granted asylum in that Member State), than 'just' the financial contribution. This aspect of burden sharing very much depends on the evidence gathered (travel tickets, passports, identity cards). This evidence is to demonstrate which Member State is responsible for a person's presence in the territory of the Member States.[161] The difficulty, however, arises in cases where the documentary evidence was destroyed in order to hide evidence of unauthorised entry. In cases

> 'where there is indicative evidence only, there is disagreement about how to treat it. The results appeared to be that in the great majority of cases, the Member State in which the

157. See also Decision No. 1/2000 of 31 October 2000 of the Committee set up by Art. 18 of the Dublin Convention concerning the transfer of responsibility for family members in accordance with Art. 3(4) and Art. 9 of that Convention, OJ L 281, 7.11.2000, 1.

158. 'Evaluation of the Dublin Convention', 5 (see *supra* 155).

159. 'Revisiting the Dublin Convention', par. 35.

160. On the financial burden-sharing (the European Refugee Fund) see further chapter 2, 2.6.2.1.

161. It should be noted that the criteria under Arts. 4 and 8 of the Dublin Convention have a different character in comparison with Arts. 5, 6 and 7. Arts. 4 and 8 do not determine the Member State's responsibility by basing it on the way of arrival/presence of an asylum seeker in the territory of a Member State. On the criteria laid down in the Dublin Convention see chapter 1, 1.5.

> asylum application was lodged is sooner or later forced to accept responsibility under Article 8 of the Convention'.[162]

According to the statistics, Article 8 of the Dublin Convention was the second most frequently applied criterion. It allocated responsibility in the absence of other criteria to the Member State which received the asylum application first.

Moreover, it seems that the allocation of responsibility to examine asylum applications, according to the Dublin Convention, mostly affected States with external borders. Especially in these cases, the practice showed an increase in the secondary movements of asylum seekers. Asylum seekers often very quickly leave the Member State in which they lodged their first asylum application. This often happens even before the procedure for determining the Member State responsible for examining the substance of the application can begin and without formally withdrawing their application, in order to continue their journey to the Member State where they wish to be.[163]

Aside from the concerns on the functioning of the Dublin Convention analysed above, there are some other issues which the Community legal instrument replacing the Dublin Convention (the 'Dublin II') should rectify. One, for example, concerns the absence of judicial protection. Since this cooperation took place outside the Community legal framework, the ECJ had no jurisdiction to interpret the Dublin Convention or to rule on disputes between the Member States in relation to it. Instead,

> 'the task of examining questions of application was entrusted to the Article 18 Committee, which does [did] not have at its disposal any instruments to ensure that its decisions are [were] applied in a consistent fashion. The Article 18 Committee has not been [was not] able to ensure the uniform application and interpretation of the Dublin Convention in the same way that the Court of Justice ensures the proper application of Community legislation'.[164]

Another concern was that the Dublin Convention applied only to applicants for asylum, who were defined as persons seeking protection under the 1951 Geneva Convention, claiming refugee status within the meaning of Article 1 of the Geneva Convention, as amended by the New York Protocol.[165] As a result, persons granted other forms of protection were indirectly excluded from the scope of the Dublin Convention.

To conclude, one can ask oneself whether it was the slow speed of the procedures or the lack of a common policy which brought about the drawbacks in the

162. 'Revisiting the Dublin Convention', par. 53.
163. 'Evaluation of the Dublin Convention', 4. See also chapter 3, 3.4.5.
164. *Supra* 162, par. 46.
165. Dublin Convention, Art. 1.

functioning of the Dublin system. Presumably if there would be a common system uniting the Member States in solving the problem of distribution of asylum applications and burden sharing, there would be a more coordinated approach expediting the whole procedure. Everything pointed to the need to adopt a new legislation and to have a functioning supervisory body, in order to make the system of determining the responsible Member State more effective.

2.2.2 New hierarchy of criteria

Article 63(1)(a) TEC specifically provides for the adoption of criteria and mechanisms for determining which Member State is responsible for considering an application for asylum submitted by a national of a third country in one of the Member States. The new legal measure, replacing the 1990 Dublin Convention, was given the form of a Council Regulation, known as 'Dublin II'. It is based on the same principles as the Dublin Convention, namely the idea that in the area within which free movement of persons is guaranteed, each Member State is responsible to all the other Member States for its actions or its failure to act concerning the entry and residence of TCNs and it must thus bear the consequences thereof. This approach is also reflected in the criteria for allocating responsibility, the effect of which is strengthened by the hierarchical order in which they shall be applied.

The Member State responsible should be determined on the basis of the situation at the time when the asylum seeker first lodged his/her application with a Member State. Special arrangements apply in cases where the applicant is an unaccompanied minor.[166] Special attention is also paid to family members, according to the principle of family unity.[167] In essence the criteria listed in the 'Dublin II' Regulation are similar to those in the Dublin Convention:[168]

1. Where the asylum seeker is in possession of a valid residence document, the Member State which issued the document is responsible for examining the application for asylum (Art. 9(1)).
2. Where the asylum seeker is in possession of a valid visa, the Member State which issued the visa is responsible for examining the application for asylum, except when the visa was issued when acting for or on a written authorisation of another Member State. In such cases the latter Member State is responsible for examining the application (Art. 9(2)).[169]

166. Dublin II, Art. 6.

167. Id., Arts. 7, 8, 14.

168. Id., Chapter III (Arts. 5–14).

169. However, when a Member State first consults a central authority of another Member State, in particular for security reasons, the latter's reply to the consultation does not constitute a written authorisation within the meaning of this provision.

3. In cases when the asylum seeker holds more than one valid residence document or visa issued by different Member States, the responsibility for examining the application for asylum is undertaken by the Member State in the following order:
   In the first place the responsibility lies with the Member State which issued the residence document conferring the right to the longest period of residency. When the periods of validity are identical, the Member State which issued the residence document having the latest expiry date is responsible.
   When the various visas are of the same type, the Member State which issued the visa having the latest expiry date has the responsibility.[170] In cases when there are visas of different types, the Member State which issued the visa having the longest period of validity is responsible for examining the application for asylum. This does not hold true in cases where their periods of validity are identical. Then the responsibility lies on the Member State which issued the visa having the latest expiry date (Art. 9(3)).
4. Where the asylum seeker is in the possession of one or more residence documents which have expired less than two years before or one or more visas which have expired less that six months before, and which enabled him actually to enter the territory of a Member State, the same criteria apply as in the three cases mentioned above. This is true unless the applicant has left the territory of the Member State(s) (Art. 9(4)).
5. Where the asylum seeker is in possession of one or more residence documents which have expired more than two years before or one or more visas which have expired more than six months before, and enabled him to enter the territory of a Member State – in cases when the applicant has not left the territories of the Member States – the Member State in which the application is lodged is responsible[171] (Art. 9(5)).
6. Where it is proved that an asylum seeker has irregularly crossed the border into a Member State by land, sea or air having come from a third country, the Member State entered in this manner is responsible for examining the application for asylum. This responsibility will cease twelve months after the date on which the irregular border crossing took place (Art. 10(1)).[172]

---

170. The 'Dublin II' Regulation distinguishes between and defines four types of visas: long-stay visa, short-stay visa, transit visa and airport transit visa (Art. 2).

171. The fact that a residence document or visa were issued on the basis of a false or presumed identity or on submission of forged, counterfeit or invalid documents, shall not prevent responsibility being allocated to the Member State which issued it. Nevertheless, the Member State issuing the residence document or visa is not responsible if it can prove that fraud was committed after the document or visa had been issued.

172. Problems which are likely to arise with this criterion concern the evidence and proof of the irregular crossings, as well as the exact date of the irregular crossing essential for counting the time limits of twelve months set by the 'Dublin II' Regulation.

7. When a Member State cannot or can no longer be held responsible – in accordance with the previous criterion – that the asylum seeker, who has entered the territories of the Member States irregularly or whose circumstances of entry cannot be established, at the time of lodging the application has been previously living for a continuous period of at least five months in a Member State, that Member State is responsible for examining the application for asylum (Art. 10(2)).
8. If the applicant has been living for periods of time of at least five months in several Member States, the Member State where he stayed most recently is responsible for examining the application (Art. 10 (2)).
9. Where entering the 'Dublin area' by a Member State for which the third-country-national does not need a visa, this State is responsible for examining the application for asylum (Art. 11).
10. If an application for asylum is made in an international transit area of an airport of a Member State by a TCN, that Member State is responsible for examining the application (Art. 12).
11. Where no Member State responsible for examining the application for asylum can be designated on the basis of the criteria listed in this Regulation, the first Member State with which the application for asylum was lodged is responsible for examining it (Art. 13).[173]

2.2.3 Evaluation of the 'Dublin II' Regulation

The purpose of this Regulation is to lay down in Community law criteria and mechanisms for determining the Member State responsible for examining an asylum application, which create mutual rights and obligations between the Member States.[174] These rights and obligations cannot be created by the Member States acting in isolation and can, in view of the scope and effects of this measure, be better achieved at Community level.[175] 'Dublin II' was designed to replace an instrument of public international law (the Dublin Convention). The instrument which meets these conditions in the Community law is a *regulation,* which according to Article 249 TEC shall have general application and shall be binding in its entirety and directly applicable in all Member States. Referring to the direct applicability in *all* Member States, there is, however, a discrepancy: Title IV TEC is not applicable in the United Kingdom and Ireland, unless these countries decide otherwise, pursuant to the provisions set out in the Protocol on the position of the United Kingdom and Ireland attached to the Treaties (TEC, TEU). Pursuant to the

173. In addition, another criterion has been established according to Art. 18 of the Temporary Protection Directive (2001/55/EC): the Member State responsible for considering an asylum application submitted by a person enjoying temporary protection shall be the Member State which has accepted his transfer into its territory.

174. Dublin II, Art. 1.

175. Id., Preamble, par. 16.

Protocol on the position of Denmark attached to the Treaties, Title IV TEC does not apply to Denmark either.

According to the Preamble to the 'Dublin II' Regulation (par. 17 and 18), the United Kingdom and Ireland gave notice of their wish to take part in the adoption and application of this Regulation. Denmark, on the other hand, did not take part in the adoption and was not bound by the Regulation or subject to its application. The Dublin Convention still applied between Denmark and the other EU Member States, as well as between Denmark and Iceland and Norway. It should be noted that the situation has changed after the conclusion of an agreement between the European Community and the Kingdom of Denmark extending to Denmark the provisions of the 'Dublin II' Regulation.[176] As a result, the provisions of 'Dublin II' together with its implementing measures shall apply to the relations between the European Community and Denmark under international law.

In comparison to the Dublin Convention, the 'Dublin II' Regulation comprises some additional criteria governing the Member States' responsibility; however the fundamental change is that this new legal instrument was adopted within the Community legal framework. The control mechanisms are therefore different from those under the Dublin Convention. Moreover, this Regulation, by being a Community legal instrument, is also closely interrelated with other Community instruments on asylum law (especially asylum procedures). By applying this Regulation, it should be more feasible to achieve coherency within the Common European Asylum System.[177]

The same set of objectives as used to evaluate the Dublin Convention, were used for the Dublin II Regulation, in order to evaluate whether the Dublin II redressed the shortcomings of the Dublin Convention.[178] The following observations are the result of this evaluation:

One of the objectives set by the Proposal for the 'Dublin II' Regulation[179] was to *prevent the abuse of asylum procedures in the form of multiple applications* submitted simultaneously or successively by the same person in several Member

176. See Council Decision of 21 February 2006 on the conclusion of the Agreement between the European Community and the Kingdom of Denmark extending to Denmark the provisions of Council Regulation (EC) No. 343/2003 establishing the criteria and mechanisms for determining the Member State responsible for examining an asylum application lodged in one of the Member States by a third-country national and Council Regulation (EC) No. 2725/2000 concerning the establishment of Eurodac for the comparison of fingerprints for the effective application of the Dublin Convention, OJ L 66, 8.3.2006, 37.

177. To give an example on the links that exist between the Community instruments dealing with asylum procedures, Art. 4(1) of the 'Dublin II' Regulation states that the process of determining the Member State responsible under this Regulation shall start as soon as an application for asylum is first lodged with a Member State. This procedure should be therefore understood as an admissibility procedure, in conformity with the Asylum Procedures Directive, since it precedes the examination of the substance of the application for asylum and should be therefore started as soon as the application is submitted. On the Asylum Procedures Directive (OJ L 326, 13.12.2005, 13) see chapter 2, 2.5.

178. See chapter 2, 2.2.1.

179. COM(2001) 447 final, 26.7.2001.

States with the sole aim of extending his/her stay in the EU. There are two possible ways how a procedure for determining the responsible Member State can be prolonged: multiple applications lodged by one asylum seeker and multiple examinations of an asylum application successively by several Member States. As far as the latter case is concerned, it can occur when a Member State makes use of its discretionary power to examine an asylum application lodged with it by a TCN, even though it is not responsible under the criteria laid down in this Regulation. Since this Member State becomes the State responsible within the meaning of the 'Dublin II' Regulation and assumes all the obligations associated with such responsibility, it has to inform the other Member States concerned. Otherwise it could happen that examination of an application is carried out simultaneously in two Member States. This can happen without any fault on the applicant's side, but as a result of the application of the 'sovereignty clause'. One innovation in this respect is that the asylum seeker's consent with the examination of his/her case by a Member State that is not responsible under the hierarchy of criteria is not required.

Still another case which could lead to multiple examinations of an asylum application successively by several Member States can arise as a consequence of the expiry of time limits, whereby the responsibility of a Member State is ended or where responsibility is assigned to the Member State on whose territory the asylum seeker is present.[180]

Taking all this into consideration, it can be concluded that the 'Dublin II' Regulation has not completely rectified the drawbacks of the Dublin Convention, regarding multiple applications lodged by asylum seekers or multiple examinations of these applications successively by several Member States. An effective prevention of multiple examinations of asylum applications does not depend entirely on the legislation in force. Efficient implementation of the legislation, as well as cooperation among the Member States (including mutual exchange of information) plays a significant role.

The Dublin Convention aimed to end the cases of the so-called 'refugees in orbit'. However, it did not manage to prevent such cases occurring outside the EU since a clear interpretation of the concept of a 'safe third country' was lacking at the time, what could increase the risk of generating this phenomenon.[181]

The diction of Article 3(5) of the Dublin Convention and of Article 3(3) of the 'Dublin II' Regulation regarding the Member States' retaining the right to send an asylum seeker to a third country (pursuant to their national laws and in compliance with the provisions of the 1951 Geneva Convention) is almost identical. A

180. For example Art. 10 of the 'Dublin II' Regulation lays down that the responsibility of the Member State whose border was crossed irregularly shall cease 12 months after the date on which the irregular border crossing took place.

181. Further see, e.g., Marx, R.: 'Adjusting the Dublin Convention: New Approaches to Member State Responsibility for Asylum Applications', *European Journal for Migration and Law* 3 (2001) 7–22.

question thus arises if there has been an improvement in preventing the problem of 'refugees in orbit' occurring outside the EU territory. In this respect Article 27 of the Asylum Procedures Directive[182] should be noted. This provision can fill in the above-mentioned gap by giving the criteria for identification of a 'safe third country'. Furthermore, it also takes into account the individual situation of an asylum applicant by assuring that where the third country does not permit the applicant for asylum in question to enter its territory, Member States should ensure that access to the procedure is given in accordance with the basic principles and guarantees described in the Asylum Procedures Directive.[183]

It is necessary to emphasise that if the system of returns and readmissions of asylum seekers is to operate reliably, a workable system of readmission agreements with 'safe third countries' must be established.[184] The Tampere Presidency Conclusions made a link between the common EU asylum and migration policy and the EU external policy (adoption of readmission agreements between the European Community and relevant third countries or groups of countries).[185] These readmission agreements should always be in line with the 'absolute respect of the right to seek asylum'[186] and also should provide a sufficient safeguard against *refoulement*.

Even though the system of returns and readmissions seems to be able to diminish the problem of 'refugees in orbit' outside the EU, at the same time it might attempt to extend the scope of the 'Dublin II' Regulation (the determination of the State responsible for examining an asylum application lodged in an EU Member State) to non-EU countries, and thus shift the responsibility of examining asylum applications to outside the EU. The return of asylum applicants to safe third countries can be carried out even when the Member States have not examined the application in substance, if the possibility of requesting refugee status exists in a safe third country.[187]

In order to achieve an effectively operating Common European Asylum System, it is necessary to speed up all procedures forming the System. First of all one has to realise that there are actually two main procedures to comply with: one

182. OJ L 326, 13.12.2005, 13.

183. Id., Art. 27(4).

184. See, e.g., Agreement between the Government of the Hong Kong Special Administrative Region of the People's Republic of China and the European Community on the Readmission of Persons Residing without Authorisation, 27 November 2002; Agreement between the Democratic Socialist Republic of Sri Lanka and the European Community on the Readmission of Persons Residing without Authorization: SEC(2003) 255, 21.3.2003; Agreement between the European Community and the Macao Special Administrative Region of the People's Republic of China on the Readmission of Persons Residing without Authorisation: OJ L 143/97, 30.4.2004; Agreement between the Republic of Albania and the European Community on the Readmission of Persons Residing without Authorisation: COM(2004) 92, 12.2.2004.

185. Tampere, par. 27.

186. Id., par. 13.

187. *Supra* 182, cf. Art. 27(1)(d).

to determine the Member State responsible for examining the asylum application and the other to examine the asylum claim in substance. The latter procedure is regulated by the national law of the responsible Member State, which should be in conformity with the minimum standards agreed within the EU. As regards the *speed of the procedures*, this very much depends on the time limits set by the laws.

The Member State responsible for examining an asylum application in substance should be determined as quickly as possible; for example, by laying down a reasonable time limit to make such a decision. Arrangements for taking charge and taking back (readmission between the Member States)[188] are similar to those in the Dublin Convention. However, there are significant differences concerning the time limits: the deadline for submitting a request to take charge is reduced from six months under the Dublin Convention, to a maximum of three months.[189] Where the request to take charge of an asylum applicant is not made within three months, responsibility for examining the application shall lie with the Member State in which the application was originally lodged. It is also possible for the requesting Member State to ask for an urgent reply. The period within which the reply is expected shall be then at least one week.

According to Article 19(3), (4) of the 'Dublin II' Regulation, the transfer of an applicant from the Member State in which the application for asylum was lodged to the Member State responsible shall be carried out in accordance with the national law of the first Member State; and as soon as practically possible after a consultation between the Member States concerned. The transfer should take place at the latest within six months of the acceptance of the request that charge be taken, or of the decision on an appeal or review, where there is suspensive effect. Where the transfer does not take place within the six-month time limit, responsibility shall lie with the Member State in which the application for asylum was lodged. The deadlines for implementing transfers can be extended up to a maximum of one year, if the transfer cannot be carried out due to imprisonment of the asylum seeker or up to a maximum of eighteen months if the asylum seeker absconds.

The deadlines for granting and withdrawing refugee status should be also consistent with the shorter procedural deadlines introduced by the 'Dublin II' Regulation. This is essential in order to ensure that applications for asylum are processed expeditiously. Concerning a speedy asylum system, it could be concluded that some progress has been achieved by the Dublin II. Nonetheless, as mentioned above, the time limits set by one legal instrument must be in line with the time limits set by other related instruments. Only in this manner uniformity within the Common European Asylum System can be expected.

---

188. Dublin II, Arts. 16–20.
189. Id., Art. 17(1).

The *unity of families* is another subject reconsidered and dealt with in the 'Dublin II' Regulation. As the discussions on the Dublin Convention pointed out, by limiting family reunification to cases where a family member was already legally residing in one of the Member States as a recognised refugee, the policy focused more on the refugee status than on the family ties.

> 'Where the asylum seeker has a family member, regardless of whether the family was previously formed in the country of origin, who has been allowed to reside as a refugee in a Member State'[190]

or

> 'whose application has not yet been the subject of a first decision regarding the substance,'[191]

that Member State shall be responsible for examining the application for asylum, provided that the persons concerned so desire. This formulation is broader than the one laid down in Article 4 of the Dublin Convention. However, regarding family reunification, the Member States should also make extensive use of their rights pursuant to Articles 3(2) and 15 of 'Dublin II',[192] to ensure the examination of asylum applications where a family member is legally residing in a Member State's territory under other grounds (e.g., temporary protection or subsidiary protection) by that Member State. Otherwise, reunification of many families might be obstructed. It should be noted that the above-mentioned restriction does not apply to unaccompanied minors. A new criterion to protect family unity was added for cases when the applicant for asylum is an unaccompanied minor. The Member State responsible for examining the application should then be the one 'where a member of his or her family is legally present, provided that this is in the best interests of the minor'.[193] The scope of this Article is therefore wider, and covers any family member legally present in a Member State. This brings about the question why this principle does not apply to all groups of asylum seekers.

The last objective to be examined concerns the *distribution of asylum applications within the EU Member States*. If only the 'responsibility criteria' of the 'Dublin II' Regulation are applied in order to determine which Member State is to examine an asylum application, it is logical that the distribution is not based on the Member State's capacity to receive a certain number of asylum applicants, but only on a set of agreed criteria. These criteria seem to be based on the idea that

190. Id., Art. 7.

191. Id., Art. 8.

192. Art. 3(2) of the 'Dublin II' Regulation corresponds with Art. 3(4) of the Dublin Convention (the 'sovereignty clause'); Art. 15 of the 'Dublin II' Regulation corresponds with Art. 9 of the Dublin Convention (the 'humanitarian clause').

193. Dublin II, Art. 6.

responsibility shall be attributed to the Member State most involved in the asylum seeker's entry into or presence in the EU territory (by granting him a residence permit or a visa, by insufficiently guarding its external borders, or by authorising entry without a visa).

The adoption of a new legal instrument on determination of the Member State responsible for examining an asylum application lodged in one of the Member States by a TCN provided a good opportunity to mend the drawbacks of the Dublin Convention. Although not much seems to have changed with the new Regulation (with the exception of, for example, the shortened time limits for requests to take charge), which largely retains the substance of the original convention; there is still room for improvements during its application.[194] The 'Dublin II' Regulation has first to be applied in practice for a reasonable time. More time is then also needed to make an accurate assessment on the 'Dublin II' mechanism. Article 28 of this Regulation states that three years after its coming into force,[195] at the latest, the Commission shall report to the European Parliament and the Council on its application and, where appropriate, shall propose necessary amendments.

2.2.4 **Eurodac**

'The European Council urges the Council to finalise promptly its work on the system for the identification of asylum seekers (Eurodac).'[196]

On 11 December 2000, the Council adopted a Regulation concerning the establishment of Eurodac for the comparison of fingerprints for the effective application of the Dublin Convention.[197] The Council Regulation establishing Eurodac is still in force. Where reference is made to the Dublin Convention, such reference should be now taken as reference made to the 'Dublin II' Regulation.[198]

Eurodac consists of a Central Unit, a computerised central database, in which data are processed for the purpose of comparing the fingerprint data of applicants for asylum and of other categories of aliens specified in the Regulation, along with means of data transmission between the Member States and the central database. In the central database only data concerning the Member State of origin, place and date of the application for asylum, fingerprint data, sex, reference number by the

194. See also Commission Regulation (EC) No. 1560/2003 of 2 September 2003 laying down detailed rules for the application of Council Regulation (EC) No. 343/2003 establishing the criteria and mechanisms for determining the Member State responsible for examining an asylum application lodged in one of the Member States by a third-country national, OJ L 222, 5.9.2003, 3.

195. The 'Dublin II' Regulation entered into force on 25 February 2003.

196. Tampere, par. 17.

197. *Supra* 52.

198. Dublin II, Art. 24.

Member State of origin,[199] the date on which the fingerprints were taken, the date on which the data were transmitted to the Central Unit, the date on which the data were entered in the central database, details in respect of the recipient of the data transmitted and the date of transmission shall be recorded.[200] After recording the data in the central database, the Central Unit shall destroy the media used for transmitting the data, unless the Member State of origin has requested their return.[201] Each set of data, as referred to in Article 5(1), shall be stored in the central database for ten years from the date on which the fingerprints were taken. Upon expiry of this period, the Central Unit shall automatically erase the data from the central database.[202]

In connection with the asylum procedures, the Eurodac system is to determine whether a person applying for asylum has already applied in one of the Member States before. The aim of the Eurodac system is to put an end to multiple asylum applications, or so-called 'asylum shopping'. It is equally essential that this system complies with human rights obligations. An independent body has therefore been established, in order to ensure that the data will not be used by police for other purposes and will not be passed on to the applicants' countries of origin.[203]

2.3 Reception

'This (Common European Asylum) System should include, in the short term, ... common minimum conditions of reception of asylum seekers, ...'[204]

To ensure asylum applicants a dignified standard of living in the EU, it proved necessary to set up minimum standards for their reception conditions. These minimum conditions were established by a 'Council Directive laying down minimum standards for the reception of asylum seekers' (the 'Reception Directive')[205] in accordance with Article 63(1)(b) TEC. Reception conditions mean the full set of

199. For the purposes of the Council Regulation 2725/2000 'Member State of origin' means:
– in relation to an applicant for asylum, the Member State which transmits the personal data to the Central Unit and receives the results of the comparison;
– in relation to an alien apprehended in connection with the irregular crossing of an external border, the Member State which transmits the personal data to the Central Unit;
– in relation to an alien found illegally present in a Member State, the Member State which transmits such data to the Central Unit and receives the results of the comparison.

200. *Supra* 52, Art. 5(1).

201. Id., Art. 5(2).

202. Id., Art. 6.

203. BBC news of 15 January, 2003; see also Commission staff working paper 'First Annual Report to the Council and the European Parliament on the activities of the Eurodac Central Unit', SEC(2004) 557, 5.5.2004.

204. Tampere, par. 14.

205. Council Directive 2003/9/EC of 27 January 2003, OJ L 031, 6.2.2003, 18. The Reception Directive entered into force on 6 February 2003; the transposition deadline was 6 February 2005.

measures that Member States grant to asylum seekers in accordance with the Directive in question. Because this legal instrument is a *directive*, it is binding as to the result to be achieved on each Member State to which it is addressed, but leaves to the national authorities the choice of form and methods.[206]

In April 2001 the Commission submitted a 'Proposal for a Council Directive on minimum standards on the reception of applicants for asylum in the Member States'.[207] As declared in the Explanatory Memorandum to this Proposal, besides other reports, studies and consultations, the 'foundation' materials used to draft the Proposal were the European Council Conclusions of December 2000;[208] the Reception Conditions Study, delivered by the Commission at the beginning of November 2000;[209] and written and oral comments expressed on the Commission's discussion paper.

The Reception Directive is composed of five main sets of rules (as was the Proposal for this Directive):

The first group concerns the most *general provisions*, including the purpose (Art. 1) and the scope (Art. 3) of this legal instrument, as well as the definitions of the concepts that are relevant for its clear understanding (Art. 2). The purpose of this Directive is to lay down minimum standards for the reception of asylum seekers in the Member States, i.e., to lay down comparable living conditions in all Member States of the EU. Regarding the scope, it should apply to all TCNs and stateless persons who make an application for asylum at the border or in the territory of a Member State, as long as they are allowed to remain in the territory as asylum seekers. This holds true also for their family members, if they are covered by such application for asylum, according to the national law of the given Member State.

On the other hand, this Directive does not apply in cases of requests for diplomatic or territorial asylum submitted to representations of the Member States abroad. Neither should it apply when the provisions of the 'Council Directive on minimum standards for giving temporary protection in the event of mass influx of displaced persons and on measures promoting a balance of efforts between Member States in receiving such persons and bearing the consequences thereof' (the Temporary Protection Directive)[210] apply.

The second set of rules focuses on the *reception conditions* that in principle should be *granted at all stages and in all asylum procedures*. These include infor-

206. Cf. Art. 249 TEC.

207. COM(2001) 181 final, 3.4.2001 (further referred to as the 'Proposal for the Reception Directive').

208. Nice European Council, 7–10 December 2000.

209. A Study on the legal framework and administrative practices in the Member States of the European Union regarding reception conditions for asylum seekers, displaced persons and other persons seeking international protection.

210. Council Directive 2001/55/EC of 20 July 2001, OJ L 212, 7.8.2001, 12. On the Temporary Protection Directive further see chapter 2, 2.6.

mation (Art. 5), documentation (Art. 6), residence and freedom of movement (Art. 7), further material reception conditions like housing, food, clothing and daily expenses allowance (Art. 13), medical care (Art. 13), unity of the family (Art. 8) and schooling and education of minors (Art. 10). Certain reception conditions, like access to labour market (Art. 11) or vocational training (Art. 12), should not be denied, when an applicant for asylum is not responsible for the length of the procedure and he has been in the procedure for a long period of time.

Pursuant to the general provisions on reception conditions, as laid down in Chapter II of the Reception Directive, state authorities must *inform* asylum applicants within fifteen days of lodging an application what their rights and obligations are, as well as information about organisations or persons who can provide legal or other assistance.[211]

Within three days after lodging the application with the competent authority of a Member State, the applicant is provided with a *document* issued on his/her own name, certifying his/her status as an asylum seeker or testifying that he/she is allowed to stay in the territory of the Member State whilst his/her application is pending or being examined. In specific cases, during the examination of an application for asylum, Member States may provide applicants with other evidence than the aforementioned document. Such document must be valid for as long as the asylum seeker is authorised to remain in the territory of the Member State concerned or at its border. When serious humanitarian reasons arise and these require the presence of the asylum seeker in another State, the Member State may provide him/her with a travel document.[212]

Asylum seekers may *move freely* within the territory of the host Member State or within an area assigned to them by that Member State, under certain conditions. When it proves necessary, for example for legal reasons or reasons of public order, Member States may confine an applicant to a particular place in accordance with their national law. Member States shall also provide for the possibility of granting applicants temporary permission to leave the place of residence.[213]

As regards families, Member States shall take appropriate measures to maintain, as far as possible, *family unity* as present within their territory. *Education of minors* shall be provided under similar conditions as for the nationals of the host Member State. Access to the education system shall not be postponed for more than three months from the date the application for asylum was lodged by the minor or the minor's parents. Regarding *employment,* Member States shall determine a period of time during which an applicant shall not have access to the labour market. This period starts from the date on which an application for asylum was submitted.[214]

---

211. Art. 5. See also the Proposal for the Reception Directive, Commentary on Art. 5.
212. Reception Directive, Art. 6.
213. Id., Art. 7.
214. Id., Arts. 8, 10, 11.

The third group of rules sets the minimum standards of some reception conditions, which were also mentioned in the previous group, namely *general rules on material reception conditions and health care*,[215] which the Member States are required to ensure. The living conditions of asylum applicants must be dignified at all times. Moreover, in cases where the applications are considered admissible or when the procedure in place takes too long, the living conditions should be improved above the minimum standards. Special needs of applicants should also be taken into consideration (e.g., minors, disabled people, elderly people, and pregnant women). Modalities for material reception conditions are set in Article 14. These are for instance when housing is provided in kind, instead of a sum of money allocated for that purpose. Such different conditions shall cover basic needs in all cases. Member States may set those modalities different from those provided for in this Article in exceptional cases and only for a reasonable period, which shall be as short as possible.

Member States may require asylum applicants to cover or contribute to the *cost of the material reception conditions* and of the health care, if the applicant has sufficient resources. Concerning *health care*, Member States shall provide the applicants with necessary health care, including at least emergency care and essential treatment of illness. Applicants, who have special needs in this respect, will be provided with other necessary medical care or other assistance.[216]

The *provisions for reducing or withdrawing access to some or all reception conditions* form the fourth group of rules.[217] They intend to ensure that the reception system is not abused. Decisions on reduction, withdrawal or refusal of reception conditions or sanctions shall be taken individually, objectively and impartially and reasons shall be given. However, access to emergency health care shall be ensured under all circumstances. Member States shall guarantee that material reception conditions are not withdrawn or reduced before a negative decision is taken. At the same time, the possibility of a review of such decisions is of the utmost importance, since the reduction or withdrawal of reception conditions can affect the standard of living of the applicants. Asylum seekers may appeal any reductions of their benefits within the procedures laid down in the national law. At least in the last instance the possibility of an appeal or a review before a judicial body must be granted.[218]

Finally, several *rules* have been outlined *to assure complete implementation of the Reception Directive*, and also the improvement of the efficiency of the reception systems. This applies to both national and Community level and covers cooperation, guidance, monitoring and control systems, training of staff and alloca-

215. Id., Art. 13.
216. Id., Arts.14, 15.
217. Id., Art.16.
218. Id., Art. 21.

tion of the necessary resources in connection with the national provisions enacted to implement this Directive.[219]

As mentioned above, the material reception conditions include daily expenses allowance, housing, food and clothing and can be provided in kind, as financial allowances or in vouchers. If the differences of reception conditions between various Member States remain too great, this could lead to overloading those Member States, which provide for reception standards that are exceptionally generous in comparison with other Member States. Although the Reception Directive sets minimum standards for the reception of asylum seekers (further referred to as 'the minimum standards for reception'); Member States retain the power to introduce or retain more favourable provisions.[220]

The harmonisation of conditions for the reception of asylum seekers among the Member States intends to limit the secondary movements of asylum seekers, caused usually by the variety of conditions for the reception of asylum seekers in different Member States.[221] Chapter VI of the Reception Directive involves actions to improve the efficiency of the reception system by establishing cooperation between the Member States and the Commission, meaning that the Member States shall regularly inform the Commission on the data concerning the number of persons, broken down by sex and age, covered by reception conditions and provide full information on the type and format of the identification documents provided for by Article 6.[222]

The United Kingdom, Ireland and Denmark, having a special position as far as Title IV TEC is concerned, gave the following notice of their wish to take part in the adoption and application of this Directive: in accordance with the special Protocols, the United Kingdom gave notice of its wish to take part in the adoption and application of this Directive; Ireland is not participating in its adoption. Consequently, its provisions do not apply to Ireland. Nor is Denmark participating in the adoption of the Reception Directive, and therefore is not bound by it or subject to its application.[223]

There are two key aims of the Reception Directive. One aim is to ensure a minimum standard to be offered in each of the EU Member States, which must not in any case be below the level set by this Directive. The other aim seems to point at the prevention of the secondary movements of asylum seekers. Secondary movement of asylum seekers occur when they, after lodging their asylum claim and whilst the Member State is examining that claim, leave the State and look for better conditions elsewhere.

---

219. Id., Chapter VI (Arts. 22–24); see also the Proposal for the Reception Directive, Explanatory Memorandum / An overview of the standards in the proposal.

220. Reception Directive, Art. 4.

221. Id., Preamble, par. 8.

222. Id., Art.22.

223. Id., Preamble, par. 19–21.

One could ask oneself which of those aims is actually the central objective of the Reception Directive. According to the formulation used in the Directive, the main purpose is to lay down minimum standards for the reception of asylum seekers in the Member States, so as to ensure them a dignified standard of living. In addition, the Preamble to the Reception Directive states that the harmonisation of conditions for the reception should help to limit the secondary movements of asylum seekers influenced by the variety of conditions for their reception in different Member States. This 'secondary' aim might seem to be more difficult to achieve since there is a natural human tendency to look for better living conditions. Even with this set of minimum standards, there possibly will be countries that would offer more favourable conditions, and this would indirectly promote the secondary movement phenomenon.

In this respect another issue is worth noting – the broad discretionary capacity that has been granted to the Member States. They are allowed to decide, for example, on the scope of the Reception Directive (if it applies also to those applying for subsidiary protection[224]),[225] on some conditions regarding schooling and education of minors,[226] on the freedom of movement and residence,[227] on asylum seekers' access to employment,[228] or on reduction or withdrawal of reception conditions.[229]

This broad discretionary power conferred upon the Member States by the Reception Directive may prevent its aim to ensure 'comparable conditions in all Member States.'[230] Besides, the current general attitude of the public towards applicants for asylum, as well as the political and social connotations of asylum-related issues might play a significant role in the quality of the asylum seekers' reception and living conditions.

2.4 QUALIFICATION

'This system should include, in the short term, ... the approximation of rules on the recognition and content of the refugee status. It should also be completed with measures on subsidiary forms of protection offering an appropriate status to any person in need of such protection.'[231]

On 29 and 30 April 2004, a JHA Council took place in Luxembourg, where the EU JHA ministers reached formal agreement on one of the key texts setting out

224. On the 'subsidiary protection' see chapter 2, 2.4.3.
225. Reception Directive, Art. 3(4).
226. Id., Art.10.
227. Id., Art.7.
228. Id., Art.11.
229. Id., Art. 16.
230. Cf. Preamble, par. 7.
231. *Tampere*, par. 14.

common rules on asylum – an instrument setting out the criteria for refugee status in the EU and for the subsidiary protection for persons who otherwise need international protection.[232] This Directive (further referred to as the 'Qualification Directive') also sets out the minimum rights and benefits for those granted refugee status or subsidiary protection.[233] The Qualification Directive, based on Article 63(1)(c) TEC, applies to all EU Member States except Denmark.[234]

This long-awaited Directive was welcomed very enthusiastically by some representatives of national governments and EU officials, considering it as an important step forward to a Common European Asylum System:

'I think we now have an important body of legislative instruments in the Union', Irish Justice Minister Michael McDowell said.[235]

'I believe it is the jewel in the crown of the first phase of the Common European Asylum System', JHA Commissioner Antonio Vitorino said, adding that the Commission was 'very happy' with the result of the negotiations.[236]

The Directive was formally adopted by the Council on 29 April 2004 and its adoption represents a further step towards the development of a Common European Asylum System, as called for in Tampere.[237] The key provisions of the Qualification Directive will now be analysed, in order to assess its conformity with the Tampere goals:

On 22 October 2002, the European Parliament generally welcomed the Directive and approved the proposal,[238] but with amendments.[239] The various recom-

232. The deadline for adopting the EU legal instruments on asylum was 1 May 2004. The 'Qualification Directive' was thus agreed on the very last moment before this deadline. Agreement on this Directive before 1 May was possible after the recent approval of a new immigration law in Germany which cleared the way for the country to negotiate on this issue.

233. The Council Directive 2004/83/EC of 29 April 2004 on minimum standards for the qualification of third country nationals and stateless persons as refugees or as persons who otherwise need international protection and the content of the protection granted (OJ L 304, 30.9.2004, 12) entered into force on 20 October 2004; transposition deadline: 10 October 2006.

234. Id., Preamble, par. 40. In accordance with Arts. 1 and 2 of the Protocol on the position of Denmark, annexed to the TEU and to the TEC, Denmark is not taking part in the adoption of this Directive and is not bound by it or subject to its application.

235. Spiteri, S.: 'EU agrees common rules on refugee status', *Euobserver*/Brussels, 31 March 2004.

236. Ibid.

237. Tampere, par. 14.

238. Proposal for a Council Directive on minimum standards for the qualification and status of third country nationals and stateless persons as refugees or as persons who otherwise need international protection, COM(2001) 510, 12.9.2001 (further referred to as the 'Proposal for the Qualification Directive').

239. See European Parliament legislative resolution on the proposal for a Council directive on minimum standards for the qualification and status of third country nationals and stateless persons as refugees or as persons who otherwise need international protection, COM(2001) 510 – C5-0573/2001 – 2001/0207(CNS); OJ C E/2003/300/ 134.

mendations for amendments were aimed principally at expanding the scope of the Directive to apply to all persons and not only to TCNs and stateless persons; the removal of a provision including 'quasi-state authorities' as agents of protection; establishing parity of treatment between refugees and beneficiaries of subsidiary protection, especially in terms of access to employment; and addressing the lack of provisions on the mechanism to track what happens to failed asylum applicants who are returned, in order to monitor the quality of decision making within the EU. However, the amendments proposed by the Parliament were not included in the Directive.[240] This is regrettable since the Parliament's proposals for amendments would have made the qualification procedure fairer and it would have allowed a quality control system for the decision making.

The *purpose* of the Qualification Directive is to establish minimum standards for the qualification of TCNs and stateless persons as refugees or beneficiaries of subsidiary protection within EU Member States; and also the minimum levels of rights and benefits attached to the protection granted.[241] The Qualification Directive only applies to persons who are TCNs or stateless persons. Family members are defined as the beneficiary's spouse or unmarried partner in a stable relationship and their unmarried and dependent minor children, who are present in the Member State where the application for international protection is made.[242] Surprisingly, to be defined as family member by this Directive, one has to be present in the same Member State in relation to the application for international protection. Considering the situation of persons, who had to flee torture or persecution, this limitation can become an obstacle for the person's family reunification.

The 'refugee' definition under Article 2 (c) reflects Article 1A(2) of the 1951 Geneva Convention on Refugees; nevertheless it is limited to a 'third-country national' and 'stateless person', contrary to 'any person' as laid down in the Geneva Convention. The Directive therefore does not include nationals of the Member States of the EU.[243] This might bring about an infringement of Article 3 of the 1951 Geneva Convention stating that 'the Contracting States shall apply the provisions of this Convention to refugees without discrimination as to race, religion or *country of origin.*' Moreover, the Tampere Presidency Conclusions called for a

240. ECRE Information Note on the Council Directive 2004/83/EC of 29 April 2004 on minimum standards for the qualification of third country nationals and stateless persons as refugees or as persons who otherwise need international protection and the content of the protection granted (IN 1/10/2004/ext/CN), 2.

241. Qualification Directive, Art. 1.

242. Id., Art. 2(h).

243. Par. 13 of the Preamble to the Qualification Directive claims that this Directive is without prejudice to the Protocol on asylum for nationals of Member States of the European Union, as annexed to the TEC. On the Protocol on asylum for nationals of Member States of the European Union see chapter 1, 1.7.3.1.

EU, fully committed to the obligations of the Geneva Convention and other relevant human rights instruments.[244]

As appears from the title of the Qualification Directive, the standards agreed on are *minimum standards* only. The Preamble and also Article 3 of this Directive encourage the Member States to introduce or retain more favourable standards for determining who qualifies as a refugee or as a person eligible for subsidiary protection, and for determining the content of international protection, in so far as those standards are compatible with this Directive.[245]

2.4.1 Assessment of applications

Article 4 reflects the assessment of facts and circumstances regarding the applicant. A positive aspect is that the assessment of applications should be carried out on an individual basis (par. 3). Member States may consider it the duty of the applicant to submit as soon as possible all elements needed to substantiate the application for international protection. In cooperation with the applicant, it is the duty of the Member State to assess the relevant elements of the application (par. 1).

> 'It is a general legal principle that the burden of proof lies on the person submitting a claim. Often, however, an applicant may not be able to support his statement by documentary or other proof; and cases in which an applicant for asylum can provide evidence of all his/her statements would be an exception rather than the rule. In most cases a person fleeing from persecution would have arrived with the barest necessities and very frequently even without personal documents. Thus, while the burden of proof in principle rests on the applicant, the duty to ascertain and evaluate all the relevant facts is shared between the applicant and the examiner. Indeed, in some cases, it may be for the examiner to use all the means at his disposal to produce the necessary evidence in support of the application. Even such independent research may not, however, always be successful and there may also be statements that are not susceptible to proof. In such cases, if the applicant's account appears credible, he/she should, unless there are good reasons to the contrary, be given the benefit of the doubt.'[246]

The recognition of the significance of individual statements is also important to note,[247] as well as the formulation that past episodes of persecution, serious harm or direct threats of such persecution or such harm, are to be interpreted as strongly indicative of the applicant's well-founded fear of persecution or real risk of suffering serious harm in the future.[248]

---

244. Tampere, par. 4; for the definition of 'person eligible for subsidiary protection' see chapter 2, 2.4.3.

245. Qualification Directive, Preamble, par. 8; Art. 3.

246. *UNHCR Handbook*, par. 196.

247. Qualification Directive, Art. 4(2).

248. Id., Art. 4(4).

Article 4(5) states that where Member States apply the principle that it is the applicant's duty to prove the application for international protection and where aspects of the applicant's statements are not supported by documentary or other evidence, those aspects shall not need confirmation, when the following conditions are met:

a. the applicant has made a genuine effort to substantiate his application;
b. all relevant elements at the applicant's disposal have been submitted, and a satisfactory explanation regarding any lack of other relevant elements has been given;
c. the applicant's statements are found to be coherent and plausible and do not run counter to available specific and general information relevant to the applicant's case;
d. the applicant has applied for international protection at the earliest possible time, unless the applicant can demonstrate good reason for not having done so; and
e. the general credibility of the applicant has been established.

Regarding the condition established in paragraph 5(b), it presumes that the applicant has provided all *relevant elements*[249] or a *satisfactory explanation in case of their absence*. The fact that this requirement allows for exceptions is positive.

International protection needs arising 'sur place' are dealt with in Article 5 of the Qualification Directive. Pursuant to the *UNHCR Handbook*,

> 'the requirement that a person must be outside his country to be a refugee[250] does not mean that he must necessarily have left that country illegally, or even that he must have left it on account of a well-founded fear. He may have decided to ask for recognition of his refugee status after having already been abroad for some time. A person who was not a refugee when he left his country but who becomes a refugee at a later date, is called a refugee *sur place*. A person becomes a refugee *sur place* due to circumstances arising in his country of origin during his absence. Diplomats and other officials serving abroad, prisoners of war, students, migrant workers and others have applied for refugee status during their residence abroad and have been recognised as refugees.'[251]

249. Pursuant to Art. 4(2) the relevant elements consist of the applicant's statements and all documentation at the applicant's disposal regarding the applicant's age, background, including that of relevant relatives, identity, nationality(ies), country(ies) and place(s) of previous residence, previous asylum application, travel routes, identity and travel documents and the reasons for applying for international protection.

250. 1951 Geneva Convention, Art. 1A(2).

251. *UNHCR Handbook*, par. 94, 95.

Article 5(3) of the Qualification Directive claims that

> '*without prejudice* to the Geneva Convention, Member States may determine that an applicant who files a subsequent application shall normally not be granted refugee status, if the risk of persecution is based on circumstances which the applicant has created by his own decision since leaving the country of origin'.

In contrast to Article 5(3), the UNHCR believes that

> 'a person may become a refugee *sur place* as a result of his own actions, such as associating with refuges already recognised, or expressing his political views in his country of residence. Whether such actions are sufficient to justify a well-founded fear of persecution must be determined by a careful examination of the circumstances. Regard should be taken in particular to whether such actions may have come to the attention of the authorities of the person's country of origin and how they are likely to be viewed by those authorities'.[252]

Article 8 of the Proposal for the Qualification Directive suggests that refugee status should be denied if the applicant engages in activities for the sole purpose of creating the necessary conditions for making an application of international protection. In contrast, however, the Commentary to the Articles observes that Member States should ensure that applicants are recognised as persons in need of international protection if the activities referred to in Article 8(2) 'may reasonably be expected to come to the notice of the authorities of the individual's country of origin, be treated by them as demonstrative of an adverse political or other protected opinion or characteristic, and give rise to a well-founded fear of being persecuted'. Moreover, a well-founded fear of persecution could also arise, when the persecutor in the country of origin knows or reasonably suspects that someone has claimed asylum abroad. The wording of Article 8 of the Proposal offered a fairer approach by requiring a presence of an ill-disposed intention to create the circumstances needed to apply for international protection.

Actors of persecution or serious harm include not only the state and parties or organisations controlling the state, or a substantial part of the territory of the state, but also non-state actors if it can be demonstrated that the state or parties controlling the state (including international organisations) are unable or unwilling to provide protection against persecution or serious harm.[253] The inclusion of the non-state actors helps this Directive to comply with the 1951 Geneva Convention (especially with Article 1A(2)), providing protection to those who do not have the protection of their country of nationality or residence.

In Article 7, referring to the *actors of protection*, the inclusion of non-state authorities (parties or organisations, including international organisations, control-

---

252. Id., par. 96.
253. Qualification Directive, Art. 6.

ling the state or substantial part of the territory of the state) in the definition, next to the states, brings about certain concerns.[254] Having accepted that it is possible to have a well-founded fear of being persecuted or of otherwise suffering serious harm at the hands of non-state agents, this Article sets out the limited conditions where non-state bodies can be considered as potential protectors, in a similar manner to recognised states. This requires that an international organisation such as the UN or NATO or a stable state-like authority controls the territory of proposed return and is willing and able to give effect to rights and to protect an individual from harm, in a manner similar to a recognised state for as long as this is necessary.[255] This justification, however, seems to overlook the fact that state-like authorities cannot be parties to international human rights instruments and therefore cannot be held accountable for non-compliance with international refugee and human rights obligations. Their lack of accountability in international law makes it impossible for persons living within their jurisdiction to hold them responsible at an international level for ensuring that human rights standards are safeguarded. Another question which arises is whether state-like authorities are in a position to ensure compliance with human rights obligations. The case of Kosovo is an example where international organisations showed ineffectiveness in maintaining peace, security and guaranteeing human rights when providing 'state protection' in conflict areas.[256]

Article 8 of the Qualification Directive refers to *internal protection*. Paragraph (1) states that as part of the assessment of the application for international protection, Member States may determine that an applicant is not in need of international protection if in a part of the country of origin there is no well-founded fear of being persecuted or no real risk of suffering serious harm and the applicant can reasonably be expected to stay in that part of the country. There are, however, no criteria for considering whether internal protection may be available for the applicant. The ECRE suggested the following criteria to be applied in assessing the reasonableness of the internal protection alternative:

- The protection must be afforded by a *de jure* not just *de facto* authority. This is necessary given that de facto authorities are under no international legal obligation and often not in a position to safeguard human rights.
- The claimant must be able to access the area of internal protection in safety and dignity and legally.
- Conditions to meet the needs of particularly vulnerable groups must be available, e.g., adequate health care for claimants with medical needs or adequate care and reception for unaccompanied minors.

254. Id., Art. 7(1)(b).

255. Proposal for the Qualification Directive, Commentary on Arts. 17, 18.

256. See Comments from ECRE on the Proposal for a Council Directive on minimum standards for the qualification and status of third country nationals and stateless persons as refugees or as persons who otherwise need international protection, 6.

- Conditions in the area of internal protection must ensure that the applicant is not forced back into the area where there is a risk of serious harm for a Convention reason, i.e., it must offer a durable protection alternative and provide effective protection from *refoulement* to the area where the person fears persecution.
- The absence of a risk of serious harm in the proposed site of internal protection must be objectively established, rather than being considered reasonably unlikely to occur.[257]

Article 8 of the Qualification Directive does not include any limitation to the effect that an assessment of an internal protection alternative is normally not relevant in cases where persecution emanates from state actors.[258] It should be therefore recommended that the Member States apply such a limitation when considering asylum claims. The wording contained in Article 10(1) of the Proposal for the Qualification Directive is missing in the final version of the Directive. It provided that in carrying out the examination whether a well-founded fear is clearly confined to a specific part of the territory of the country of origin, there shall be a strong presumption against finding internal protection to be a viable alternative to international protection, if the agent of persecution is, or is associated with, the national government.

Article 8(3) of the Qualification Directive allows the Member States to apply paragraph (1) of the same Article, notwithstanding technical obstacles to return to the country of origin. One could ask whether, in case a person cannot in reality return to his country of origin, he is then 'able to avail himself of the protection of the country of his nationality or his habitual residence'.[259] Otherwise this would be contrary to the 1951 Geneva Convention. It should be noted that no similar provision was contained in the Commission Proposal.

2.4.2 **Refugee**

Chapter III of the Qualification Directive determines the requirements for the qualification for being a refugee. Article 9(1) defines the necessary components of *acts of persecution*, within the meaning of Article 1A of the 1951 Geneva Convention. Paragraph (1)(a) holds that the seriousness of the act can be measured by either qualitative assessment (*nature* of acts) or a quantitative assessment (*repetition* of acts). Paragraph (1)(b) is based on the concept that accumulation of various

257. *Supra* 240, at 7–8.

258. See also UNHCR annotations for Arts. 1–19 of the draft Council Directive on minimum standards for the qualification of third country nationals and stateless persons as refugees or as persons who otherwise need international protection and the content of the protection granted, December 2002.

259. 1951 Geneva Convention, Art. 1A(2).

measures which would not in isolation amount to persecution, can give rise to a well-founded fear of persecution.

Article 9(2) enumerates the possible forms of acts of persecution. The 'list' is quite extensive and includes acts of a gender-specific and child-specific nature; acts of physical or mental violence, including acts of sexual violence; prosecution or punishment, which is disproportionate or discriminatory; prosecution or punishment for refusal to perform military service in a conflict, where performing military service would include crimes or acts falling under the exclusion clauses.[260] Unfortunately, the wording of the Proposal for the Qualification Directive, which also allowed refusal of military service based on specific individual circumstances, for example if the participation in military activities would be irreconcilable with the applicant's deeply held moral, religious or political convictions, or other valid reasons of conscience, has not been retained in the final version of the Qualification Directive.[261]

Another important provision included in the Proposal, but not retained in the final version provided that 'it is immaterial whether the applicant comes from a country in which many or all persons face the risk of generalised oppression'.[262] The Preamble to the Qualification Directive in paragraph 26 states that 'risks to which a population of a country or a section of the population is generally exposed do normally not create in themselves an individual threat which would qualify as a serious harm'. If one would take the wording of this paragraph strictly, persons who belong to a group that is being persecuted but who have not yet endured an 'individualised' threat might not qualify for international protection. Hopefully, the vagueness of this wording will not be in practice interpreted so strictly by the Member States.

Article 10 of the Qualification Directive outlines those elements which the Member States should take into account when assessing the *reasons for persecution.* Paragraph (1) contains definitions of the concepts of race, religion, nationality, particular social group and political opinion. Paragraph (2) stipulates that when assessing if an applicant has a well-founded fear of being persecuted it is immaterial whether the applicant actually possesses the racial, religious, national, social or political characteristic which cause the persecution, provided that such a characteristic is attributed to the applicant by the actor of persecution. The inclusion of paragraph (2) into Article 10 of the Qualification Directive, in contrast to the Proposal, is an important addition to the *reasons for persecution*, since it includes circumstances likely to occur in places where persecution exists.

The *cessation* of a TCN or a stateless person from being a refugee is described in Article 11. The grounds on which these persons can cease to be refugees broadly reflect Article 1C of the 1951 Geneva Convention. However, Article 11

260. On 'exclusion clauses' see the Qualification Directive, Art. 12.
261. Proposal for the Qualification Directive, Art. 11(1)(d).
262. Id., Art. 11(2)(c).

of the Qualification Directive does not include the 'compelling reasons arising out of previous persecution for refusing to avail himself of the protection of the country of nationality'[263] in paragraph (1)(e) and the 'compelling reasons arising out of previous persecution for refusing to return to the country of his habitual residence'[264] in paragraph (1)(f).

The *UNHCR Handbook* states that Article 1C(5) of the 1951 Geneva Convention refers to 'circumstances' (fundamental changes) in the country, which can be assumed to remove the basis of the fear of persecution. The second paragraph of this clause contains an exception to the cessation provision contained in the first paragraph. It deals with the special situation where a person may have been subjected to very serious persecution in the past and will not therefore cease to be a refugee, even if fundamental changes have occurred in his country of origin. It is frequently recognised that a person who (or whose family) has suffered under atrocious forms of persecution should not be expected to repatriate. Even though there may have been a change of regime in his country, this may not always produce a complete change in the attitude of the population, nor, in view of his past experiences, in the mind of the refugee.[265]

Article 1C(6) of the 1951 Geneva Convention, the last cessation clause,[266] is actually parallel to the above-mentioned cessation clause. The difference, nevertheless, is that this clause deals exclusively with stateless persons who are able to return to the country of their former habitual residence. 'Circumstances' should be interpreted in the same way as Article 1C(5). One should remember that apart from the changed circumstances in his/her country of former habitual residence, the person must be able to return there. This possibility, however, does not always exist for stateless persons.[267] Although the 'compelling reasons' are missing in Article 11(1) of the Qualification Directive, it should be stressed that paragraph (2) encourages the Member States in considering points (e) and (f) of paragraph (1) to have regard to whether the change of circumstances is of such a significant and non-temporary nature that the refugee's fear of persecution can no longer be regarded as well-founded.

Exclusion from refugee status is discussed in Article 12 of the Qualification Directive, which is broadly based on the exclusion clauses of the 1951 Geneva Convention (Art. 1 D, E and F).[268] On the other hand, there are considerable differences between Article 12 of the current Directive and Article 14 of the Proposal for this Directive. Since the application of this specific provision may limit the right for asylum, it is relevant to make a comparison between the content of the proposed and the current Article. Article 14 of the Proposal reiterates the principle

---

263. 1951 Geneva Convention, Art. 1C(5).
264. Id., Art. 1C(6).
265. *UNHCR Handbook*, par. 135, 136.
266. On the 'cessation clauses', as laid down in the 1951 Geneva Convention, see chapter 1, 1.2.
267. *UNHCR Handbook*, par. 137–139.
268. On the 'exclusion clauses', as laid down in the 1951 Geneva Convention, see chapter 1, 1.2.

that a person who comes within the terms of one of the exclusion clauses in Article 1D, E, F of the Geneva Convention is excluded from refugee status. Exclusion can also occur where the facts requiring exclusion become known after the recognition of international protection. The Proposal therefore established that the Directive would not apply to an applicant who comes within the following situations:

a. assistance or protection of the United Nations (this paragraph refers to the exclusion clause in Article 1D of the 1951 Geneva Convention);
b. rights in country of residence (this paragraph relates to situations covered by Article 1E of the 1951 Geneva Convention);
c. applicants not deserving international protection (this paragraph obliges the Member States, in order to maintain the integrity and credibility of the 1951 Geneva Convention, not to grant refugee status to an applicant in the situations covered by Article 1F of the Geneva Convention).[269]

Article 14(2) of the Proposal further states that the grounds for exclusion shall be based solely on the personal and knowing conduct of the person concerned. Paragraph (3) ensured that the person excluded from refugee status was entitled to lodge a legal challenge in the Member State concerned.[270] Paragraph (4) states, that the obligation not to grant refugee status to those undeserving of it, is without prejudice to Member States' obligations under international law.[271]

Although the current Article 12 of the Qualification Directive does not provide that the grounds for exclusion must be based solely on the personal and knowing conduct of the person concerned (as was the case in the Proposal); paragraph (3) of Article 12 includes persons who instigate or otherwise participate in the commission of crimes or acts mentioned in paragraph (2). Excluding persons who encourage crimes against peace, war crimes and/or crimes against humanity from international protection could be seen as a constructive improvement in comparison with the Proposal.

Article 13 of the Qualification Directive imposes an obligation on Member States to grant *refugee status* to TCNs and stateless persons who qualify as refugees in accordance with the previously mentioned requirements. This legally binding provision to grant asylum complies with the obligation laid down in Article II-78 of the Charter of Fundamental Rights of the Union.[272] This should be assessed positively as no similar provision existed in the Proposal for this Directive.

---

269. See also the Proposal for the Qualification Directive, Comentary on Art. 14, at 24–25.
270. The relevant procedural standards can be found in the Council Directive on minimum standards on procedures in Member States for granting and withdrawing refugee status, OJ L 326, 13.12.2005, 13; see also chapter 2, 2.5.
271. See also the Proposal for the Qualification Directive, Comentary on Art. 14, at 25–26.
272. See the Treaty establishing a Constitution for Europe, OJ C 310, 16.12.2004, Part II.

The *grounds for revoking, ending, or refusing to renew refugee status* are outlined in Article 14 of the Qualification Directive. According to paragraph (1) Member States *shall* revoke, end or refuse to renew the refugee status granted by a governmental, administrative, judicial or quasi-judicial body, if the person has ceased to be a refugee. The Member State which has granted refugee status shall on an individual basis demonstrate that the person concerned has ceased to be or has never been a refugee.[273] Member States *shall* revoke, end or refuse to renew refugee status if it is established by the Member State concerned that:

- he/she should have been or is excluded from being a refugee;
- his/her misrepresentation or omission of facts, including the use of false documents, were decisive for the granting of refugee status.[274]

Member States *may* revoke, end or refuse to renew the status granted to a refugee by a governmental, administrative, judicial or quasi-judicial body, providing that:

- there are *reasonable grounds* for regarding him/her as a danger to the security of the Member State in which he or she is present;
- he/she, having been convicted by a final judgement of a particularly serious crime, constitutes a danger to the community of that Member State.[275]

The inclusion of *national security concerns*, as grounds for not granting refugee status, constitutes a widening of the exclusion provisions of the 1951 Geneva Convention. Nevertheless, Article 33(2) of the 1951 Geneva Convention similarly allows for an exception to the prohibition of *refoulement* for reasons of national security or where an individual poses a danger to the community following conviction for a particularly serious crime. Taking this into consideration it could be said that in practice both the Qualification Directive and the 1951 Geneva Convention allow for a form of exclusion from international protection in cases when national security is a concern.

Article 14(5) authorises that in situations described in paragraph (4), Member States may decide not to grant status to a refugee, where such decision has not yet been taken. Article 14(6), nonetheless, entitles the persons to whom paragraphs (4) or (5) apply, the rights set out in the 1951 Geneva Convention, Articles 3 (non-discrimination), 4 (religion), 16 (access to courts), 22 (public education), 31 (unlawful presence in the country of refuge), 32 (protection against expulsion) and 33 (*non-refoulement*).

273. Qualification Directive, Art. 14(2); this is without prejudice to the duty of the refugee in accordance with Art. 4(1) to disclose all relevant facts and provide all relevant documentation at his/her disposal.

274. Id., Art.14(3).

275. Id., Art.14(4).

2.4.3 Subsidiary protection[276]

The regime of subsidiary protection, including the rights and benefits deriving therefrom is intended to establish a harmonised system of protection by EU Member States for those in need of international protection but not covered by the 1951 Geneva Convention.[277] Persecutions on the basis of gender or sexual orientation; or threats to person's life under specific circumstances in situations of armed conflicts (war refugees), are examples of possible grounds for an application for subsidiary protection. In such cases the 1951 Geneva Convention would not apply, because the above-mentioned reasons are not contained in the definition of the term 'refugee'.[278]

Since the 1950s, most of the 15 EU Member States (i.e., those with EU membership before 1 May 2004) had some form of complementary protection, known by names as '*de facto* refugee status', 'B status' and 'humanitarian protection'. As the variety of names suggests, there was no single idea of what complementary protection entailed. In some Member States (Austria, Luxembourg, Spain), it was simply an obligation not to remove a person, whereas in others (Greece, Italy, Sweden) such a protection required the granting of a residence permit of some kind.[279]

The qualification for subsidiary protection is dealt with in Chapter V of the Qualification Directive. Article 2 defines a 'person eligible for subsidiary protection' as a

> 'third-country national or a stateless person who does not qualify as a refugee but in respect of whom substantial grounds have been shown for believing that the person concerned, if returned to his or her country of origin, or in the case of a stateless person, to his or her country of former habitual residence, would face a real risk of suffering serious harm, as defined in Article 15, and to whom Article 17(1) and (2) [the exclusion clauses] do not apply, and is unable, or, owing to such risk, unwilling to avail himself or herself of the protection of that country'.

The elements of serious harm, which are enumerated as grounds for qualification for subsidiary protection in Article 15, are as follows:

---

276. During discussions in the EU, Commission Services described subsidiary protection as an asylum issue that was 'more of a political nature'. See further Council of the European Union Note from Commission Services 'Horizontal Issues in the Asylum Proposals' 13636/01 ASILE 53 (9 November 2001).

277. On subsidiary protection further see e.g., Piotrovicz, R., Eck, C. van: 'Subsidiary Protection and Primary Rights', *International and Comparative Law Quarterly* 53(1) (January 2004), 107–138.

278. Cf. 1951 Geneva Convention, Art. 1A(2); see also chapter 1, 1.2.

279. Bouteillet-Paquet, D.: 'General Presentation of the Odysseus Comparative Study: What Lessons Should be Drawn from the EU Member States' Experience?', paper presented at the conference Subsidiary Protection: Improving or Degrading the Right of Asylum in Europe?, Brussels, 16–17 November 2001.

a. death penalty or execution; or
b. torture or inhuman or degrading treatment or punishment of an applicant in the country of origin; or
c. serious and individual threat to a civilian's life or person by reason of indiscriminate violence in situations of international or internal armed conflict.

It should be noted that in the Proposal for the Qualification Directive the grounds for subsidiary protection went beyond 'serious harm' and included violations of human rights, reflecting the content of Article 3 of the ECHR.[280] In addition, the Commentary to the Proposal referred to the ECHR and the case law of the European Court of Human Rights as 'legally binding framework, which informed of the choice of categories of beneficiary in this Proposal'. The categories and definitions of persons listed in the Proposal did not intend to create completely new classes of persons that Member States are obliged to protect but represented a clarification and codification of existing practice.[281]

The Tampere Conclusions called for an open and secure EU, fully committed to the obligations of the 1951 Geneva Convention and other relevant human rights instruments.[282] It should be presumed that the ECHR is one of the 'relevant human rights instruments'; therefore the omission of a reference to this convention in Article 15 of the Qualification Directive could be seen as a loss.

Article 16 of the Qualification Directive refers to the *cessation* of subsidiary protection. It states that the Member States shall have regard to whether the circumstances that led to the granting of subsidiary protection no longer exist and that this change of circumstances is significant and non-temporary in nature; so the person eligible for subsidiary protection no longer faces a real risk of serious harm.

Provisions on *exclusion* from subsidiary protection status, as laid down in Article 17 of the Qualification Directive, differ from a number of similar provisions of the Proposal for this Directive. The formulation that the commission of a serious non-political crime prior to the applicant's admission as a refugee[283] is one of the reasons for exclusion, has been modified to a commitment of a serious crime.[284] The new wording thus widens the grounds for exclusion from subsidiary protection. A new ground for exclusion was also added to the Qualification Directive: if an applicant for asylum constitutes a danger to the community or to the security of the Member State in which he or she is present.[285]

280. Art. 3 of the ECHR (Prohibition of Torture) reads: 'No one shall be subjected to torture or to inhuman or degrading treatment or punishment.'

281. Proposal for the Qualification Directive, Commentary on Art. 15, at 26.

282. Tampere, par. 4.

283. Proposal for the Qualification Directive, Art. 17(1)(b).

284. Qualification Directive, Art. 17(1)(b).

285. Id., Art. 17(1)(d).

Other modifications, in comparison to the Proposal, concern the deletion of the safeguard which provided that 'the application of the exclusion shall not in any manner affect obligations that Member States have under international law',[286] a safeguard concerning access to court proceedings to challenge exclusion,[287] as well as the requirement that the grounds for exclusion be based solely on the personal and knowing conduct of the person concerned.[288] In addition, two new provisions were included in the Qualification Directive: Article 17(2) provides that the grounds for exclusion apply to persons who instigate or otherwise participate in the commission of crimes or acts mentioned (in the previous paragraph); paragraph (3) provides that Member States may exclude a TCN or a stateless person from being eligible for subsidiary protection, if he/she prior to his/her admission to the Member State has committed one or more crimes, outside the scope of paragraph (1), which would be punishable by imprisonment if the crimes had been committed in the Member State concerned, and if he or she left his/her country of origin solely in order to avoid sanctions resulting from these crimes.

TCNs and stateless persons eligible for subsidiary protection shall be granted such protection by the Member States. Following the formulation of Article 18 of the Qualification Directive, there is an express obligation for the Member States to grant subsidiary forms of protection. This should be regarded as a significant step forward towards a Common European Asylum System, 'completed with measures on subsidiary forms of protection offering an appropriate status to any person in need of such protection'.[289]

The provision on revocation of, ending of or refusal to renew subsidiary protection status, as laid down in Article 19, in its substance corresponds with the provisions of Article 14 concerning refugee status. However, there is no reference to the principle of *non-refoulement* in Article 19. It would have been more appropriate to include an expression similar to Article II-79(2) of the Charter of Fundamental Rights of the Union, which determines that 'no one may be removed, expelled or extradited to a State where there is a serious risk that he or she would be subjected to the death penalty, torture or other inhuman or degrading treatment or punishment'.[290]

2.4.4 **Content of International Protection**

The content of international protection (applicable to both refugees and persons eligible for subsidiary protection, unless otherwise indicated)[291] is provided in Chapter VII of the Qualification Directive. Article 20 contains *general rules* and

286. Proposal for the Qualification Directive, Art.17(4).
287. Id., Art. 17(3).
288. Id., Art. 17(2).
289. Tampere, par. 14.
290. See *supra* 272.
291. Qualification Directive, Art. 20(2).

states that when implementing Chapter VII, Member States shall take into account the specific situation of vulnerable persons (such as minors, unaccompanied minors, disabled people, elderly people, pregnant women, single parents with minor children and persons who have been subjected to rape, torture or other serious forms of psychological, physical or sexual violence). Article 20 also acknowledges the rights laid down in the 1951 Geneva Convention.[292]

Article 21 of the Qualification Directive encompasses provisions on protection from *refoulement.* Paragraph (1) provides that Member States shall respect the principle of *non-refoulement,* in accordance with their international obligations. Paragraph (2) says that Member States may *refoule* a refugee, whether formally recognised or not, where not prohibited by the international obligations, when:

a. there are reasonable grounds for considering him/her as a danger to the security of the Member State in which he/she is present; or
b. he/she, having been convicted by a final judgement of a particularly serious crime, constitutes a danger to the community of that Member State.

The sole dedication of Article 21 to the principle of *non-refoulement* emphasises its importance for the context of international protection. Nevertheless, the failure to include protection from *refoulement* also in Article 19 (related to the revocation of, ending of or refusal to renew subsidiary protection status) is cause for concern.

The Tampere Presidency Conclusions made a direct link between the Common European Asylum System based on the full and inclusive application of the 1951 Geneva Convention and the principle of *non-refoulement*[293] by granting this protection to refugees. The Tampere Conclusions also stipulate that this System should be completed with measures on subsidiary forms of protection.[294] Taking this into consideration, it could be logically deduced that because the subsidiary forms of protection are part of the Common European Asylum System, persons eligible for such protection should also benefit from the principle of *non-refoulement.*

The content of international protection, as laid down in Chapter VII of the Qualification Directive, further includes provisions on the maintenance of family unity, residence permits, travel documents, access to employment, access to education, social welfare, health care, unaccompanied minors, access to accommodation, freedom of movement within the Member States, access to integration facilities and repatriation.[295]

Chapter VIII deals with the *administrative cooperation.* Article 36 ('Staff') provides that Member States shall ensure that the authorities and other organisations

---

292. Id., Art. 20(1), (6).
293. Cf. Tampere, par. 13.
294. Id., par. 14.
295. Qualification Directive, Arts. 23–34.

implementing the Qualification Directive have received the necessary training. Article 37 calls for a review by the Commission of the application of the Directive within 18 months following its transposition into the national laws of the Member States.[296]

Subsidiary protection seekers do not have the appellate rights that the 'Convention refugees' have. Taking into account that the Qualification Directive provides a status for those claiming to be refugees, as well as for those in need of a subsidiary form of protection; they should receive the same rights and procedural guarantees. In addition, for applications for international protection, Member States provide subsidiary protection more frequently than protection based on the 1951 Geneva Convention.[297]

At the time of the adoption of the Qualification Directive that defines refugee- and subsidiary protection status, problems remained with respect to procedural guarantees related to international protection. In order to complete successfully the first stage of the Common European Asylum System, this 'protection gap' had to be resolved. However, the Asylum Procedure Directive was formally adopted only in December 2005 despite the fact that the deadline for its adoption was set at 1 May 2004.

2.5 Procedures

'...This system should include, in the short term,...common standards for a fair and efficient asylum procedure...In the longer term, Community rules should lead to a common asylum procedure and a uniform status for those who are granted asylum valid throughout the Union.'[298]

The main purpose of the asylum procedure could be defined as to establish whether an applicant for asylum is in need of international protection. It is vital at this point to remember that a person is a refugee within the meaning of the 1951 Geneva Convention as soon as he/she fulfils the criteria contained in the definition.[299] An asylum procedure must ensure asylum seekers access to protection by

---

296. Art. 38(1) reads: 'The Member States shall bring into force the laws, regulations and administrative provisions necessary to comply with this Directive before 10 October 2006. They shall forthwith inform the Commission thereof.'

297. Communication from the Commission to the Council and the European Parliament, 'A More Efficient Common European Asylum System: The Single Procedure as the Next Step', COM(2004) 503 final, 15.7.2004, par. 11.

298. Tampere, par. 14, 15.

299. On the definition of 'refugee' according to the Qualification Directive see chapter 2, 2.4.2. On the declaratory nature of refugee status determination further see *UNHCR Handbook*, par. 28.

enabling them to present the merits of their claim to a clearly identified authority, responsible for taking a decision in their asylum claim.[300]

The achievement of a consensus on the 'Council Directive on minimum standards on procedures in Member States for granting and withdrawing refugee status' (further referred to as the Asylum Procedures Directive)[301] pursuant to Article 63(1)(d) TEC, has been particularly difficult:

The European Commission presented its first Proposal for a Council Directive on minimum standards on procedures in Member States for granting and withdrawing refugee status in September 2000.[302] The Proposal was sent to the Council, the European Parliament and the Economic and Social Committee. The Economic and Social Committee delivered a favourable opinion in April 2001.[303] On 20 September 2001 the European Parliament adopted its Opinion in plenary, approving the Commission's proposal subject to amendments and calling on the Commission to amend the Proposal accordingly. On the basis of a report presented to the plenary by Mr. Watson, chairperson of the Committee on Citizen's Freedoms and Rights, JHA, the European Parliament has adopted 106 amendments.[304]

The declaration of the Laeken European Council requested the Commission to bring forward a modified proposal.[305] On this base the Commission presented an 'Amended Proposal for a Council Directive on minimum standards on procedures in Member States for granting and withdrawing refugee status'.[306]

300. See Comments from the ECRE on the Amended proposal for a Council Directive on minimum standards on procedures in Member States for granting and withdrawing refuge status, 4; The determination of refugee status, although mentioned in the 1951 Geneva Convention (Art. 9), is not specifically regulated. In particular, the Convention does not indicate what types of procedures are to be adopted for the determination of refugee status. It is therefore left to each Contracting State to establish the procedure that it considers most appropriate, having regard to its particular constitutional and administrative structure. In view of this situation and of the unlikelihood that all states bound by the 1951 Geneva Convention and 1967 New York Protocol could establish identical procedures, the Executive Committee of the High Commissioner's Programme, at its 28th session in October 1977, recommended that procedures should satisfy certain basic requirements; further see *UNHCR Handbook*, par. 189–194.

301. OJ L 326, 13.12.2005, 13; the Asylum Procedures Directive entered into force on 2 January 2006; transposition deadline: 1 December 2007. The United Kingdom and Ireland have notified their wish to take part in the adoption and application of this Directive. Denmark does not take part in the adoption of this Directive and is not bound by it or subject to its application.

302. COM(2000) 578 final, OJ C62 E, 27.02.2001, 231. An earlier initiative concerning minimum guarantees for asylum procedures was already taken on the basis of the Treaty on European Union (Treaty of Maastricht), namely Art. K.1 thereof (see Council Resolution of 20 June 1995 on minimum guarantees for asylum procedures, OJ C 274, 19.09.1996, 13).

303. Doc. CES 530/2001.

304. A5-0291/2001, OJ C 77E, 28.03.2002, 94.

305. Presidency Conclusions, Laeken European Council, 14 and 15 December 2001, par. 41.

306. COM(2002) 326 final/2, 03.07.2002.

During the JHA Council meeting of 29 and 30 April 2004, the minimum standards on procedures in Member States for granting and withdrawing refugee status were among the debated items again.[307] The Council, subject to parliamentary scrutiny and reservations by certain delegations, and after a number of further amendments, agreed on a 'general approach' to the Amended Proposal for the Procedures Directive.

Taking the very good European Commission's draft as a starting point, the long process of inter-state negotiations resulted in an 'Amended Proposal to the Asylum Procedures Directive', which contained no binding commitment to satisfactory procedural standards, allowing scope for Member States to adopt or continue worse practices in determining asylum claims.[308] On 1 December 2005, 19 months after the deadline set for the adoption, the Asylum Procedure Directive was finally adopted.

For the purpose of this study the structure provided in the Asylum Procedures Directive will be used:
- General provisions;
- Basic principles and guarantees;
- Procedures at first instance;
- Procedures for the withdrawal of refugee status;
- Appeal procedures.

2.5.1 General provisions

The *purpose* of the Asylum Procedures Directive, as laid down in Article 1, is to establish minimum standards on procedures in Member States for granting and withdrawing refugee status.

Article 3 sets the *scope* of this Directive. It shall apply to all applications for asylum made in the territory, including at the border, or in the transit zones of the Member States and to the withdrawal of refugee status.[309] It shall also apply in cases where Member States employ or introduce a procedure in which asylum applications are examined both as applications on the basis of the 1951 Geneva Convention and as applications for other kinds of international protection, as defined by Article 15 of the Qualification Directive.[310] In addition, Member States

307. At this JHA Council meeting the Qualification Directive (OJ L 304, 30.09.2004) on the criteria for awarding refugee or subsidiary protection status in the EU Member States was adopted without debate.

308. Doc. number 8771/04, interinstitutional file 2000/0238 (CNS), subject matter ASILE 33, document date: 30.4.2004. See also UNHCR News: 'UNHCR regrets missed opportunity to adopt high EU asylum standards', 30 April 2004; available at: www.unhcr.ch.

309. *Asylum Procedures Directive*, Art. 3(1).

310. Id., Art. 3(3); on the grounds for qualification for a subsidiary protection (Art. 15) see chapter 2, 2.4.3.

may decide to apply this Directive in procedures for deciding on applications for any kind of international protection.[311] This Directive shall not apply in cases of request for diplomatic or territorial asylum submitted to representations of Member States.[312]

2.5.2 Basic principles and guarantees

It is of central importance for an effective right to asylum to have *access to an asylum procedure* in the country, where the asylum application was submitted. The Asylum Procedures Directive states that Member States may require that applications for asylum be made in person and/or at a designated place[313] and they shall ensure that each adult having legal capacity has the right to make an application for asylum on his/her own behalf.[314] With regards to minors, Member States may determine in national legislation those cases in which a minor can make an application on his/her own behalf, cases in which the application of an unaccompanied minor has to be lodged by a representative, as well as cases in which the lodging of an application for asylum is deemed to constitute also the lodging of an application for asylum for any unmarried minor.[315]

Authorities likely to be addressed by someone who wishes to make an asylum application should be able to advise that person how and where he/she may make such an application and/or may require these authorities to forward the application to the competent authority.[316] It is welcomed that the obligation of Member States to ensure that asylum claims are lodged with the right authority has been included in the Asylum Procedures Directive.[317] Otherwise, if there is a risk of failure to

311. Id., Art. 3(4).

312. Id., Art. 3(2).

313. Id., Art. 6(1).

314. Id., Art. 6(2).

315. Id., Art. 6(4); the Convention on the Rights of the Child specifically informs that 'State Parties shall take appropriate measures to ensure that a child who is seeking refugee status or who is considered a refugee in accordance with applicable international or domestic law and procedures shall, whether unaccompanied or accompanied by his or her parents or by any other person, receive appropriate protection and humanitarian assistance in the enjoyment of applicable rights set forth in the present Convention and in other international human rights or humanitarian instruments to which the said States are Parties'. See the Convention on the Rights of the Child, Art. 22 (adopted by resolution 44/25 of 20 November 1989, entered into force on 2 September 1990, United Nations, Treaty Series, vol. 1577, 3); all EU Member States are Parties to this Convention.

316. Asylum Procedures Directive, Art. 6(5).

317. Pursuant to the UNHCR's 'basic requirements' the competent official (e.g., immigration officer or border police officer) to whom the applicant addresses himself/herself at the border or in the territory of a Contracting State should have clear instructions for dealing with cases which might come within the purview of the relevant international instruments. He/she should be required to act in accordance with the principle of *non-refoulement* and to refer such cases to a higher authority. See Official Records of the General Assembly, 32nd Session, Supplement No. 12 (A/32/12/Ad.1), par. 53(6)(e).

lodge an asylum claim due to a possible ignorance of the firstly addressed national authorities, the whole asylum procedure could be jeopardised.

In order to prevent cases of *refoulement* (when persons are sent back to a third country, where they could suffer persecution), the inclusion of a provision which allows applicants for asylum to remain in the territory of the Member State until the determining authority makes a decision, should be received very positively. The right to remain, however, does not necessarily constitute an entitlement to a residence permit.[318]

The Asylum Procedures Directive permits considering a *late application* as one, though not the sole, ground for rejecting its examination.[319] There is, however, no criterion setting time limits for a 'late' application. Besides, the reasons for a late application may not only be valid (e.g., in cases of psychological trauma) but also, not related at all to the merits of the application. It could be therefore recommended to expand this paragraph by a general safeguard to the effect that the filing of an application for asylum shall not be subject to any prior formality.[320] A late application should not be considered as a ground for rejecting an application for asylum. Member States shall ensure that all applicants for asylum enjoy the following guarantees:

- they must be informed, in a language which they may reasonably be supposed to understand, of the procedure to be followed and of their rights and obligations during the procedure; and the possible consequences of not complying with their obligations and not co-operating with the responsible authorities;[321]
- they must receive the services of an interpreter for submitting their case to the competent authorities;[322]
- they must not be denied the opportunity to communicate with the UNHCR or with any other organisation working on behalf of the UNHCR on the territory of the Member State, pursuant to an agreement with that Member State;[323]
- they must be given notice in reasonable time of the decision by the determining authority on their application for asylum;[324]
- they must be informed about the result of the decision by the determining authority in a language that they may reasonably be supposed to understand when they are not assisted or represented by a legal officer or other counsellor

318. Asylum Procedures Directive, Art. 7(1); Art. 7(2) allows for certain exceptions. Pursuant to the UNHCR's 'basic requirements' the applicant should be permitted to remain in the country pending a decision on his/her initial request by the competent authority, unless it has been established by that authority that his/her request is clearly abusive. See Official Records of the General Assembly, 32nd Session, Supplement No. 12 (A/32/12/Ad.1), par. 53(6)(e).

319. Asylum Procedures Directive, Art. 8(1).

320. See Comments from the ECRE on the Amended Proposal for a Council Directive on minimum standards on procedures in Member States for granting and withdrawing refugee status, 4.

321. Asylum Procedures Directive, Art. 10(1)(a).

322. Id., Art. 10(1)(b).

323. Id., Art. 10(1)(c).

324. Id., Art. 10(1)(d).

and when free legal assistance is not available; information on how to challenge a negative decision shall also be provided.[325]

These guarantees comply with the 'basic requirements' as recommended by the Executive Committee of the High Commissioner's (for Refugees) Programme:

> '(ii) The applicant should receive the necessary guidance as to the procedure to be followed.
> (iii) There should be a clearly identified authority – wherever possible a single central authority – with responsibility for examining requests for refugee status and taking a decision in the first instance.
> (iv) The applicant should be given the necessary facilities, including the services of a competent interpreter, for submitting his case to the authorities concerned. Applicants should also be given the opportunity, of which they should be duly informed, to contact a representative of UNHCR.
> (v) If the applicant is recognised as a refugee, he should be informed accordingly and issued with documentation certifying his refugee status…'.[326]

Article 12 of the Asylum Procedures Directive spells out the general principle that before a decision is taken by the determining authority, the applicant for asylum shall be given an opportunity of a personal interview on his/her application for asylum with a person competent under national law to conduct such an interview.[327] Paragraph (2) lists a number of exceptions to the general principle by allowing Member States to omit a personal interview in certain cases, namely:

- when the determining authority is able to take a positive decision on the basis of evidence available; or
- the competent authority has already had a meeting with the applicant for the purpose of assisting him/her with filling his/her application and submitting the essential information regarding the application (in terms of Article 4(2) of the Qualification Directive); or
- the determining authority, on the basis of a complete examination of information provided by the applicant, considers the application as unfounded.[328]

A personal interview should be construed as an essential asylum-procedure-right and therefore asylum applicants should not be deprived of it; except in cases when the competent authority considers it possible to grant refugee status on the basis of written information submitted, and also in specific cases of persons with medical or psychological problems.[329]

---

325. Id., Art. 10(1)(e).
326. *UNHCR Handbook*, par. 192.
327. Asylum Procedures Directive, Art. 12(1).
328. The application is considered as unfounded in cases where the circumstances specified in Art. 23(4)(a), (c), (g), (h) and (j) of the Asylum Procedures Directive apply.
329. Asylum Procedures Directive, Art. 12(3).

Cases of *detention* are dealt with in Article 18 of the Asylum Procedures Directive. Paragraph (1) provides that Member States shall not hold a person in detention for the sole reason that he/she is an applicant for asylum.[330] Paragraph (2) obliges the Member States to ensure that where an applicant for asylum is held in detention, there must be a possibility of speedy judicial review. Nonetheless, a clear list of grounds for detention of applicants for asylum is lacking.[331] Detention should be justified only as a measure of last resort if there is a repeated and unjustified failure to comply with reporting requirements imposed by the authorities.[332] A list of grounds for detention should be exhaustive and its interpretation should be narrow in order to prevent possible cases of arbitrary detention of asylum applicants. Moreover, one has to bear in mind that persons genuinely seeking international protection could have already gone through persecution and detention before they were able to lodge their asylum claim in the country of asylum. Therefore the detention of persons seeking asylum should always be well-considered and appropriately justified.

So far the asylum applicants' rights were discussed. The Asylum Procedures Directive also includes *obligations of the applicants for asylum.*[333] The wording of the provisions ('Member States may…') contained in Article 11 suggests that a large extent of discretion is left to the Member States in this respect. Member States may impose upon applicants for asylum obligations to co-operate with the competent authorities, insofar as these obligations are necessary for the processing of the application.[334] In particular, Member States may provide that:

a. applicants for asylum are required to report to the competent authorities or to appear before them in person, either without delay or at a specified time;
b. applicants for asylum have to hand over the documents in their possession relevant to the examination of the application, such as their passports;
c. applicants for asylum are required to inform the competent authorities of their current place of residence or address and of any changes thereof as soon as possible. Member States may provide that the applicant shall have to accept any communication at the most recent place of residence or address which he/she indicated accordingly;

---

330. Examples of international documents referring to the conditions of detention are: the 1951 Geneva Convention, Art. 25 and 31; the Universal Declaration of Human Rights [GA Res. 217A(III) of 10 December 1948], Art. 9; the International Covenant on Civil and Political Rights [GA Res. 2200A (XXI) of 16 December 1966], Art. 9; ECHR (Art. 5).

331. See also ExCom Conclusion No. 44(XXXVII)-1986, Detention of Refugees and Asylum Seekers, UNHCR Guidelines on Applicable Criteria and Standards relating to the Detention of Asylum-Seekers (1999).

332. Further see, e.g., ECRE's position on the detention of asylum seekers, April 1996.

333. Asylum Procedures Directive, Art. 11.

334. Id., Art. 11(1).

d. the competent authorities may search the applicant and the items he/she carries with him/her;
e. the competent authorities may take a photograph of the applicant;
f. the competent authorities may record the applicant's oral statements, provided he/she has previously been informed thereof.[335]

With the presumption that these obligations would be imposed in a fair manner by the national authorities, the above-mentioned obligations might deter non-genuine asylum seekers from applying for refugee status in a Member State; specially those persons who utilise the asylum procedure as means to 'buy time' in order to remain in the Member State's territory.

Other provisions, part of the basic principles and guarantees in relation to the asylum procedure, which will be discussed are the procedures in cases of explicit withdrawal of the application, or in cases of implicit withdrawal or abandonment of the application and the data protection:

Clear and precise standards under national laws should be guaranteed in cases when the applicant withdraws his/her application. Article 19 of the Asylum Procedures Directive refers to 'explicit withdrawal of an asylum application'. Member States shall ensure that the determining authority takes a decision either to discontinue the examination or to reject the application.[336] Member States may also decide that the determining authority can make a decision to discontinue the examination without taking a decision. In such cases, Member States shall ensure that the determining authority shall enter a notice in the applicant's file.[337] Member States may thus decide which approach to adopt in their national laws in the situations pictured above. The most appropriate response of the determining authorities in cases when the applicant withdraws his/her asylum application seems to be a discontinuation of the procedure and placing a notice into the file of the applicant, which allows appropriate consideration of the facts around the withdrawal during a potential future reopening of his/her case. Rejection of the application would most probably require taking a decision on the substance of an application. Nonetheless, this does not seem to be necessary once the application has been explicitly withdrawn.[338]

Article 20 of the Asylum Procedures Directive refers to procedures in case of 'implicit withdrawal or abandonment of an asylum application'. This Article foresees a possibility not only to discontinue but also to reject an application for asylum in those cases, when there is a 'reasonable cause to consider' that an applicant for asylum has implicitly withdrawn or abandoned his/her application and therefore has not established an entitlement to refugee status in accordance with

335. Id., Art. 11(2).
336. Id., Art. 19(1).
337. Id., Art. 19(2).
338. *Supra* 320, at 13.

the Qualification Directive.[339] Member States may assume that the applicant has implicitly withdrawn or abandoned his/her asylum application in particular when it is ascertained that:

a. he/she failed to respond to requests to provide information essential to his/her application in terms of Article 4 of the Qualification Directive or has not appeared for a personal interview [...], unless the applicant demonstrates within a reasonable time that his/her failure was due to circumstances beyond his/her control;
b. he/she has absconded or left without authorisation the place where he/she lived or was held, without contacting the competent authority within a reasonable time or he/she has not within a reasonable time complied with reporting duties or other obligations to communicate.[340]

Member States shall also ensure that the applicant who reports again to the competent authority after a decision to discontinue is taken, is entitled to request that his/her case be reopened, unless the request is examined as a subsequent application[341] or is examined in accordance with the procedural rules.[342] Member States may provide for a time limit after which the applicant's case can no longer be reopened. On the other hand, Member States may also allow the determining authority to take up the examination at the stage, at which the application was discontinued.[343] It is important to note that the Asylum Procedures Directive requires the Member States to ensure that asylum applicants are not removed contrary to the principle of *non-refoulement.*[344]

As regards the *collection of information on individual cases*, Member States shall not directly disclose the information regarding individual applications for asylum, or the fact that an application has been made, to the alleged actor or actors of persecution of the applicant. At the same time, the Member States shall not obtain information from such person(s) in a manner that would result in them being informed of the fact that an application has been made by the applicant; and which would jeopardise the physical integrity of the applicant and his/her dependants, or the liberty and security of his/her family members still living in the country of origin.[345]

Article 21 of the Asylum Procedures Directive emphasises the role of the UNHCR, which should have access to applicants for asylum, including those in detention and in airport or port transit zones; access to information on individual

339. Asylum Procedures Directive, Art. 20(1), 1st subpar.
340. Id., Art. 20(1), 2nd subpar.
341. On cases of subsequent applications see Art. 32.
342. On procedural rules see Art. 34.
343. Asylum Procedures Directive, Art. 20(2), 1st, 2nd and 4th subpar.
344. Id., Art. 20(2), 3rd subpar.
345. Id., Art. 22.

applications for asylum, on the course of the procedure and on the decisions taken (provided that the applicant for asylum agrees). The UNHCR should be able to present its views to any competent authorities regarding individual applications for asylum at any stage of the procedure under Article 35 of the 1951 Geneva Convention.[346] Paragraph (2) extends access to applicants and information on their cases to organisations which work in the territory of the Member State on behalf of the UNHCR pursuant to an agreement with that Member State. The terms 'on behalf of the UNHCR' and 'pursuant to an agreement with that Member State' might be perceived as limitations in regards to other organisations (e.g., NGOs), which could also valuably contribute to the protection of asylum applicants.[347]

2.5.3 **Procedures at first instance**

The third group of provisions to be discussed regards procedures at first instance. The following provisions will now be discussed:

- provisions on examination procedure and criteria for prioritisation and acceleration of any examination procedure;
- cases of inadmissible and unfounded applications;
- application of the concept of first country of asylum;
- safe third country concept;
- safe country of origin concept; and
- border procedures.

Article 23 of the Asylum Procedures Directive refers to the examination procedure.[348] Member States shall process applications for asylum in an examination procedure in accordance with the basic principles and guarantees discussed above. Member States shall ensure that an examination procedure is concluded as soon as possible, without prejudice to an adequate and complete assessment. When no decision can be taken within six months, the applicant concerned shall either be informed of the delay or receive, upon his/her request, information on the time frame within which the decision on his/her application is to be expected. Nevertheless, such information shall not constitute an obligation for the Member State towards the applicant concerned to take a decision within that time-frame.[349]

---

346. Id., Art. 21(1). Art. 35 of the 1951 Geneva Convention lays down the obligation of the national authorities of the Contracting States to co-operate with the UNHCR.

347. *Supra* 320, at 14.

348. Par. 11 of the Preamble to the Asylum Procedures Directive states: 'It is in the interest of both the Member States and applicants for asylum to decide as soon as possible on applications for asylum. The organisation of the processing of applications for asylum is left to the discretion of the Member States, so that they may, in accordance with their national needs, prioritise or accelerate the processing of any application, taking into account the standards in this Directive.'

349. Asylum Procedures Directive, Art. 23(1), (2).

The provisions of Article 23(1) and (2) should be welcomed, as they emphasise the importance of a procedure that is concluded 'as soon as possible'. On the other hand, the release from obligation for the Member States to comply with a time frame (set by the Member States themselves) within which the decision has to be taken will most probably not help to ensure an expedite procedure. Member States may lay down that an *examination procedure*, in accordance with the basic principles and guarantees, be *prioritised or accelerated* if:[350]

a. the applicant in submitting his/her application and presenting the facts, has only raised issues that are not relevant or of minimal relevance to the examination of whether he/she qualifies as a refugee; or
b. the applicant clearly does not qualify as a refugee or for refugee status in a Member States; or
c. the application for asylum is considered to be unfounded (because the applicant comes from a safe country of origin or a country which is not a EU Member State and is considered to be a safe third country for the applicant); or
d. the applicant has misled the authorities by presenting false information or documents or by withholding relevant information or documents with respect to his/her identity and/or nationality that could have had a negative impact on the decision; or
e. the applicant has filed another application for asylum stating other personal data; or
f. the applicant has not produced information establishing with a reasonable degree of certainty his/her identity or nationality, or, it is likely that, in bad faith he/she has destroyed or disposed of an identity or travel document that would have helped establish his/her identity or nationality; or
g. the applicant has made inconsistent, contradictory, improbable or insufficient representations which make his/her claim clearly unconvincing in relation to his/her having been an object of persecution; or
h. the applicant has submitted a subsequent application which does not raise any relevant new elements with respect to his/her particular circumstances or to the situation in his/her country of origin; or
i. the applicant has failed without reasonable cause to make his/her application earlier, having had opportunity to do so; or
j. the applicant is making an application merely in order to delay or frustrate the enforcement of an earlier or imminent decision which would result in his/her removal; or

350. Id., Art. 23(4)(a)–(o).

k. the applicant failed without good reason to comply with obligations referred to in Article 4(1), (2) of the Qualification Directive[351] or in Articles 11(2)(a)[352] and (b)[353] and 20(1)[354] of this Directive; or
l. the applicant entered the territory of the Member State unlawfully or prolonged his/her stay unlawfully and, without good reason, has either not presented himself/herself to the authorities and/or filed an application for asylum as soon as possible given the circumstances of his/her entry; or
m. the applicant is a danger to the national security or the public order of the Member State; or the applicant has been forcibly expelled for serious reasons of public security and public order under national law; or
n. the applicant refuses to comply with an obligation to have his/her fingerprints taken in accordance with relevant Community and/or national legislation; or
o. the application was made by an unmarried minor (in cases when the lodging of an application for asylum is deemed to constitute also the lodging of an application for asylum for any unmarried minor),[355] after the application of the parents or parent responsible for the minor has been rejected by a decision and no relevant new elements were raised with respect to his/her particular circumstances or to the situation in his/her country of origin.[356]

Moreover, Member States may prioritise or accelerate any examination in accordance with the basic principles and guarantees, including where the application is likely to be well-founded or where the applicant has special needs.[357]

The provisions regarding the accelerated or prioritised examination procedure seem to be made to quickly exclude the non-genuine asylum seekers from the procedure resulting in the granting of refugee status. This is positive, as it might minimise the number of bogus asylum applications; and based on this, one could presume that the remaining genuine asylum applications will be processed as quickly as possible. On the other hand, according to paragraph 12 of the Preamble to the Asylum Procedures Directive, 'The notion of public order may cover a conviction for committing a serious crime.' This addendum is quite worrisome since it is very vague: it does not specify if the conviction was made in the country of

351. Art. 4(1), (2) of the Qualification Directive refers to the submitting, as soon as possible, of all elements needed to substantiate the application, i.e., applicant's statements and all documentation at the applicant's disposal regarding age, background, relevant relatives, identity, nationality, country and place of previous residence, previous asylum applications, travel routes, identity and travel documents and the reasons for applying for international protection.

352. This provision refers to an applicant's obligation to report to the competent authorities or to appear there in person, either without delay or at a specified time.

353. This provision refers to an applicant's obligation to hand over documents in their possession relevant to the examination of the application.

354. This provision refers to cases of implicit withdrawal or abandonment of asylum applications.

355. Asylum Procedures Directive, Art. 6(4)(c).

356. Id., Art. 23(4).

357. Id., Art. 23(3).

origin/previous residence, in a third country or in the Member State, 'a serious crime' is not defined and also one has to remember that by being convicted of a serious crime an applicant should not automatically be considered a non-genuine asylum seeker, unless Article 12 of the Qualification Directive applies.[358]

If an asylum application is *inadmissible,* the national authorities do not have to consider its merits at all. Therefore even though the situation of the asylum seeker in the country of origin may be dreadful, with the result that his case for refugee status may be well-founded, the authorities will not even examine the application. Inadmissible cases concern situations where it is believed that the asylum seeker should have applied somewhere else, or where the asylum seeker already has protection somewhere else.[359]

The Asylum Procedures Directive applies this principle to cases when a person already received protection elsewhere or is subject to the 'Dublin II' Regulation, which allocates responsibility to another Member State for considering his/her asylum application. Furthermore, Member States are not required to examine whether the applicant qualifies as a refugee in accordance with the Qualification Directive when an application may be considered inadmissible according to Article 25 of the Asylum Procedures Directive. Member States *may* consider an application for asylum as inadmissible if:

a. another Member State has granted refugee status;
b. a country which is not a Member State is considered as a first country of asylum for the applicant;
c. a country which is not a Member State is considered as a safe country for the applicant;
d. the applicant is allowed to remain in the Member State concerned on some other grounds and as result of this he/she has been granted a status equivalent to the rights and benefits of the refugee status by virtue of the Qualification Directive;
e. the applicant is allowed to remain in the territory of the Member State concerned on some other grounds which protect him/her against *refoulement* pending the outcome of the procedure for the determination of status pursuant to point (d);
f. the applicant has lodged an identical application after a final decision;
g. a dependant of the applicant lodges an application, after he/she has consented to have his/her case be part of an application made on his/her behalf (in accordance with Article 6(3)) and there are no facts relating to the dependant's situation which justify a separate application.

---

358. Art. 12 of the Qualification Directive, regarding causes of exclusion from refugee status, is broadly based on Art. 1F of the 1951 Geneva Convention.

359. Statewatch analysis: 'EU law on asylum procedures: An assault on human rights?'.

Article 28 deals with cases of *unfounded applications*,[360] referring to applications for asylum when the determining authority has established that the applicant does not qualify for refugee status according to the Qualification Directive.[361] Member States *may* also consider an application as manifestly unfounded when the following cases are so defined in their national legislation:

- the applicant does not clearly qualify as a refugee according to the Qualification Directive;[362] or
- when the applicant is submitting facts that are not relevant or have minimum relevance to the examination of whether he/she qualifies as a refugee by virtue of the Qualification Directive;[363] or
- when the applicant comes from a safe country of origin; or because the country which is not a Member State is considered to be a safe third country for the applicant;[364] or
- when the applicant is an unmarried minor who applies after the application of his parents has been rejected by a decision and no new relevant elements were raised with respect to his/her circumstances or to the situation in his/he country of origin;[365] or in other cases of unfounded applications for asylum in which any of the relevant circumstances apply.[366]

The most discussed provisions of the Amended Proposal Directive are the provisions regarding the concepts of *safe third country, first country of asylum* and *safe country of origin*. These concepts are given as grounds for considering an application for asylum as inadmissible or unfounded. A variety of terms are used as synonyms of what has become generally known as a 'safe third country'. These include 'country of first asylum', 'host third country', 'country responsible for examining the asylum application'. The terms are, however, not perfectly identical; and the vocabulary has been developing over the last decade of application and implementation of this principle.[367] For example the UNHCR sees a clear dis-

---

360. On the definition of 'manifestly unfounded applications' see Resolution on Manifestly Unfounded Applications for Asylum, Conclusions of the meeting of the ministers responsible for immigration Doc. 10579/92 IMMIG (London, 30 Nov.-1 Dec. 1992); on the definition of 'manifestly unfounded' and 'clearly abusive' asylum claims see also UNHCR Executive Committee Conclusions, The Problem of Manifestly Unfounded or Abusive Applications for Refugee Status or Asylum (No. 30 (XXXIV)-1983).

361. Asylum Procedures Directive, Art. 28(1).

362. Id., Art. 23(4)(b).

363. Id., Art. 23(4)(a).

364. Id., Art. 23(4)(c).

365. Id., Art. 23(4)(o).

366. Id., Art. 23(4)(d) to (n).

367. See, e.g., the paper by Selm, J. van: 'Access to Procedures, "Safe Third Countries", "Safe Countries of Origin" and 'Time Limits"' (2001), commissioned by UNHCR and the Carnegie Endowment for International Peace as a Background paper for the Third Track discussions held in Geneva in June 2001 as part of the Global Consultations on International Protection in the context of the 50th anniversary of the 1951 Convention relating to the Status of Refugees, 7, par. 15.

tinction between a 'first country of asylum' – a place where protection has been granted, and where the level of protection remains satisfactory; and a 'safe third country' – a place with which an asylum seeker has some connection, e.g., transit, and in which the State applying the principle believes the person could have requested protection. This implies that the 'first country of asylum' has accepted responsibility for the protection of the individual in question, but a 'safe third country' has not done so. UNHCR considers that any analysis of the issue must be based on the understanding that the responsibility for examining an asylum request lies primarily with the State to which it has been submitted. While that State may be relieved from such responsibility if it ensures that another State will consider the request, it is essential that any arrangements that may be concluded to this end be consistent with the imperatives of refugee protection.[368]

One discussion of the terminology is particularly interesting in the light of the European developments discussed below. In 1995 the United Kingdom Delegation in Geneva wrote a note explaining the terminology as follows:

- 'safe third country' – meaning a country other than the country of origin or the one where the applicant is seeking asylum which is 'safe' in that the applicant would not 'face treatment contrary to Article 33 of the 1951 Geneva Convention, or other violations of human rights';
- 'host third country' (the term used in the London Resolution)[369] entails the following: 'The word "host" means that the asylum applicant has been in a third country before arriving in the country in which he or she has applied for asylum.'

A 'safe third country', the note says, is broader: the applicant does not need to have been in the 'safe' State in question, but can safely be sent there. The London Resolution was given the title of dealing with 'host third countries'. In fact, as will be pointed out below, the development of the concept means it is actually about 'safe third countries' according to the above definitions.[370]

Pursuant to Article 27(1) of the Asylum Procedures Directive, Member States may apply the safe third country concept only where the competent authorities are satisfied that a person seeking asylum will be treated in accordance with the following principles in the third country concerned:

a. life and liberty are not threatened on account of race, religion, membership of a particular social group or political opinion; and

368. See in this regard the position stated in 'Revisiting the Dublin Convention, Some reflections by UNHCR in response to the Commission staff working paper', 2.

369. Resolution of 30 November and 1 December 1992 of the ministers of the Member States of the EC responsible for immigration on a harmonised approach to questions concerning host third countries, SN 4823/92 WGI 1283 AS 147.

370. *Supra* 367, at 8, par.17.

b. the principle of *non-refoulement* in accordance with the Geneva Convention is respected; and
c. the prohibition of removal, in violation of the right to freedom from torture and cruel, inhuman or degrading treatment as laid down in international law, is respected; and
d. the possibility exists to request refugee status and, if found to be a refugee, to receive protection in accordance with the Geneva Convention.

All four above-mentioned conditions must be fulfilled simultaneously, in order to establish a third country as 'safe' for the asylum applicant. Paragraph (2) provides additional rules that shall be laid down in the national legislation of the Member States regarding the application of the safe third country concept:

a. rules requiring a connection between the person seeking asylum and the third country concerned on the basis of which it would be reasonable for that person to go to that country;
b. rules on the methodology by which the competent authorities satisfy themselves that the safe third country concept may be applied to a particular country or to a particular applicant. Such methodology shall include case-by-case consideration of the safety of the country for a particular applicant and/or national designation of countries considered to be generally safe;
c. rules, in accordance with international law, allowing an individual examination of whether the third country concerned is safe for a particular applicant which, as a minimum, shall permit the applicant to challenge the application of the safe third country concept on the grounds that he/she would be subjected to torture, cruel, inhuman or degrading treatment or punishment.

When implementing a decision, which is solely based on Article 27, Member States shall inform the applicant for asylum accordingly and provide him/her with a document informing the authorities of the third country, in the language of that country, that the applicant has not been examined in substance.[371]

One can say that the whole applicability of the safe-third-country concept stands or falls with Article 27(4). This provision regulates the need for admission on the territory of the alleged safe third country. If the third country concerned does not agree on the application of the concept, then the Member State in question is still obliged to process the application for international protection in full accordance with the basic principles and guarantees as laid down in the Asylum Procedures Directive.[372] This provision should protect asylum seekers from being

371. Asylum Procedures Directive, Art. 27(3).

372. JHA Council – 'Analysis of the Asylum Procedures Directive' (MEMO/04/98), Brussels, 28 April 2004.

sent to third countries not willing to provide them with protection; and by this also help to avoid the problem of refugees in orbit.

Article 26 of the Asylum Procedures Directive states that a country can be considered a *first country of asylum* for a particular applicant for asylum if:

a. he/she has been recognised in that country as a refugee and he/she can still avail himself/herself of that protection; or
b. he/she otherwise enjoys sufficient protection in that country, including benefiting from the principle of *non-refoulement*;

provided that he/she will be readmitted to that country.[373]

A key development in the concept of safe countries of origin was the 'Conclusion on countries where there is generally no serious risk of persecution', agreed by the European Community in London in November 1992.[374] The EU Immigration Ministers defined a safe country of origin as a country

> 'which can clearly be shown, in an objective and verifiable way, normally not to generate refugees or where it can be clearly shown, in an objective and verifiable way, that circumstances which might in the past have justified recourse to the 1951 Convention have ceased to exist'.

The Conclusions of the EU Immigration Ministers provide that a safe country of origin determination by a Member State should not be an automatic bar to all asylum applications from that State, but may be used instead as justification for directing applicants into expedited procedures with sharply curtailed legal safeguards.[375]

The Council *shall*, acting by a qualified majority on a proposal from the Commission and after consulting the European Parliament, adopt a minimum common list of third countries which shall be regarded by Member States as safe countries of origin in accordance with Annex II to the Asylum Procedures Directive.[376]

The Council *may*, acting in the same way as mentioned above, amend the minimum common list by adding or removing third countries, in accordance with Annex II. The Commission shall examine any request made by the Council or by a Member State that it submits a proposal to amend the minimum common

---

373. Asylum Procedures Directive, Art. 26. In applying the concept of the first country of asylum to the particular circumstances of an applicant for asylum, Member States may take into account the content of Art. 27(1) on the safe-third-country concept.

374. Conclusions of 30 November and 1 December 1992 of the Ministers of the Member States of the EC responsible for immigration on countries in which there is generally no serious risk of persecution, SN 4821/92 WGI 1281 AS 145.

375. Byrne, R., Shacknove, A.: 'The Safe Country Notion in European Asylum Law', *Harvard Human Rights Journal* 9 (Spring 1996), 193–194.

376. Asylum Procedures Directive, Art. 29(1).

list.[377] When making its proposal, the Commission shall make use of information from the Member States, its own information and, *where necessary*, information from UNHCR, the Council of Europe and other relevant international organisations.[378]

Concerning the removing of a third country from the minimum common list, the following possibilities are further envisaged by the Asylum Procedures Directive:

– Where the Council requests the Commission to submit a proposal for removing a third country from the minimum common list, the obligation of Member States pursuant to Article 31(2) shall be suspended with regard to this third country as of the day following the Council decision requesting such a submission.[379]
– Where a Member State requests the Commission to submit a proposal to the Council for removing a third country from the minimum common list, that Member State shall notify the Council in writing of the request made to the Commission. The obligation of this Member State pursuant to Article 31(2) shall be suspended with regard to the third country as of the day following the notification to the Council.[380]

The European Parliament shall be informed of cases of the above-mentioned suspensions.[381] Such suspensions shall end after three months, unless the Commission makes a proposal, before the end of this period, to withdraw the third country from the minimum common list. The suspensions shall in any case end when the Council rejects a proposal by the Commission to withdraw the third country from the list.[382] Upon request by the Council, the Commission shall report to the Council and the European Parliament on whether the situation in a country listed on the minimum common list, is still in conformity with Annex II.[383] It should be taken into account that in order to have an always updated common list of 'safe countries of origin', the system of adding to and removing from such a list should be very flexible; because the political situation in many countries tends to change quite frequently.

Annex II to the Asylum Procedures Directive relates to the designation of safe countries of origin for the purposes of Articles 29 and 30(1): a country is considered as a safe country of origin where

377. Id., Art. 29(2).
378. Id., Art. 29(3).
379. Id., Art. 29(4).
380. Id., Art. 29(5).
381. Id., Art. 29(6).
382. Id., Art. 29(7).
383. Id., Art. 29(8).

> 'on the basis of the legal situation, the application of the law within a democratic system and the general political circumstances, it can be shown that there is generally and consistently no persecution (as defined in Article 9 of the Qualification Directive), no torture or inhuman or degrading treatment or punishment and no threat by reason of indiscriminate violence in situations of international or internal armed conflict'

In making this assessment, account shall be taken, *inter alia*, of the extent to which protection is provided against persecution or mistreatment through:

a. the relevant laws and regulations of the country and the manner in which they are applied;
b. observance of the rights and freedoms laid down in the ECHR and/or the International Covenant for Civil and Political Rights and/or the Convention against Torture, in particular the rights from which derogation cannot be made under Article 15(2) of the said ECHR;
c. respect of the *non-refoulement* principle according to the Geneva Convention;
d. provision for a system of effective remedies against violations of these rights and freedoms.

The Council first released a draft common list of safe countries of origin in March 2004. It included ten countries: Benin, Botswana, Cape Verde, Chile, Costa Rica, Ghana, Mali, Mauritius, Senegal and Uruguay. In addition, Bulgaria and Romania were considered 'safe' because of their status as EU candidate states. On the other hand one wonders why countries with a tradition of respect for human rights (e.g., Canada, New Zealand) do not appear on the list. A more logical approach would be, for example, to make two lists: one listing the countries considered safe and the other one listing the countries not considered to be safe. By this way all countries would be included in either the positive or the negative list, similar to the EU visa lists approach. The exclusion of a third country from the common list of safe countries of origin is a politically very sensitive issue and this might be one of the biggest obstacles encountered in the adoption of the Asylum Procedures Directive. Moreover why this list of safe countries was not included rather in the Qualification Directive which deals with the criteria for admissibility?

Article 30 on 'national designation of third countries as safe countries of origin' provides that without prejudice to Article 29, Member States *may* retain or introduce legislation that allows, in accordance with Annex II, for the national designation of third countries other than those appearing on the minimum common list, as safe countries of origin for the purpose of examining applications for asylum. This may include designation of part of a country as safe where the conditions in Annex II are fulfilled in relation to that part.[384]

384. Id., Art. 30(1).

By derogation from the previous paragraph, Member States *may* retain legislation in force at the time of adoption of the Asylum Procedures Directive (i.e., 1 December 2005) that allows for the national designation of third countries, other than those appearing on the minimum common list, as safe countries of origin for the purposes of examining applications for asylum where they are satisfied that persons in the third countries concerned are generally[385] neither subject to:

a. persecution, as defined in the Qualification Directive;[386] nor
b. torture or inhuman or degrading treatment or punishment.[387]

Member States may also retain legislation in force at the time of the adoption of the Asylum Procedures Directive that allows for the *national designation of part of a country as safe* or a country or part of a country as safe for a specified group of persons in that country where the conditions mentioned above are fulfilled in relation to that part or group.[388]

In assessing whether a country is a safe country of origin in accordance with the previous paragraphs (as regards the retaining of the national legislation in force at the time of adoption of this Directive…), Member States shall have regard to the legal situation, the application of the law and the general political circumstances in the third country concerned.[389]

The assessment of whether a country is a safe country of origin in accordance with Article 30, shall be based on a range of sources of information, including *in particular* information from other Member States, the UNHCR, the Council of Europe and other relevant international organisations. Member States shall notify the Commission of the countries that are designated as safe countries of origin pursuant to the provisions of Article 30A (i.e., the national designation of third countries as safe countries of origin).[390]

The difference between the requirements to consider a country of origin 'safe' in the minimum common list of third countries (Art. 29) and in the national desig-

385. Par. 21 of the Preamble to the Asylum Procedures Directive states: 'The designation of a third country as a safe country of origin for the purposes of this Directive cannot establish an absolute guarantee of safety for nationals of that country. By its very nature, the assessment underlying the designation can only take into account the general civil, legal and political circumstances in that country and whether actors of persecution, torture or inhuman or degrading treatment or punishment are subject to sanction in practice when found liable in the country concerned. For this reason, it is important that, where an applicant shows that there are serious reasons to consider the country not to be safe in his/her particular circumstances, the designation of the country as safe can no longer be considered relevant for him/her.'

386. On the 'acts of persecution' see the Qualification Directive, Art. 9.

387. Asylum Procedures Directive, Art. 30(2).

388. Id., Art. 30(3).

389. Id., Art. 30(4).

390. Id., Art. 30(5), (6).

nation of third countries as safe countries of origin (Art. 30) is worth noting. The main difference concerns the role of the UNHCR, the Council of Europe and other relevant international organisations. Art. 29(3) states that when making its proposal the Commission shall make use of information from the Member States, its own information and, *where necessary*, information from the UNHCR, the Council of Europe and other relevant international organisations. In contrast Article 30 (5) provides that the assessment shall be based on a range of sources of information, including *in particular* information from other Member States, the UNHCR, the Council of Europe and other relevant international organisations. The wording used in Article 29(3) (*'where necessary')* might seem to give a more supplementary role to the above-mentioned organisations, despite the fact that the UNHCR is the guarantor of the 1951 Geneva Convention and main expert in global asylum matters. In addition, the Tampere Conclusions stressed the importance of consulting the UNHCR and other international organisations.[391]

Having regard to the possibility of various lists of 'safe countries of origin' within the EU, allowed by the Asylum Procedures Directive (minimum common list, national lists), this might create a potential risk of divergence within the Common European Asylum System, when applying the 'safe country of origin' concept. Especially when Member States may retain their national lists of 'safe countries of origin' adopted before the introduction of the minimum common list, and these national lists could have been made using different criteria.

Regarding the application of *the safe country of origin concept*, Article 31 provides that a third country designated as a safe country of origin either in accordance with the provisions of Article 29 or 30 may, after an individual examination of the application, be considered as a safe country of origin for a particular applicant for asylum only if:

a. he/she has the nationality of that country, or
b. he/she is a stateless person and was formerly habitually resident in that country;

and he/she has not submitted any serious grounds for considering the country not to be a safe country of origin in his/her particular circumstances in terms of his/her qualification as a refugee in accordance with the Qualification Directive.

Applications for asylum made by nationals coming from third countries, which are on an EU common list of 'safe countries of origin', shall be considered unfounded.[392] Accordingly, accelerated procedures would apply, denying applications without substantively considering the claim. The UNHCR does not object in

391. Tampere, par. 14.
392. Asylum Procedures Directive, Art. 31(2).

principle to the notion of designating countries as 'safe countries of origin', based on criteria establishing a general presumption of safety, which the individual should be able to disprove. 'Such considerations must, however, be limited to the actual country of origin or, in the case of stateless persons only, the country of habitual residence. They cannot be extended to any country in which the claimant may be entitled to reside.'[393] The UNHCR takes the position that the 'safe country of origin' notion does not have, per se, to be a barrier to access to procedures. Its implementation prior to any further substantive determination of the asylum claim means it is perceived as a barrier. However, the UNHCR suggests that if applied not to admissibility, but to the substantive determination of the claim, the principle would not necessarily be so problematic. During the substantive determination of the claim, the individual would have the opportunity to 'rebut a general presumption of safety in his/her individual case.'[394]

Article 35 of the Asylum Procedures Directive regards cases of *border procedures*. Paragraph 16 of the Preamble provides that: 'Border procedures should mainly apply to those applicants who do not meet the conditions for entry into the territory of the Member States.' There is no further clarification on what the conditions for entry are. Considering that the entry of TCNs into the territory of the Member States is in principle conditional on possessing valid travel documents and valid visas, where required;[395] one might assume that the proposed recital refers to these conditions and points to irregular crossings of the external border of the EU by persons seeking asylum.

Despite the irregularity of such crossings, the fact that a person is in genuine need of international protection should always take priority. The prevention and control of irregular economic immigration into the EU Member States have long been considered essential elements of the emerging common immigration and asylum policy of the Union. To this end the European Commission issued the Communication on a common policy on illegal immigration, setting out a comprehensive Action Plan.[396] The Communication provides that 'measures relating

---

393. UNHCR, 'Note on key issues of concern to UNHCR on the draft Asylum Procedures Directive', March 2004, available at http://www.unhcr.ch/news/290304Qua.pdf.

394. UNHCR, Asylum Processes (Fair and Efficient Asylum Procedures), Global Consultations on International Protections, 2nd Meeting; EC/GC/01/12, 31 May 2001, par. 40.

395. See Council Regulation (EC) No. 574/1999 of 12 March 1999 determining the third countries whose nationals must be in possession of visas when crossing the external borders of the Member States, OJ L 072, 18.03.1999, 2; and its amending acts: Council Regulation (EC) No. 539/2001 of 15 March 2001 listing the third countries whose nationals must be in possession of visas when crossing the external borders and those whose nationals are exempt from that requirement, OJ L 81, 21.3.2001, 1; Council Regulation (EC) No. 2414/2001 of 7 December 2001, OJ L 327, 12.12.2001, 1 and the Council Regulation (EC) No. 453/2003 of 6 March 2003, OJ L 69, 13.3.2003, 10.

396. Communication from the Commission to the Council and the European Parliament on a common policy on illegal immigration, COM(2001) 672 final, not published in the OJ.

to the fight against illegal immigration have to balance the right to decide whether to accord or refuse admission to the territory to TCNs and the obligation to protect those genuinely in need of international protection.'[397] This reflects what was proclaimed by the European Council summit in Tampere, that 'the freedom of movement of persons should not be regarded the exclusive preserve of the Union's own citizens. It would be in contradiction with Europe's traditions to deny such freedom to those whose circumstances lead justifiably to seek access to the EU territory.'[398] In addition, irregular crossings of borders by asylum seekers have been qualified as one of the criteria according to which the State responsibility for examining an asylum application is determined.[399]

Article 35(1) of the Asylum Procedures Directive says that

> 'Member States may provide for procedures, in accordance with the basic principles and guarantees of Chapter II, in order to decide at the border or transit zones of the Member State on the applications made at such locations'. However, 'when procedures as set out in paragraph (1) do not exist, Member States may maintain, subject to the provisions of this Article and in accordance with the laws or regulations in force at the time of the adoption of this Directive, procedures derogating from the basic principles and guarantees described in Chapter II, in order to decide, at the border or in transit zones, as to whether applicants for asylum who have arrived and made an application for asylum at such locations, may enter their territory.'[400]

It is only logical and fair that all asylum seekers irrespective of whether they apply at the border (including sea and air ports), or further inside the country, benefit from the same basic principles and guarantees.[401] It should be noted with great concern that the provisions of Article 17 (in Chapter II) regarding the conditions of detention, do not apply on cases of border procedures. As a result, applicants for asylum who irregularly crossed the EU borders might be detained for up to four weeks 'for the sole reason of being asylum seekers' and without 'the possibility of speedy judicial review'.[402]

Article 35A of the Amended Proposal to the Asylum Procedures Directive introduced the concept of super safe third countries,[403]according to which Member States might provide that

---

397. Id., par. 3.2.

398. Tampere, par. 3.

399. Dublin II, Art. 10(1).

400. Asylum Procedures Directive, Art. 35(2).

401. UNHCR, 'Note on key issues of concern to UNHCR on the draft Asylum Procedures Directive', March 2004, cf. Chapter II ('Basic principles and guarantees') and Art. 35(3).

402. Cf. Art. 18(1), (2) and Art. 35(3), (4).

403. The term 'super safe' country was not used in the (Amended) Proposal to the Asylum Procedures Directive itself. However, it was used for example by the ECRE: ECRE's Memorandum to the Irish Presidency, 20 January 2004; the Commission (EU): 'Minimum standards for Member States' procedures for granting and withdrawing refugee status in the EU – Political agreement in the Council'; Statewatch: 'Call for withdrawal of the Asylum Procedures Directive'; UNHCR: 'UNHCR re-

> 'no, or no full examination of the asylum application and of the safety of the applicant in his/her particular circumstances (as described in Chapter II of the Amended Proposal Directive) takes place in cases where a competent authority has established, on the basis of the facts, that the applicant for asylum is seeking to enter or has entered illegally into the territory from a safe third country'.[404]

In the current text of the Asylum Procedures Directive the same concept can be found in Article 36 under the heading 'The European safe third countries concept'. For the purpose of Article 36 a third country can only be considered as a safe third country when:

a. it has ratified and observes the provisions of the Geneva Convention without any geographical limitations;
b. it has in place an asylum procedure prescribed by law;
c. it has ratified the ECHR and observes its provisions, including the standards relating to effective remedies; and
d. it has been so designated by the Council in accordance with paragraph 3 (i.e., acting by qualified majority on a proposal from the Commission and after consultation of the European Parliament).[405]

Despite the fact that the above-mentioned provisions are restricted to very specific cases, it should not justify a possible unfairness towards persons genuinely seeking asylum. Moreover, if one takes into consideration that the European safe third countries must have ratified the ECHR, the scope gets narrower and implicitly points to the EU neighbouring countries.[406] Supposing that the provisions of Article 36 will apply, Member States would have no obligation to examine such applications for asylum.

The reference to an *illegal entry* into the territory of a Member State, as a condition for the application of Article 36 (which allows to exclude a Member States from the obligation to examine applications for asylum in cases of asylum applicant's illegal entry) might raise the question of compliance with the notion of Article 31 of the 1951 Geneva Convention. The provision of Article 31 prohibits the imposition of penalties on account of illegal entry or presence of asylum seekers/refugees.

Paragraph (4) of Article 36 of the Asylum Procedures Directive mandates Member States to lay down in their national laws modalities for implementing the

---

grets missed opportunity to adopt high EU asylum standards' (UNHCR Press Release of 30 April 2004); when referring to the concept of Art. 35A.

404. The Amended Proposal Directive, Art. 35A(1).

405. Asylum Procedures Directive, Art. 36(2).

406. All of the EU neighbouring countries, except for Belarus, are parties to the ECHR. Belarus is a candidate for membership in the Council of Europe; Belarus applied for membership on 12 March 1993.

provisions of the European safe third countries concept. These modalities should be in compliance with the principle of *non-refoulement* and also should provide for exceptions from the application of Article 36 for humanitarian or political reasons; or for reasons of public international law.

It might seem rather difficult to respect the principle of *non-refoulement* when there is the option given to Member States of not examining an asylum application at all. The call for compliance with the principle of *non-refoulement* is very positive, nevertheless, the option of not examining at all an asylum application provided for in paragraph (1), should be seriously reconsidered. On the other hand, the provision guaranteeing that where a European safe third country does not readmit the applicant for asylum in question, Member States shall ensure that access to a procedure is given in accordance with the basic principles and guarantees (laid down in Chapter II of the Proposal Directive)[407] should be received positively.

The Council shall, acting by qualified majority on a proposal from the Commission and after consultation of the European Parliament, adopt or amend a common list of third countries that shall be regarded as the *European safe third countries*.[408] Member States which already have designated third countries as safe in accordance with the criteria set in this Article before the date of the adoption of this Directive, may apply the provisions of paragraph (1) (no examination or no full examination of asylum applications) to these third countries until the Council adopts the above-mentioned common list.[409]

2.5.4 Procedures for the withdrawal of refugee status

As regards withdrawal of a refugee status already granted in a Member State to a TCN, Member States shall ensure that an examination to withdraw the refugee status of a particular person may start when new elements or findings arise indicating that there are reasons to reconsider the validity of his/her refugee status.[410] Member States shall ensure that where the competent authority is considering to withdraw the refugee status of a TCN or a stateless person,[411] the person concerned shall enjoy the following guarantees:

a. to be informed in writing that the competent authority is reconsidering his or her qualification for refugee status and the reasons for such a reconsideration; and

---

407. Asylum Procedures Directive, Art. 36(6).
408. Id., Art. 36(3).
409. Id., Art. 36(7).
410. Id., Art. 37.
411. See the Qualification Directive, Art. 14.

b. to be given the opportunity to submit, in a personal interview[412] or in a written statement, reasons as to why his/her refugee status should not be withdrawn.

In addition, Member States shall ensure that within the framework of such a procedure:

a. the competent authority is able to obtain precise and up-to-date information from various sources, such as, where appropriate, information from the UNHCR, as to the general situation prevailing in the countries of origin of the persons concerned; and
b. where information on an individual case is collected for the purposes of reconsidering the refugee status, it is not obtained from the actor(s) of persecution in a manner that would result in such actor(s) being directly informed of the fact that the person concerned is a refugee whose status is under reconsideration, nor jeopardise the physical integrity of the person and his/her dependants, or the liberty and security of his/her family members still living in the country of origin.[413]

A withdrawal of a refugee status is interrelated with the 'cessation clauses', laid down in Article 14 of the Qualification Directive and also in Article 1C(1) to (6) of the 1951 Geneva Convention. The cessation clauses 'spell out the conditions under which a refugee ceases to be a refugee. They are based on the consideration that international protection should not be granted where it is no longer necessary or justified.'[414] Contrary to the asylum determination procedure, where a person's status as a refugee is decided, the procedure for the withdrawal of refugee status commences once a recognised refugee comes within the terms of one of the cessation clauses (reflecting changes in the situation of the refugee and/or changes in the country where persecution was feared, because the reasons for a person becoming a refugee have ceased to exist).[415]

The decision of a competent authority of a Member State to withdraw the refugee status must be given in writing and the reasons in fact and in law have to be stated in the decision. Furthermore, information on how to challenge the decision shall be given in writing.[416] Member States may also decide that the refugee status lapses by law in case of cessation if a TCN or a stateless person, who is a refugee, has voluntarily reavailed himself/herself of the protection of the country of his/her nationality (or habitual residence); or having lost his/her nationality, has voluntarily reacquired it; or has acquired a new nationality, and enjoys the protection of the country of his/her new nationality; or has voluntarily re-established himself/

412. See Asylum Procedures Directive, Art. 10(1)(b) and Arts. 12–14.
413. Id., Art. 38.
414. *UNHCR Handbook*, par. 111.
415. Id., par. 112–115.
416. Asylum Procedures Directive, Art. 38(2).

herself in the country which he/she left or outside which he/she remained owing to fear of persecution;[417] or if the refugee has evidently renounced his/her recognition as a refugee.[418]

2.5.5 Appeal procedures[419]

Article 39(1) of the Asylum Procedures Directive provides that Member States shall ensure that applicants for asylum have the right to an effective remedy before a court or tribunal, against the following:

a. a decision taken on their application for asylum;[420]
b. a refusal to reopen the examination of an application after its discontinuation;[421]
c. a decision not to further examine the subsequent application;[422]
d. a decision refusing entry within the framework of the border procedures;[423]
e. a decision to withdraw of refugee status.[424]

The Member States *shall* provide for time limits and other necessary rules for the applicant to exercise his/her right to an effective remedy;[425] they *may* also lay down time limits for the court or tribunal to examine the decision of the determining authority.[426] Having regard to the fact that Member States should ensure that applicants for asylum have the right to an *effective remedy* before a court or tribunal; then the determination of time limits to examine a decision should not be left fully to the discretion of the Member States.[427]

---

417. Qualification Directive, Art. 11(1)(a)–(d).
418. Asylum Procedures Directive, Art. 38(4).
419. Par. 27 of the Preamble to the Asylum Procedures Directive states that: 'It reflects a basic principle of Community law that the decisions taken on an application for asylum and on the withdrawal of refugee status are subject to an effective remedy before a court or tribunal in the meaning of Art. 234 of the Treaty. The effectiveness of the remedy, also with regard to the examination of the relevant facts, depends on the administrative and judicial system of each Member State seen as a whole.'
420. According to Art. 39(1)(a) a decision taken on their application for asylum includes a decision: i) to consider an application inadmissible pursuant to Art. 25(2); ii) taken at the border or in the transit zones of a Member State as described in Art. 35(1); iii) not to conduct an examination pursuant to Art. 36.
421. See Asylum Procedures Directive, Arts. 19, 20.
422. Id., Arts. 32, 34.
423. Id., Art. 35(2).
424. Id., Art. 38.
425. Id., Art. 39(2).
426. Id., Art. 39(4).
427. The first Proposal for a Council Directive on minimum standards on procedures in Member States for granting and withdrawing refugee status (COM(2000) 578 final) laid down some time limits within the appeal procedures: e.g., the time limit for filing the grounds of appeal in regular cases should not be in any case less that 20 working days (Art. 34(1)); in cases where an application

One of the most striking provisions of this Directive is to be found in Article 39 (3). It provides that Member States shall, *where appropriate*, provide for rules in accordance with their international obligations dealing with:

a. the question of whether the remedy shall have the effect of allowing applicants to remain in the Member State concerned pending its outcome;
b. the possibility of legal remedy or protective measures where the remedy does not have the effect of allowing applicants to remain in the Member State concerned pending its outcome. Member States may also provide for an ex officio remedy; and
c. the grounds for challenging a decision in cases when an application for asylum is considered as inadmissible, if a country is considered as a safe third country for the applicant,[428] in accordance with a set methodology.[429]

Member States may lay down in national legislation the conditions under which it can be assumed that an applicant has implicitly withdrawn or abandoned his/her remedy.[430] The Asylum Procedures Directive further states that when an applicant has been granted a status, which offers the same rights and benefits under national and Community law as the refugee status by virtue of the Qualification Directive, the applicant may be considered to have an effective remedy where a court or tribunal decides that the remedy pursuant to Article 39(1) is inadmissible or unlikely to succeed on the basis of insufficient interest on the part of the applicant in maintaining the proceedings.[431]

The introduction of the notion of an effective remedy is a significant element in the completion of the first stage of the Common European Asylum System. According to Article 43 of the Asylum Procedures Directive, by 1 December 2007 Member States shall bring into force the laws, regulations and administrative provisions necessary to comply with this Directive. All asylum decisions in the systems of 24 EU Member States will be subject to judicial scrutiny for the first time (with the exception of Denmark). This will have a real impact on national judges and on the ECJ, as well. What is, however, alarming is the non-application of the suspensive effect (the right of the asylum applicants/refugees, to remain in the Member State pending their appeal). It is difficult to believe that a remedy will be considered 'effective' even if it does not allow applicants with a disputable claim to remain in the Member State pending their appeal. And what is more, it would increase considerably the possibility of persons being returned to persecution in violation of the principle of *non-refoulement.*

---

was found to be inadmissible or manifestly unfounded, the reviewing body should take a decision within 65 working days after notice of appeal has been given (Art. 35(1)).

428. Asylum Procedures Directive, Art. 25(2)(c).

429. Id., Art. 27(2)(b), (c).

430. Id., Art. 39(6).

431. Id., Art. 39(5).

In this context, it is important to bear in mind that in some European countries negative decisions in 30 to 60% of the claims are overturned on appeal.[432] An exception to the general rule could be considered in strictly limited categories ('manifestly unfounded' and 'clearly abusive' claims). In such cases, nevertheless, there must still be access to the possibility of an independent review of the decision to remove the person pending appeal. Such a review could be simplified and fast, taking into account the chances of an appeal.[433]

The part of the Asylum Procedures Directive dealing with appeal procedures seems to be one of the most problematic to agree on among the Member States: the most substantial changes in relation to the first Proposal of the Commission can be found in this part. For example, the original obligation to introduce a two-level appeal system, in which a court of law would have to be competent at least once to review a decision,[434] has been replaced by the right of every applicant for asylum to have an effective remedy before a court of law against the decision of his application, leaving the institutional arrangements for review or appeal to national discretion.[435]

The long process of negotiations in the Council on this legal instrument resulted in the elimination of several provisions that guaranteed more satisfactory procedural standards for asylum applicants. Taking into account that the 'absolute respect of the right to seek asylum'[436] and the commitment of the EU Member States 'to work towards establishing a Common European Asylum System based on full and exclusive application of the 1951 Geneva Convention, thus ensuring that nobody is sent back to persecution'[437] were agreed by the heads of state or government of the Member States in Tampere. It is rather disappointing that the Member States have failed to follow the commitments they made themselves at the beginning of the harmonisation process. In addition, the Member States reaffirmed that 'this System should include a common standards for a fair and efficient asylum procedure'.[438]

The Asylum Procedures Directive regulates how decisions on asylum claims are made in the Member States. Following the analysis of the Directive, it could be concluded that the most worrisome provisions in this respect are:

---

432. See 'UNHCR regrets missed opportunity to adopt high EU asylum standards' (UNHCR Press Release of 30 April 2004).

433. See also UNHCR, 'Note on key issues of concern to UNHCR on the draft Asylum Procedures Directive', March 2004; available at: http://www.unhcr.ch/news/290304Qua.pdf; JHA Council, 'Analysis of the Asylum Procedures Directive', MEMO/04/98, Brussels, 28 April 2004.

434. The Proposal (Procedures) Directive, Art. 38.

435. Asylum Procedures Directive, Art. 39(1); on harmonisation of asylum procedures see, e.g., Hailbronner, K.: Asylum 'Law in the Context of a European Migration Policy', in Walker, N. (ed.): *Europe's Area of Freedom, Security and Justice* (Oxford 2004), 41–88.

436. Tampere, par. 13.

437. Ibid.

438. Id., par. 14.

- the rules on designation of the so-called 'safe third countries', to which asylum seekers may be returned;
- the approach taken on the 'safe country of origin' concept (Arts. 29–31), does not encourage the approximation of decision practices in the Member States;
- a possibility to deny altogether access to asylum procedure in the EU if a person is seeking to enter or has entered illegally the territory of a Member States through the so-called 'European safe third country';
- the rules which allow countries to deport rejected asylum seekers before the results of their appeals are known, and thus infringing their right to an effective remedy in case of error during the asylum determination procedure;
- the fact that Member States have too much discretionary power to decide on many provisions in the Asylum Procedures Directive may not help the harmonisation of the Common European Asylum System.

The idea of harmonising the asylum procedures within the EU should be received positively. Moreover, the Asylum Procedures Directive sets minimum procedural rules and encourages Member States to introduce or maintain more favourable standards on procedures for granting and withdrawing refugee status insofar as compatible with this Directive.[439] This should hold true especially for those Member States which are already applying higher standards. Nevertheless, in this same harmonisation of asylum procedures, there is a possible risk of inserting less beneficial and somewhat controversial practices from one Member State to the others, especially through inter-state negotiations.

2.6 Temporary protection and burden sharing

'The European Council urges the Council to step up its efforts to reach agreement on the issue of temporary protection for displaced persons on the basis of solidarity between Member States. The European Council believes that consideration should be given to making some form of financial reserve available in situations of mass influx of refugees for temporary protection. The Commission is invited to explore the possibilities for this.'[440]

Article 63(2) TEC provides that the Council has to adopt measures relating to refugees and displaced persons in the following areas:

a. minimum standards for giving temporary protection to displaced persons from third countries who cannot return to their country of origin and for persons who otherwise need international protection;

439. Asylum Procedures Directive, Art. 5.
440. Tampere, par. 16.

b. promoting a balance of effort between Member Sates in receiving and bearing the consequences of receiving refugees and displaced persons.

Temporary protection in the event of a mass influx should not be understood as a third form of protection, alongside the protection granted on the basis of the 1951 Geneva Convention and under subsidiary protection. In fact, a set of minimum standards for giving temporary protection in the event of a mass influx (further referred to as the temporary protection) and measures promoting a balance of efforts between the Member States on a basis of solidarity form one of the components of the asylum system. Moreover they are a tool enabling the system to operate smoothly and not collapse under a mass influx.[441]

The concept and the legal framework for temporary protection have been developed by several Member States as a response to the large-scale movement of people fleeing conflict in the former Yugoslavia. The system of temporary protection requires special provisions able to speed up the decision making related to temporary admission so as to avoid the application of the lengthier procedures laid down for the 'regular' asylum requests.

As far as the EU *acquis* regarding temporary protection is concerned, in the context of the Treaty of Maastricht, EU Member States adopted two instruments, stimulated by the influx of displaced persons from former Yugoslavia in the early 1990s:

- Council Resolution of 25 September 1995 on burden sharing with regard to the admission and residence of displaced persons on a temporary basis based on Article K.1 TEU,[442] and
- Council Decision of 4 March 1996 on an alert and emergency procedure for burden sharing with regard to the admission and residence of displaced persons on a temporary basis based on Article K.3 (2)(a) TEU.[443]

None of these instruments was implemented, not even in the context of the Kosovo crisis in spring 1999. Nevertheless, the Kosovo conflict prompted the Member States to take additional national measures and to co-ordinate their actions. There were also initiatives from the Commission, proposing two joint actions. One, based on Article K.3 (2)(b) TEU concerning temporary protection of displaced persons of 5 March 1997,[444] and the other one an amended proposal for the previous joint action with a second proposal for a further joint action, separate

441. See Proposal for a Council Directive on minimum standards for giving temporary protection in the event of a mass influx of displaced persons and on measures promoting a balance of efforts between Member States in receiving such persons and bearing the consequences thereof, COM(2000) 303 final, 24.5.2000, Explanatory Memorandum.

442. OJ C 262, 7.10.1995, 1.

443. OJ L 063, 13.3.1996, 10.

444. See Bulletin EU 3-1997, JHA cooperation (1/2), [COM(97)93].

from, but parallel to the first, concerning solidarity in the admission and residence of beneficiaries of the temporary protection of displaced persons.[445]

On 1 May 1999, when the Treaty of Amsterdam entered into force, the legal grounds changed. The discussion on the issues in question continued, a good example of this being the discussion under the Finnish Presidency on all questions relating to temporary protection and solidarity in the light of the experience of the Member States responding to the crisis in Kosovo.

On the basis of the Amsterdam 'timetable' set by Article 63 TEC and also on the basis of the Tampere Conclusions, the Commission initiated a 'Proposal for a Council Directive on minimum standards for giving temporary protection in the event of a mass influx of displaced persons and on measures promoting a balance of efforts between Member States in receiving such persons and bearing the consequences thereof'.[446] The central objectives of this Commission Proposal were:

- 'to implement the Treaty (of Amsterdam), the Vienna Action Plan, the Presidency Conclusions of Tampere special European Council and the scoreboard presented to the Council and Parliament in March 2000;
- to avoid a total bottleneck in national asylum systems in the event of a mass influx, which would have a negative effect on the Member States, the persons concerned and other persons seeking protection outside the context of a mass influx and thereby supporting the viability of the Common European Asylum System;
- to make immediate protection and fair rights available to the persons concerned;
- to clarify the link between temporary protection and the 1951 Geneva Convention, safeguarding the full application of the Convention;
- to contribute to achieving balance between the efforts made by the Member States to receive the persons concerned by offering coordination facilities in the event of a mass influx in the EU and in implementing temporary protection;
- to give practical expression to solidarity in the reception of the persons concerned by means of financial solidarity and the double voluntary action in the reception of them.'[447]

To achieve the above-mentioned objectives, the Commission presented a 'package' in a single Directive, based on Article 63(2)(a), (b) TEC. The United Kingdom gave notice of its wish to take part in the adoption and application of this Directive. Ireland and Denmark are not participating in its adoption and therefore the following provisions do not apply to them. On 21 July 2001 the Council adopted a 'Directive on minimum standards for giving temporary protection in

445. COM(1998) 372 final/2, 3.7.1998.
446. COM(2000) 303 final, 24.5.2000.
447. Id., Explanatory Memorandum, par. 5.1.

the event of a mass influx of displaced persons and on measures promoting a balance of efforts between Member States in receiving such persons and bearing the consequences thereof' (further referred to as the Temporary Protection Directive).[448] This Directive thus joins together both tasks listed in Article 63(2) TEC (minimum temporary protection standards and burden sharing).[449] The standards and measures are linked and they have been enacted in a single legal instrument according to the Preamble to the Directive, for reasons of effectiveness, coherence and solidarity.

Regarding the nature of these provisions – setting up the minimum standards, the Member States may introduce or maintain more favourable provisions for the persons concerned.[450] The preparation of a common policy on asylum is a constituent part of the EU's objective of establishing progressively an area of freedom, security and justice. As mentioned above, temporary protection is to be offered to those who, forced by circumstances, legitimately seek protection in the EU. As it happened during the conflict in Kosovo, it proved necessary to set up exceptional schemes, in order to offer to displaced persons immediate temporary protection.

The 'exceptionality' of this procedure is therefore based on the fact that 'in a case of need' the action held by Member States has to be immediate; and the protection granted is supposed to last temporarily. These features distinguish the procedure from the 'regular' procedure on examining (and granting) refugee status or subsidiary forms of protection. Temporary protection could be therefore characterised as a procedure of an exceptional, immediate and temporary character, which aims at a specific group of people – *displaced persons* from third countries, who are unable to return to their country of origin, for example because of an ongoing war conflict. The *exceptionality* of this procedure then means that temporary protection can be applied only in an event of a mass influx or imminent mass influx of displaced persons and it is applied to avoid the possible collapse of the 'regular' asylum system.[451] The *immediacy* could be explained by means of an urgently taken action, in order to handle the situation. Therefore the procedure is supposed to be speedier in comparison with the standard asylum procedure. Finally, the *temporary character* of such action points out that temporary protection is granted only for a limited period of time, in comparison with the refugee status (and subsidiary forms of protection), which provides for a lasting protection, unless the circumstances change substantially.

---

448. Council Directive 2001/55/EC of 20 July 2001, OJ L 212, 7.8.2001, 12; entered into force on 7 August 2001; transposition deadline: 31 December 2002.

449. The minimum standards for giving temporary protection were to be fulfilled within the five-year-transitional period, commenced on 1 May 1999. Pursuant to the 3rd subparagraph of Art. 63(4) TEC, measures on burden-sharing were not subject to the transitional period.

450. Temporary Protection Directive, Preamble, par. 12.

451. Id., Art. 2(a).

For the sake of a better understanding of the Temporary Protection Directive, the concept of temporary protection will be explained first, and then the concept of solidarity between the Member States. Following the order of the Directive, the key elements of temporary protection will be discussed.

2.6.1 Temporary protection

In order to determine the target group of persons who qualify for temporary protection, criteria for the exclusion of certain persons from such protection will be specified. Article 28 enables Member States to exclude individuals from the benefit of temporary protection by setting reasons for exclusion. The first paragraph specifies the grounds applicable for exclusion (e.g., if the person has committed a crime against peace or a war crime) while the second paragraph lays down the limits within which these grounds become effective (the grounds for exclusion must be based exclusively on the personal conduct of the person concerned).

The duration of temporary protection shall be one year. Unless terminated, it may be extended automatically by six monthly periods for a maximum of one year. The total duration is then two years. Where reasons for temporary protection persist, the Council may decide to extend the protection up to one year further.[452]

The existence of a mass influx of displaced persons is established by a Council Decision. The Council Decision has the effect of introducing temporary protection for displaced persons to which it refers, in all the Member States, in accordance with the provisions of this Directive. Such Decision has to include at least the following information:

- a description of the specific groups of persons to whom the temporary protection applies;
- the date on which the temporary protection will take effect;
- information received from the Member States on their reception capacity; and
- information from the Commission, the UNHCR and other relevant international organisations.[453]

When the maximum duration of the temporary protection has been reached or at any time by a Council Decision, the protection comes to an end. The situation in the country of origin must be such as to permit a safe and durable return of those granted the temporary protection. Human rights and fundamental freedoms, and the Member States' obligations regarding *non-refoulement* must always be respected.[454] The European Parliament has to be informed of the Council Decision on activating and on terminating temporary protection.

452. Id., Art. 4.
453. Id., Art. 5(3).
454. Id., Art. 6.

From the previous paragraphs we know that it is the Council, which makes the decision on the introduction of temporary protection, its termination, and also its extension, if it shows necessary. The decision making is the same for all above-mentioned situations: the Council decides by a qualified majority, on a proposal from the Commission, which shall also examine any request by a Member State that it submits a proposal to the Council.[455]

Once temporary protection has been initiated, the Member States have to adopt measures necessary to provide persons enjoying temporary protection with a residence permit for the entire duration of the protection. Since displaced persons may come from countries where its nationals must be in possession of visas when entering the EU, the Member States have to provide and facilitate the necessary visas to these persons to be admitted to their territory for the purposes of temporary protection. By reason of the urgency of the situation, formalities must be reduced to a minimum (e.g., regarding costs, visas should be free of charge or their cost must be reduced to a minimum).[456]

Person enjoying temporary protection can be engaged in employed or self-employed activities, as well as in activities such as educational opportunities for adults, vocational training or practical workplace experience. However, for reasons of labour market policies, Member States *may* give priority to EU citizens and citizens of States bound by the Agreement on the European Economic Area or to legally resident TCNs who receive unemployment benefits.[457] The possible limitation of the opportunity to be employed, while the temporary protection lasts, seems to be an expression of the policy atmosphere in the Member States at the time, rather than a rule.

The Member States shall further ensure that persons enjoying temporary protection have access to suitable accommodation or receive the means to obtain housing. Medical care, necessary assistance in terms of social welfare and means of subsistence must be provided if the beneficiaries do not have sufficient resources. People with special needs, such as unaccompanied minors or persons who had to undergo torture, rape or other serious forms of psychological, physical or sexual violence, should be provided with necessary medical or other necessary assistance. Access to educational system to persons under 18 years of age should be granted under the same conditions as to the nationals of the host Member State. Regarding family reunification, it is also a part of the obligations of the Member States towards the beneficiaries of temporary protection.[458]

One could ask whether there is any link between temporary protection in the event of a mass influx and the 'standard' asylum procedure. There is, indeed, access to the asylum procedure in the context of temporary protection. Temporary

455. Id., Arts. 4–6 on the basis of Art. 67 TEC.
456. Id., Art. 8.
457. Id., Art. 12.
458. Id., Arts. 13–15.

protection should not, therefore, prejudice recognition of refuge status under the 1951 Geneva Convention,[459] as displaced persons may fall within the scope of its Article 1A and thus have the right to apply for a durable protection, if they fulfil the required criteria.

Article 17 of the Temporary Protection Directive explicitly provides that persons enjoying temporary protection must be able to lodge an application for asylum at any time. The examination of any asylum application, not processed before the end of the period of temporary protection, shall be completed after the end of that period. The criteria and mechanisms, contained in the 'Dublin II' Regulation for deciding which Member State is responsible for considering an asylum application apply. The Member State responsible for examining an asylum application submitted by a person enjoying temporary protection pursuant to this Directive will be the Member State which has accepted his transfer into its territory.[460]

It is on Member States' own discretion ('the Member States *may*') to provide that temporary protection may not be enjoyed concurrently with the status of asylum seeker while applications are under consideration. Where, after an asylum application has been examined, refugee status or, where applicable, other kind of protection is not granted to a person eligible for or enjoying temporary protection, the Member State shall (unless there are grounds for exclusion from temporary protection) provide for that person to enjoy or to continue to enjoy temporary protection for the remainder of the period of this protection.[461]

As soon as the grounds for temporary protection regime elapse, the protection comes to an end. The Member States then apply the general laws on asylum and on the entry and residence of aliens. The end of temporary protection does not mean that the Member States have no responsibility anymore in this respect. The issues concerning returns and measures which would apply following temporary protection must be dealt with. It should be ensured that 'after the temporary protection, and on the occasion of decisions to return or expel an asylum seeker whose application has been rejected, or a person having benefited from temporary protection, the Member State must examine whether there are compelling humanitarian reasons for applying a subsidiary form of protection, a degree of tolerance, pending expulsion or a lasting solution such as resettlement or a permanent or long-term residence permit. This may be the case, for example, where there is persistent armed conflict or persistent serious infringements of human rights, where the prospects of return are unrealistic because the individual or group of individuals belongs to a particular ethnic or other grouping, or where return is

---

459. Id., Art. 3.
460. Id., Art. 18.
461. Id., Art. 19.

impossible as the persons concerned face the risk of torture or cruel or inhuman treatment.'[462]

A voluntary return is obviously the most preferable solution. Candidates for voluntary return 'must be informed of the conditions in which they will return. Member States may use exploratory visits as a way of helping the candidates'. Since 'a voluntary return, on the basis of a programme organised with the host Member State and/or an international organisation, may take some time to implement', the Directive allows Member States to extend personally to the individuals concerned the rights provided for under the terms of temporary protection until the actual date of return.[463]

2.6.2 Solidarity between Member States (burden sharing)

Even though the link between the temporary protection in the event of a mass influx of displaced persons and the solidarity between Member States has been strongly emphasised, in particular by joining these two issues in a single directive, solidarity should not be associated exclusively with temporary protection. If the Common European Asylum System as a whole is to run in a fair manner, it should be based on solidarity between all EU Member States, and apply to all forms of international protection.

The Commission also considered, given the background, that such solidarity 'must be capable of being expressed through a clear, transparent and predictable financial mechanism' and 'the question of physical distribution must be settled by Community legislation'. This is something that the Member States have called for, mainly those most affected by mass influx in recent years. 'But only a physical distribution based on the voluntary action of the Member States and the displaced persons themselves will found a consensus in the European Union'.[464]

2.6.2.1 *European Refugee Fund*

The Treaty of Amsterdam presented in Article 63(2)(b) TEC an objective of promoting a balance of efforts between Member States in receiving and bearing consequences of receiving refugees and displaced persons. Regarding financial solidarity, the Temporary Protection Directive simply refers to the Council Decision

462. Proposal for the Temporary Protection Directive, Comment on Art. 20.

463. Id., Comment on Art. 21. In addition, families with children, who are minors and attend school in a Member State, may be allowed to stay until the children complete the current school period. Member States should also take account of persons who have enjoyed temporary protection and who cannot, for instance in view of their state of health, reasonably be expected to travel.

464. Proposal for the Temporary Protection Directive, Explanatory Memorandum, par. 6.1.

establishing a European Refugee Fund (ERF).[465] This Council Decision makes it clear that it is not only when a case of emergency measures occurs, when the ERF may be used. The ERF was established in order to support and to encourage the efforts made by the Member States in receiving and bearing the consequences of receiving refugees and displaced persons.[466] To achieve this objective, the ERF shall support Member States' actions relating to conditions for reception, integration of persons whose stay in a Member State is of a lasting and/or stable nature, as well as to repatriation, provided that the persons concerned have not acquired a new nationality and have not left the territory of the Member State.[467]

The resources are to be distributed according to the scheme set up in Article 10 of the Council Decision. Pursuant to this Article, for the years 2000 to 2004 each Member State should have received a fixed amount of the ERF's annual allocation. The remainder of the available resources will be distributed proportionally between the Member States in accordance with a fixed scheme.[468]

In order to support and encourage the efforts made by the Member States in receiving and bearing the consequences of receiving refugees and displaced persons, the following period (1 January 2005 to 31 December 2010) will be regulated by a Council Decision of 2 December 2004 establishing the ERF for the period 2005 to 2010 ('ERF II').[469] For the purpose of this Decision groups targeted by the actions shall comprise:

- any TCNs or stateless persons having the status defined by the 1951 Geneva Convention and the 1967 Protocol, who are allowed to reside as refugees in one of the Member States;
- any TCNs or stateless persons enjoying a form of subsidiary protection (within the meaning of the Qualification Directive);
- any TCNs or stateless persons who have applied for one of the forms of protection described above;
- any TCNs or stateless persons enjoying temporary protection within the meaning of the Temporary Protection Directive.[470]

The 'ERF II' shall support actions in the Member States related to the reception conditions and asylum procedures; integration of persons (see above the groups targeted by the actions) whose stay in a Member State is of a lasting and stable nature; voluntary returns of persons who have not acquired a new nationality and

465. Council Decision 2000/596/EC of 28 September 2000 establishing a European Refugee Fund, OJ L 252, 6.10.2000, 12. See also Proposal for a Council Decision creating a European Refugee Fund, COM(1999) 686 final, OJ C 116 E, 26.4.2000, 72.

466. Council Decision establishing a European Refugee Fund, Art. 1.

467. Id., Art. 4.

468. Id., Art. 10.

469. OJ L 381, 28.12.2004, 52; see also Proposal for a Council Decision establishing the European Refugee Fund for the period 2005–2010, COM(2004) 102 final, 12.2.2004.

470. Council Decision establishing European Refugee Fund II, Art. 3.

have not left the territory of Member States. The aforementioned actions shall, in particular, promote the implementation of the provisions of the relevant existing and future Community legislation in the field of the Common European Asylum System.[471]

As regards the responsible authorities, these should be appointed by each Member State and should handle all communication with the Commission.[472] Actions in the Member States shall be implemented on the basis of two multi-annual-programme phases, each lasting three years (2005 to 2007 and 2008 to 2010).[473] The Commission shall carry out regular monitoring on the 'ERF II' in cooperation with the Member States. The ERF II shall be evaluated regularly by the Commission in partnership with the Member States in order to assess the relevance, effectiveness and impact of the actions.[474]

In accordance with Article 3 of the Protocol on the position of the United Kingdom and Ireland, annexed to the TEU and to the TEC, the United Kingdom and Ireland notified their wish to take part in the adoption and application of the Decision establishing the ERF for the period 2005 to 2010. On the other hand, in accordance with Articles 1 and 2 of the Protocol on the position of Denmark, Denmark is not taking part in the adoption of this Decision and is not bound by it or subject to its application.

The Temporary Protection Directive provides for a reasonable standard of rights to be granted to persons enjoying temporary protection. Nonetheless, there are some provisions which should be improved. The duration of the temporary protection may be extended up to three years. This seems to be too long, considering that the rights provided for by this Directive are not equal to the rights granted to persons applying for the 'regular' refugee status. It was pointed out that the right to employment may be restricted. Taking into account that the temporary protection may last up to three years, the Member States should consider granting free access to their labour markets. As far as the freedom of movement of persons granted temporary protection is concerned, there is no reference to it in the Temporary Protection Directive. It could be assumed that it is at the Member States' discretion whether they grant this right under their national legislation and in this manner improve the standards set by the Temporary Protection Directive.

No doubt, it is not easy to create a fair system of burden sharing among 25 Member States. However, the financial aspect seems to be the less problematic. It appears to be easier to agree on a common fund and on a system of contributions from each participating State than to share a burden of the actual number of asylum applicants; especially since the issues related to asylum and immigration

471. Id., Art. 4(1), (2).
472. Id., Art. 13.
473. Id., Art. 15.
474. Id., Art. 27.

are politically very sensitive and often seen negatively by public opinion.[475] It is not surprising that this system of burden sharing has been ironically referred to as 'burden shifting',[476] meaning the shifting of responsibility from one Member State to another. In addition, the secondary movements of asylum seekers make the whole system even more difficult to manage.

2.7 Other Directives

'The European Union must ensure fair treatment of third-country nationals who reside legally on the territory of its Member States. A more vigorous integration policy should aim at granting them rights and obligations comparable to those of EU citizens...The legal status of third-country nationals should be approximated to that of Member States' nationals. A person, who has resided legally in a Member State for a period of time to be determined and who holds a long-term residence permit, should be granted in that Member State a set of uniform rights which are as near as possible to those enjoyed by EU citizens; e.g. the right to reside, receive education, and work as an employee or self-employed person, as well as the principle of non-discrimination vis-à-vis the citizens of the State of residence... .'[477]

Although there is a very close link between immigration and asylum,[478] they cannot always be dealt with by the same legal instruments: not all immigrants seek international protection and not all of them would be eligible for such protection and the rights related to it. On the other hand, persons granted asylum (or other forms of international protection) in a Member State, should enjoy the same rights like other TCNs, lawfully residing in that Member State. In this respect, two Directives will be briefly discussed: the 'Family Reunification Directive' and the 'Directive on Long-Term Residents', insofar they can influence the rights of persons in need of international protection.

---

475. See, e.g., 'The image of migrants, refugees and asylum seekers in the media, a motion for a recommendation', Parliamentary Assembly of the Council of Europe, 20 September 2004, Doc. 10280.

476. See, e.g., Kumin, J.: 'Asylum in Europe: Sharing or Shifting the Burden', *World Refugee Survey*, 1995; available at: http://www.refugees.org/world/articles/europe_wrs95.htm.

477. Tampere, par. 18–21.

478. The Tampere Conclusions also refer to the issues of asylum and immigration as 'separate but closely related issues'. Id., par. 10.

2.7.1 **Family reunification**

The Family Reunification Directive[479] was the first of two proposals put forward by the Commission aiming at integration of TCNs into the community of the host Member State and ensuring them a fair treatment. This Directive provides that a TCN residing lawfully in the territory of a Member State, holding a residence permit issued by a Member State valid for a year or more, with reasonable prospects of obtaining the right of permanent residence ('the sponsor') can apply for family reunification (usually while the family members are outside the territory).[480] The Directive makes a distinction between those family members who *must* be admitted (spouse and minor children) and those for whom the Member States have a *discretion* whether to admit or not (first-degree relatives in the direct ascending line, where they are dependent on the TCN or his or her spouse and do not enjoy proper family support in the country of origin, and adult unmarried children where they cannot support themselves).[481]

The right to family reunification is, nonetheless, dependent on evidence of the existence of 'normal' accommodation for a comparable family in the same region, sickness insurance for the TCN and the family members, and stable and regular resources which are higher than or equal to the level of resources which are sufficient to maintain the sponsor and the family members.[482] In order to ensure the integration of the family members, the Directive also provides for family members to enjoy access to employment and self-employment, education and vocational training. Member States may delay the exercise of employment or self-employment rights for up to 12 months.[483]

Article 3(2) contains provisions excluding from its scope persons, where the sponsor is:

- applying for recognition of refugee status (whose application has not yet given rise to a final decision);
- authorised to reside in a Member State on the basis of temporary protection or applying for authorisation to reside on that basis and awaiting a decision on his/her status;
- authorised to reside in a Member State on the basis of a subsidiary form of protection in accordance with international obligations, national legislation or

479. Council Directive 2003/86/EC of 22 September 2003 on the right to family reunification, OJ L 251, 3.10.2003, 12; entered into force on 3 October 2003; transposition deadline: 3 October 2005; legal basis: Art. 63(3)(a) TEC. The UK, Ireland and Denmark are not participating in the adoption and are not bound by this Directive.

480. Family Reunification Directive, Art. 5(3).

481. Id., Art. 4.

482. Id., Art. 7.

483. Id., Art. 14; further see, e.g., Barnard, C.: *The Substantive Law of the EU (The Four Freedoms)*, (Oxford 2004), 446.

the practice of the Member States; or applying for authorisation to reside on that basis and awaiting a decision on his/her status.

The above-mentioned provisions of Article 3 give reasons for concern, particularly, given that TCNs already enjoying temporary protection or a subsidiary form of protection in a Member State can be excluded from the scope of the Family Reunification Directive; and for that reason deprived of rights granted by this Directive.[484] Persons granted subsidiary forms of protection should not be disadvantaged in comparison to the 'Convention refugees' (those granted protection on the basis of the 1951 Geneva Convention). The same applies for those granted temporary protection, which can last up to three years (a period of time reasonably long to justify that a family should be unified).

The Family Reunification Directive contains specific provisions for the family reunification of recognised refugees.[485] Nevertheless, Member States may confine the application of these provisions to refugees whose family relationships predate their entry.[486] According to Article 5(4) of the Family Reunification Directive, the competent authorities of the Member States shall give to a person, who has submitted the application, written notification of the decision as soon as possible; in any case no later than nine months from the date on which the application was lodged. In exceptional cases this time limit may be extended. However, there is no specific time limit for the extension laid down in the Directive, what can bring about uncertainty for the refugee and his/her family.[487]

Provisions of Article 12(1) and (2) lay down a preferential treatment of refugees, in comparison to other TCNs to whom this Directive applies: refugees are exempted from meeting the general requirements for the application of the right to family reunification;[488] by derogation from Article 8 of the Directive, refugees are exempted from the general requirement of having a residence in the Member State for a certain period of time before having their family members join them. This favourable treatment of refugees is positive, especially taking into account persecution (or a well-founded fear of being persecuted) they had to suffer and also the fact that they had to flee from their country of origin or residence.

Articles 4 and 10 of the Family Reunification Directive strictly limit the family members who can join the sponsor in a Member State to nuclear family members only. These very restrictive provisions can weaken an effective integration of refugees in the society of a Member State. Furthermore, these provisions raise issues

484. It should be noted that the Dublin II Regulation seeks to preserve the family unity of asylum seekers (Preamble, par. 6); the Temporary Protection Directive grants the right to family reunification to displaced persons in the events of a mass influx (Art. 15).

485. Family Reunification Directive, Chapter V (Arts. 9–12).

486. Id., Art. 9(2).

487. Pursuant to Art. 11(1), Art. 5 applies to the submission and examination of the application applicable to refugees.

488. Cf. Art. 7.

under international human rights instruments such as the European Convention on Human Rights and Fundamental Freedoms (ECHR; Article 8), the Convention on the rights of the Child, and also under Article II-67 of the Charter of Fundamental Rights of the Union. These issues have resulted in the European Parliament challenging the validity of this Directive before the ECJ. MEPs argued, for example, that Article 4(1) of the Family Reunification Directive, allowing verification on children aged over 12 years, who arrive independently from the rest of their family, before authorising their entry and residence, contradicts Article 8 of the 1950 ECHR.[489]

Although the sponsor's family members shall be entitled to access to education, employment and self-employed activities, as well as to vocational guidance and training, Member States *may* restrict access to employment or self-employed activity to first-degree relatives in the direct ascending line or adult unmarried children. Moreover, Member States *may* decide, according to their national law, the conditions under which family members shall exercise these activities.[490] The aforementioned limitations do not seem to help with the integration of TCNs and their families into the host society.

2.7.2 Long-term residents[491]

The aim of the Directive on Long-Term Residents is to establish a common status of long-term residents for those TCNs who have resided 'legally and continuously' for five years in the territory of the Member State concerned. A long-term residence permit, valid for at least five years, will be granted where the TCN has adequate resources and sickness insurance,[492] and is automatically renewable on expiry. Long-term residents should enjoy equal treatment with nationals regarding a number of areas, like access to employment, education, and training (including study grants), recognition of diplomas, social protection and social assistance (including social security), and access to goods and services.[493] An individual can be

---

489. On 2 December 2003, the Legal Affairs Committee of the European Parliament agreed to ask the European Court of Justice (ECJ) to review legality of the Family Reunification Directive, due to infringement of the ECHR and the Charter of Fundamental Rights of the Union. Moreover the European Parliament (EP) stated that the procedure leading to the adoption of this Directive was reached before the EP gave its opinion (therefore infringing Art. 67 TEC). An action against the Council of the European Union was brought before the ECJ on 22 December 2003 by the EP (see C-540/03). According to the information from the Ministry of Justice of the Netherlands, a request for an accelerated procedure was not granted.

490. Family Reunification Directive, Art. 14.

491. Council Directive 2003/109/EC of 25 November 2003 concerning the status of third-country nationals who are long-term residents, OJ L 16, 23.1.2004, 44; entered into force on 23 January 2004; transposition deadline: 23 January 2006; legal basis: Art. 63(3), (4) TEC. The United Kingdom, Ireland and Denmark are not participating in the adoption and are not bound by this Directive.

492. Id., Art. 5.

493. Id., Art. 11.

expelled only on the grounds of personal conduct but not, apparently, lack of resources.[494]

Not only will long-term residents (and their families) enjoy the benefits of the status of long-term resident in the state of their residence, but for the first time, they will also enjoy the rights of free movement to other Member States. This Directive provides that long-term residents (and their families) can reside in the territory of another Member State for more than three months if they are exercising an economic activity as employed or self-employed persons or studying there and have adequate resources and sickness insurance; or simply having adequate resources and sickness insurance.[495] This goes beyond the rights already provided by the Schengen *acquis*, which merely gives rights to move for up to three months. This Directive demonstrates the increasing parallelism between the rights of legally resident TCNs and those of nationals of the Member States who are citizens of the Union.[496]

Refugees are defined in this Directive as TCNs enjoying refugee status within the meaning of the Geneva Convention, as amended by the New York Protocol.[497] Article 3 of the Long-Term Residents Directive expressly excludes from its scope those TCNs who are authorised to reside in a Member State on the basis of temporary protection or have applied for authorisation to reside on that basis and are awaiting a decision on their status,[498] those authorised to reside in a Member State on the basis of a subsidiary form of protection[499] and also refugees and those who have applied for recognition as refugees and whose application has not yet been finally decided.[500]

The rights conferred on the TCNs; including the free movement (see above) therefore do not apply to persons granted international protection in the EU. It brings one to the conclusion that even though they would reside legally and continuously in a Member State, where the refugee status was granted to them, for the required period of time (five years), they would not be treated equally with those TCNs falling under the scope of this Directive. One should note that the Action Plan implementing the Hague Programme[501] provides that a 'Proposal for long-term resident status for beneficiaries of international protection' should be launched during the second phase of development of the Common European Asylum System.

494. Id., Art. 12.
495. Id., Arts. 14–15.
496. See Barnard, C.: *The Substantive Law of the EU* (Oxford 2004), 446–447.
497. Long-Term Residence Directive, Art. 2(f).
498. Id., Art. 3(2)(b).
499. Id., Art. 3(2)(c).
500. Id., Art. 3(2)(d).
501. On the (draft) Action Plan see chapter 4, 4.4.3.

2.8 Conclusions

The final deadline of 1 May 2004 set by the Treaty of Amsterdam, in view to complete the first stage of the creation of a Common European Asylum System, already passed. All the relevant Community legal instruments, except for the Asylum Procedures Directive, were formally adopted before the above-mentioned deadline; however, not in every case meeting the individual deadlines.[502] By summing up the work done by the Commission and the Council, together with the European Parliament, the compliance with the goals set in October 1999 in Tampere has been examined.

On the 'Council Regulation establishing the criteria and mechanisms for determining the Member State responsible for examining an asylum application lodged in one of the Member States by a third-country national' ('Dublin II' Regulation), it can be said that the hierarchy of the criteria is clear. Regarding its workability not much can be said at this moment, although the three-year-period given to the Commission to report on the 'Dublin II' application has already lapsed.[503]

Regarding the 'Council Directive laying down minimum standards for the reception of asylum seekers' (the Reception Directive), the aims of Tampere were fulfilled; although the extensive discretional powers given to the Member States for example in the fields of education, access to employment and freedom of movement might lead to measures being incongruous with the 1951 Geneva Convention.[504]

The 'Council Directive on minimum standards for the qualification of third-country nationals and stateless persons as refugees or as persons who otherwise need international protection and the content of the protection granted' (the Qualification Directive) approximated the rules on the recognition and content of the refugee status among the EU Member States and included measures on subsidiary forms of protection, offering appropriate status to persons in need of such protection. However, the number of derogations included in the chapter on the content of international protection (e.g., benefits for family members, duration of residence permits, entitlement to social welfare benefits, access to employment), which make a distinction between persons granted refugee status and persons granted subsidiary forms of protection, might be a cause for concern; especially since the guarantees given to the 'Convention refugees' seem to be more favourable and also taking into account that subsidiary protection is granted more fre-

---

502. Following the adoption of the Tampere Conclusions in 1999, the Commission, at the request of the European Council, drew up a scoreboard to review progress every six months. See COM(2000) 167; COM(2000) 782; COM(2001) 278; COM(2001) 628; COM(2002) 261; COM(2002) 738; COM (2003) 291; COM(2003) 812. The achievements of the Tampere programme are to be found in the final report adopted on 2 June 2004 (COM(2004) 401 final).

503. Cf. Dublin II, Art. 28.

504. Cf. Reception Directive, Art. 10 and the 1951 Geneva Convention, Art. 22 (education); Art. 11 and Arts. 17–19 (employment); Art. 7 and Art. 26 (freedom of movement).

quently. This difference of guarantees offered is also present in the Family Reunification Directive. This state of affairs is regrettable; the grounds on which the international protection is granted should be the only difference distinguishing these two groups of persons in need of international protection.

Concerning the 'Council Directive on minimum standards on procedures in Member States for granting and withdrawing refugee status' (the Asylum Procedures Directive), Tampere called for common standards for a fair and efficient asylum procedure. The application of the concepts of 'safe third country', 'safe country of origin' and 'the European safe third countries', for instance, might raise doubts regarding the proposed fairness of the procedures. Regarding efficiency, one can say that the lacking of clear time limits and the provisions on appeals without suspensive effect do not contribute positively in this respect. The late adoption of this Directive proved the enormous difficulties in reaching common grounds on asylum issues between the Member States.

As far as the 'Council Directive on minimum standards for giving temporary protection in the event of a mass influx of displaced persons and on measures promoting a balance of efforts between Member States in receiving such persons and bearing the consequences thereof' (the Temporary Protection Directive) is concerned, Member States reached an agreement on this issue. Nevertheless, the shortcomings of the provisions on employment and freedom of movement of displaced persons are worth noting. Moreover, the status of temporary protection (which may last up to three years) is excluded from the rights derived from the Family Reunification Directive.

Regarding the financial burden sharing amongst the Member States, the creation of the ERF provides for the allocation of resources needed for the reception, procedure and integration of persons in need of international protection and also the return of persons not eligible of such protection. On the other hand, there is no scheme available, according to which the 'physical' burden sharing (i.e., the distribution of the actual number of asylum applications lodged in all EU Member States) would apply.

Whilst analysing the EU legislation on asylum and comparing it with the goals set in Tampere in 1999, a number of discrepancies emerged. Nevertheless, the core of the first phase setting up the Common European Asylum System (the adoption of the European asylum legislation) has been completed in December 2005 by adopting the Asylum Procedures Directive. This phase has now to be followed by the implementation of the legal measures. It is a crucial task, which has to be carried out by the Member States in order to achieve an efficiently working and fair Common European Asylum System.

Chapter 3

THE PERSPECTIVE OF A NEW MEMBER STATE: SLOVAKIA

'The countries applying for membership of the European Union are well aware that Justice and Home Affairs will have a special significance for their application. However, the JHA acquis is different in nature from other parts of the Union's acquis. Much still needs to be done and the acquis will therefore constantly develop over the pre-accession years.'[505]

3.1 INTRODUCTION

In order to assess the state of affairs of the Common European Asylum System, it proved necessary to evaluate the implementation in practice of the EU asylum legislation. It was therefore essential to analyse this implementation at a national level in at least one of the Member States. Slovakia was chosen as an example due to the specific circumstances with its geographical location (at the EU external border), its newly acquired EU membership and the extreme increase of asylum applications lodged in the previous years.[506]

Although Slovakia is still considered to be mainly a transit country of migration flows rather than a 'final destination' country, the increased number of asylum applications lodged indicates a potential change in this tendency. This change is certainly linked to the accession of Slovakia to the EU on 1 May 2004.[507] In addition, while in other EU countries a decrease of asylum applicants was observed in the course of 2004 (20%), Slovakia experienced the highest number of asylum applications lodged in its history.

Slovakia, by having the geographical location on the eastern external border of the EU, is one of those Member States focused particularly on the safeguarding of

505. Vienna Action Plan, par. 21.

506. Although in 2005 a significant decrease of asylum applications was observed (70%), in comparison to the neighbouring countries, also new EU Member States (Hungary, Poland, the Czech Republic), the number of applications for asylum lodged in Slovakia was still quite high. Based on information from the UNHCR BO, Bratislava.

507. Comparing the statistics (regarding the first-instance decisions) for years 1992, 2004 and 2005, the results vary considerably: in 1992, 87 persons in total applied for asylum, and the refugee status was granted in 56 cases (31 cases were still pending); there was no case of termination of the procedure. It means the acceptance rate was 100%. In contrast to this, in 2004 there were 11,391 persons applying for asylum, but only 15 were granted refugee status (3,147 cases were pending); there were 11,586 terminated cases. The acceptance rate in 2004 was 1.14%. In 2005, there were 3,549 applications, only 25 persons obtained asylum (acceptance rate in 2005 was 2.9%). There were 1,467 pending and 2,923 terminated cases by the end of 2005. Based on the Statistical Report from the Migration Office of the Ministry of Interior of the Slovak Republic.

the borders. Before Slovakia's accession, the dealing with border issues like security, migration, including the crossing of the borders by asylum seekers, was for the most part of national interest. As from the moment of accession to the EU, Slovakia's borders became also EU borders, either internal (borders with Austria, the Czech Republic, Hungary and Poland) or external (border with Ukraine).[508]

Since 1 May 2004, the 'Dublin II' Regulation and the Eurodac system started to apply in Slovakia. It was expected that Austria, the Czech Republic and other EU countries would return a number of asylum applicants who transferred through Slovakia westwards, which would mean a considerable burden on the existing system. The most frequently used criteria for determining Slovakia as the Member State responsible for examining asylum applications (on the basis of 'Dublin II') were expected to be the ones under Article 10 (where an asylum seeker has irregularly crossed the border into a Member State) and Article 13 (the first Member State with which the application for asylum was lodged).[509] In 2005, there were in total 2,715 incoming requests from other EU countries for transfers; in 1,995 cases, the requests were based on the information received from Eurodac.[510]

3.2 EU-Slovakia relations before joining the EU[511]

Before discussing the evolution of the Slovak asylum legislation, a brief overview of the EU-Slovakia relations is given, in order to outline at least some of the main events on the way towards Slovakia's membership in the EU and to better understand the circumstances under which the institution of asylum has been integrated into the Slovak legal order.

The diplomatic relations between the Czech and Slovak Federal Republic (CSFR) and the EC started in December 1989. On 16 December 1991 the European Agreement on Association of the CSFR to the EC (Association Agreement) was signed between the CSFR and the EC.[512] As a result of the division of the

508. The length of the Slovak border with Austria: 105. 512 km; with the Czech Republic: 251.8 km; with Hungary: 667.850 km; with Poland: 547.164 km and with Ukraine: 97.6 km.

509. This was assumed by the representatives of the UNHCR in Slovakia, the Migration Office and the Institute for the Approximation of the Law of the Slovak Government, during the interviews held in September 2004 in Bratislava.

510. Based on information from the UNHCR BO, Bratislava.

511. This part of chapter 3 is based on information received during interviews at the UNHCR BO, Bratislava and at the Institute for the Approximation of the Law of the Slovak Government in September 2004 in Bratislava and also on information from the Representation of the European Commission in the Slovak Republic web-site (www.europa.sk).

512. Europe Agreement establishing an association between the EC and their Member States, of the one part, and the CSFR, of the other part was signed on 16 December 1991 in Brussels, but it never entered into force. Not published in the *Official Journal*.

CSFR, it could not be ratified and therefore was not valid. On 4 October 1993 the European Agreement on Association was drawn up between the EU Member States and the Slovak Republic in Luxembourg (Association Agreement).[513] 'The White Book' – Preparation of the associated countries of Central and Eastern Europe for integration in the Union's internal market[514] – was delivered to the Slovak government in November 1995. On 27 June 1995 Slovakia submitted the application for the membership in the EU to Jacques Chirac, the then President of the European Council.[515]

At the beginning of November 1996 the Slovak government received a *démarche* from the EU and on 17 November a Resolution of the European Parliament on the necessity to respect human rights and democracy in Slovakia was adopted in Strasbourg.[516] The Slovak government adopted its own statement on the Resolution. This was not a positive sign for Slovakia on its journey to the EU and it postponed its progress in this respect for a period of time and also cooled down the relations with the Union.

On 16 July 1997 the European Commission submitted to the European Parliament in Strasbourg its statement concerning the applications of ten Central European and Baltic countries and recommended to start discussions with six of them: the Czech Republic, Cyprus, Estonia, Hungary, Poland and Slovenia. The Council confirmed the position of the Commission to start the negotiations with this group of applicant countries. The negotiations started at the end of March 1998. Relations with the other countries, including Slovakia, continued in a form of individual Partnerships for Joining, aimed above all at supporting those areas, in which these countries lagged behind.[517]

The Vienna European Council summit of December 1998 did not recommend direct negotiations on joining the EU with any of the 'second group' candidate countries (Romania, Slovakia, Latvia, Lithuania and Bulgaria). Nevertheless, it evaluated positively the progress in preparation for accession negotiations in these countries.[518] The Council noted the particular progress made by Latvia and Lithuania and the new situation in Slovakia following the elections which augurs

513. The Europe Agreement establishing an association between the EC and their Member States, of the one part, and the Slovak Republic, of the other part (OJ L 359, 31.12.1994) entered into force on 1 February 1995. See also Europe Agreement on Association between the European Communities and the Slovak Republic, Slovak Chamber of Trade and Industries (Bratislava, 1994).

514. The Commission of the EC: *Preparation of the Associated Countries of Central and Eastern Europe for Integration to the Internal Market to the Union*, Vol. 1 and 2, (Brussels 1995).

515. Based on information from the Representation of the European Commission in the Slovak Republic.

516. Ibid.

517. Based on an interview at the Institute for the Approximation of the Law of the Slovak Government on 31 August 2004, Bratislava.

518. Presidency Conclusions, Vienna European Council, 11 and 12 December 1998, par. 60.

well for its integration into European structures.[519] The Council asked the Commission to elaborate new evaluation Reports on candidate countries for the Helsinki European Council meeting in December 1999.[520]

The 1999 Regular Report on Slovakia, which mentioned substantial progress in many areas, actually put Slovakia along the 'first group' candidate countries. At the Helsinki European Council Slovakia was accepted as a candidate for EU membership.[521] The official negotiations on accession started in Brussels on 15 February 2000 by the opening of the IGC on Accession of the Slovak Republic to the EU. The Chief Negotiator for Slovakia, Mr. Ján Figel', delivered in Brussels position documents on eight Negotiation Chapters for Slovakia's accession to the EU. This step actually started the negotiations on the accession.

At the European Council meeting in Laeken in December 2001 the EU's enlargement was considered irreversible. Slovakia was mentioned among those countries, which, provided they successfully conclude accession negotiations by the end of 2002, become new Member States of the EU in 2004.[522] At the Copenhagen European Council of December 2002, Slovakia officially finished the pre-accession negotiations.[523]

On 9 April 2003, the European Parliament approved the accession of ten countries, including Slovakia, to the EU by adopting the Treaty of Accession.[524] The Slovak Parliament agreed upon the Treaty of Accession to the EU in July. This was preceded by a referendum on the accession to the EU, held on 16 and 17 May 2003, with a positive outcome.[525] On 1 May 2004 Slovakia became, along with the other nine European countries, a Member State of the EU.[526]

3.3 The challenges of harmonisation

When the negotiations for accession to the EU began, the differences between the EU *acquis* and the Slovak legislation were apparent. One of the most evident discrepancies was in the area of JHA, including asylum law. It was a difficult task to harmonise the national legislation with the EU *acquis*; and not just because of the

519. Id., Annex III (Council Conclusions on the EU Enlargement, General Affairs Council, 7 December 1998).

520. Id., par. 58.

521. Presidency Conclusions, Helsinki European Council, 10 and 11 December 1999, par. 10.

522. Presidency Conclusions, Laeken European Council, 14 and 15 December 2001, par. 1, 7–12.

523. Presidency Conclusions, Copenhagen European Council, 12 and 13 December 2002, par. 3; Negotiation Chapter 24: Cooperation in the field of justice and home affairs (which includes asylum), was successfully closed on 11 July 2002.

524. OJ L 236, 23.9.2003.

525. The turnout was 52.15%. 92.46 % of the votes cast were pro the accession to the EU, 6.20% were against. See for example 'Shaky EU 'yes' for Slovakia' by J. Kliphuis, 19 May 2003 available at: http://www.rnw.nl/hotspots.

526. On the history of the EU – Slovakia relations further see www.europa.sk.

enormous number of legal acts to be adopted, amended and also translated, but in particular due to the fact that the sensitive concepts of asylum and human rights needed to be brought in line with the views of the EU.[527]

The alignment with the EU *acquis* was a challenging task for all candidate countries. The harmonisation of legislation did not simply mean taking over the texts prepared and adopted by the Institutions in Brussels. One has to realise that this process required substantial changes in the policy, legislation and both to be reflected in the implementation process in practice. Essential reforms were also required in the institutional framework.[528]

Nonetheless, conflicts did not exist merely between the candidate countries' legislation and the relevant EU *acquis*, but also between the legal systems of the Member States and the EU *acquis*. One example of this type of 'conflict' is the (partial) opting out from Title IV TEC of the United Kingdom, Ireland and Denmark. As already discussed before,[529] Title IV TEC is not applicable to the United Kingdom, Ireland and Denmark, unless they decide otherwise, in accordance with the procedure laid down in the Protocols annexed to the EC and EU Treaties. It should be recalled that some parts of the Schengen *acquis* are determined to have a legal basis in Title IV TEC.

However, for the purpose of the EU enlargement the Member States decided to present the EU/Schengen *acquis* as a single block to be taken over in its entirety by the applicant countries. The applicants thus did not have the choice to possibly opt out from any provision.[530] It is clear from Article 8 of the Protocol Integrating the Schengen *acquis* into the framework of the EU that this issue was not negotiable. Countries applying for EU membership had to accept it *en bloc*. As indicated above, difficulties may occur after the accession, when the new Member States will feel to be in a 'more equal' position. However, even after completing the accession process, there will be a transitional period on the full implementation of the Schengen *acquis*.[531] And again, this will form a temporal diversity, but this time at the EU level, among the old and the new Member States.

---

527. Based on interviews at the Institute for the Approximation of the Law of the Slovak Government on 31 August 2004 and at the UNHCR BO, Bratislava, on 2 September 2004.

528. On the reforms required see e.g., the Regular Reports from the Commission on the progress towards accession; see also chapter 3, 3.5.

529. See chapter 1, 1.7.3.2.

530. Art. 8 of the Protocol Integrating the Schengen *acquis* into the framework of the European Union reads: 'For the purposes of the negotiations for the admission of new Member States into the European Union, the Schengen *acquis* and further measures taken by the institutions within its scope shall be regarded as an *acquis* which must be accepted in full by all States candidates for admission.'

531. The *acquis* in the field of Justice and Home Affairs (JHA) had to be implemented before the date of accession, with the exception of some parts of the Schengen *acquis*. This was due to the fact that the lifting of internal border controls did not occur upon accession, but will happen later, following a separate decision by the Council. For this purpose, the Schengen *acquis* has been divided into two parts. The majority of provisions had to be applied upon accession (Category I), leaving only those provisions closely linked to the lifting of the internal border controls (Category II) to be implemented simultaneously with the lifting of internal border controls. See the Accession Treaty, OJ 236

3.4 Evolution of the Slovak Asylum Legislation

One of the main objectives of the EU laid down in Article 2 TEU is 'to maintain and develop the Union as an area of freedom, security and justice'; and also 'to maintain in full the *acquis communautaire* and build on it with a view to considering to what extent the policies and forms of cooperation introduced by this Treaty may need to be revised with the aim of ensuring the effectiveness of the mechanisms and the institutions of the Community'. Slovakia as a new Member State has to comply with the common policy objectives of the Union. From the legislative point of view the main aim has been an entire harmonisation of the national legislation with the Community/Union *acquis*, which was in fact one of the conditions for the EU membership. The harmonisation of the asylum legislation has been a long and challenging process. Many substantial reforms were expected, although at the beginning of the process of harmonisation there was a lack of due experience in this field.

The legislation on JHA in general is an area in which the differences between the EU *acquis* and the national legislation of the candidate countries were visible more than in other fields.[532] The reasons were, for instance, the previous political regime and the different functioning of the competent national institutions. Nonetheless, when following the Regular Reports from the Commission on Slovakia's progress towards the accession, the progress in aligning to the *acquis* was considerable year after year.

At the time of joining the EU on 1 May 2004, Slovakia had adopted all the EU legislation on asylum in force at that time. It can be therefore said that Slovakia acceded to the Union on the same footing as the 'old' Member States. However, the process of transposition of the EU legislation on asylum is still taking place. For example a new law was adopted in Slovakia in December 2004, amending the Slovak Asylum Law currently in force, in order to comply with the EU asylum *acquis*.[533]

A more detailed analysis of the Slovak asylum legislation is necessary to better understand the evolution of the national asylum system. The main reason to analyse the legislation is due to the significant revisions carried out since the first Refugee Law was adopted. Each of these revisions meant a reform to the institution of asylum in Slovakia. Some of the changes meant nothing more than introducing a new terminology or simply a slight alteration of the structure of a certain law. Other changes, however, implied significant modifications in this field. It

---

of 23 September 2003, Annex 1. It should be noted that on 6 April 2005, the EU Commissioner for Justice, Freedom and Security, Mr. Franco Frattini, announced that the new EU Member States will fully join the Schengen area in October 2007.

532. On diversity in the area of justice and home affairs further see e.g., Monar, J.: 'Enlargement – related diversity in EU justice and home affairs: challenges, dimensions and management instruments', WWR working document (The Hague, December 2000).

533. Law No. 1/2005 of 2 December 2004 entered into force on 1 February 2005.

should be borne in mind that the institution of asylum was practically unknown to the Slovak legal order for a number of years.[534]

The whole process leading to the accession of Slovakia (and the other nine countries) to the EU was subject to the accession criteria adopted at the Copenhagen European Council in 1993. Concerning the timing, the European Council stated that

> 'accession will take place as soon as an associated country is able to assume the obligations of membership by satisfying the economic and political conditions required.'[535]

At the same time, the European Council defined the membership criteria, which are often referred to as the 'Copenhagen criteria'. Membership criteria required that the candidate country must have achieved:

- stability of institutions guaranteeing democracy, the rule of law, human rights and respect for and protection of minorities,
- the existence of a functioning market economy as well as the capacity to cope with competitive pressure and market forces within the Union,
- the ability to take on the obligations of membership including adherence to the aims of political, economic and monetary union.[536]

3.4.1 The beginnings of the Slovak asylum law

The first legislative act dealing with asylum on the territory of the former CSFR (or Czechoslovakia), following the political changes at the end of the 1980s, was the Refugee Law of 16 November 1990, No. 498.[537] Its adoption was of vital importance, as it was necessary to establish this essential institute of the international and humanitarian law. After the separation of Czechoslovakia, this Law was revoked in Slovakia and replaced by the Refugee Law of 14 November 1995, No. 283.[538]

---

534. The CSFR acceded to the 1951 Geneva Convention and the 1967 Protocol on 26 November 1991. After the separation, Slovakia succeeded to the Convention and the Protocol on 4 February 1993. Source: UNHCR.

535. Presidency Conclusions, Copenhagen European Council, 21 and 22 June 1993, Section 7(A) iii.

536. Ibid.

537. It was adopted by the Parliament of the CSFR on 16 November 1990 and entered into force on 1 January 1991. Rights and duties of aliens in general were at that time still regulated by the Law on the Stay of Aliens on the Territory of the Czech and Slovak Socialistic Republic (No. 68 of 1965), Art. 1(3).

538. As from 1 January 1993 two new states were established: the Czech Republic and the Slovak Republic (Slovakia). Initially, both countries succeeded to the legal order of the CSFR; gradually they started to adopt their own legislation, where necessary in conformity with the developments in each of the two counties. Nevertheless, due to the harmonisation of their national legislation with the *acquis communautaire*, their national legislation does not differ to a large extent. The Slovak Refugee

Part II of the Slovak Constitution[539] lays down the fundamental rights and freedoms provided for Slovak nationals, and for persons residing in the territory of the Slovak Republic. In the context of this study, Article 53 is of a particular importance. It stipulates that 'the Slovak Republic shall grant asylum to aliens persecuted for the exercise of political rights and freedoms. Such asylum may be denied to those who have acted to violate the fundamental human rights and freedoms. Details shall be provided by law'.

In the following paragraphs, the structure and the content of the 283/1995 Refugee Law will be examined:

The main objective of the 283/1995 Refugee Law was to establish procedures of state authorities on the process of determination of refugee status in Slovakia and to define the rights and duties of aliens who applied for refugee status or who were granted refugee status in the territory of the Slovak Republic (Art. 1(1)). A new paragraph was added, in comparison with the federal Law of the former Czechoslovakia, stipulating that the scope of the new Refugee Law covers also those aliens who were granted temporary protection on the territory of the Slovak Republic (Art. 1(2)).

The procedures for determination of refugee status were dealt with in Part II of the 283/1995 Refugee Law. Participants in this procedure were aliens who applied for such recognition in the territory of the Slovak Republic. The procedure for determination of refugee status started when an alien declared his intention to apply for asylum, in writing or orally. The alien could do so either at a border crossing point at the time of entry into the territory of the Slovak Republic (at the border police department), or within *24 hours* after crossing the borders at a police department, save when there were serious obstacles for doing so.[540]

If a third country national decided to apply for asylum within the period of his/her permitted stay in the territory of the Slovak Republic, he/she could do so at the police department at the place of his/her stay. The police department, where the alien could express his intention to apply for asylum, was obliged to prepare a written record about it and send it to the Ministry of the Interior without delay. According to Article 4, the procedure for the determination of the refugee status in the territory of the Slovak Republic was under the competence of the Ministry of the Interior (hereafter referred to as the Ministry). The '24-hour-rule' for lodging an asylum claim limited the access to the asylum procedure and could result in the *bona fide* asylum seekers being treated as illegal immigrants once the time limit expired. They were thus exposed to a detention rather than being given an

Law 287/1995 came into force on 1 January 1996. In comparison with the former federal Refugee Law, it was not only more extensive, but its content was much more elaborated.

539. The Constitution of the Slovak Republic of 3 September 1992 (including the Amendments of 14 July 1998 and 14 January 1999) is available at: www.government.gov.sk.

540. The Law, however, did not specify what could have been considered as 'serious obstacles'.

opportunity for a proper consideration of their case in the procedure determining their possible refugee status.

Article 4(8) the 283/1995 Law comprised the principle of *non-refoulement*, the most essential component of refugee status and of asylum as such, since it protects against a return to a country where a person has reasons to fear persecution.[541]

Questions concerning the granting of refugee status to an asylum seeker, refusal to grant the status, cancellation of the status, accelerated procedure, suspension of the procedure, termination of the procedure, decision on granting the refugee status and an appeal procedure will now be examined. A more detailed analysis will be pursued in order to pinpoint the changes introduced by the later asylum laws. In addition to this, it is important to note that preceding the accession to the EU, the most striking discrepancies were observed in the provisions regarding asylum procedure.[542]

According to the 283/1995 Law, the Ministry should *grant* refugee status to an alien who, in the country of his nationality, had a well-founded fear of being persecuted for reasons of race, religion, nationality, for his political opinion or membership of a particular social group and he was unable or, owing to such fear, was unwilling to go back to the country of his origin.[543] The same applied to a stateless person who was outside the country of his/her former habitual residence. Refugee status could be also granted for humanitarian reasons (Art. 7).

The Ministry *denied* refugee status to an alien in the following cases:

- if the applicant did not meet the conditions for granting refugee status;
- he/she committed a crime against peace or a crime against humanity;
- he/she was coming from a safe third country to which he/she could be readmitted or from a safe country of origin; this did not apply if the alien provided facts which would imply that despite the general situation in these countries he/she was in danger of persecution;[544]
- in cases when the applicant was finally sentenced for committing a particularly serious intentional crime according to the Slovak Penal Code or sentenced for acts against the UN Charter objectives and principles.[545]

---

541. The principle of *non-refoulement* has been defined in a number of international instruments relating to refugees, both at the universal and regional levels. On the universal level a mention has already been made of the 1951 Geneva Convention on Refugees, Art. 33(1).

542. During the interviews, which took place in August and September 2004 in Bratislava, the representatives of the UNHCR BO, Bratislava and of the Institute for the Approximation of the Law of the Slovak Government agreed that the harmonisation of the asylum procedures was one of the most problematic parts in the pre-accession period.

543. Cf. 1951 Geneva Convention, Art. 1 A(2).

544. The principle of *non-refoulement* is laid down here.

545. Cf. 283/1995 Law, Art. 8 and the 1951 Geneva Convention, Art. 1F.

The Ministry *cancelled* an already granted refugee status if the recognised refugee committed a serious intentional crime according to the Slovak Penal Code for which he had been finally sentenced. The Ministry could also cancel the refugee status if the decision on recognition of refugee status was based on false or incomplete facts or forged documents (Art. 9).

If an alien's refugee status *ceased*, the Ministry secured his departure from the territory of the Slovak Republic, while co-operating with the office of the UNHCR. The refugee status ceased in cases when the applicant:

- voluntarily availed himself of protection which had been provided for him by the country of his nationality;
- after the prior loss of his nationality he reacquired his original nationality;
- he had acquired a new nationality and accepted the protection of the country of his new nationality;
- he refused without justification to avail himself of the protection of the country of his nationality even though the circumstances on the basis of which he had been granted the refugee status had ceased to exist;[546] or
- if he had voluntarily re-established himself in the country which he left owing to fear of persecution. [547]

When an alien applied for granting a refugee status and his/her claim was considered as manifestly unfounded, the Ministry had to decide within seven days from starting of the procedure (*accelerated procedure*). The decision of the Ministry could be appealed with a suspensive effect within three working days from the moment it was delivered. This accelerated procedure could be adequately used in cases dealing with the refusal of refugee status to an alien (Art. 10).

The Ministry could *suspend the procedure* upon a request of an applicant for serious reasons and for not more than thirty days. It was possible to appeal against a decision on the suspension of the procedure (Art. 11).

The Ministry *terminated the procedure* for determining refugee status if the applicant:

- cancelled his application;
- voluntarily left the territory of the Slovak Republic; or
- deceased during the asylum-determination procedure.

If the procedure was legally terminated in cases of applicant's cancellation of his/her application or his/her voluntary departure from the territory of the Slovak Republic, the Ministry decided on granting a refugee status to this alien (if he/she

546. This did not apply to refugees who were able to evoke compelling reasons arising out of previous persecution for refusing to avail themselves of the protection of the country of their nationality.

547. Cf. 283/1995 Law, Art. 14 and the 1951 Geneva Convention, Art. 1C.

would apply repeatedly) only if he/she submitted a new asylum application. However, this application would only be considered, if it contained relevant facts necessary for granting refugee status (Art. 12).

The Ministry had to take a *decision* in the procedure determining refugee status within ninety days from the day of its commencement. The Minister of the Interior could in justifiable cases extend this time limit. Such extension of the time limit had to be announced to the applicant in writing. On the other hand, the 283/1995 Refugee Law did not specify a maximum time limit, neither the consequences of exceeding such a limit. In contrast to the federal Refugee Law of the former Czechoslovakia, which only granted the refugee status for a period of five years (what cannot be considered as a lasting protection),[548] decisions on granting the refugee status according to the 283/1995 Refugee Law were issued for an indefinite period (Art. 13). Decision of the Ministry on the procedure for the determination of refugee status could be *appealed* to the authority which issued the decision within the time period of 15 days from the delivery of the decision. The Minister had to decide within sixty days and a court according to the Civil Code could review this decision (Art. 15).

The most significant improvement brought about by the 283/1995 Refugee Law obviously was the introduction of the indefinite duration of the asylum status. On the contrary, the most criticised provisions were the provision establishing the '24-hour-rule' for applying for asylum and the provision on the appeal procedure, since they did not comply with the EU requirements.[549]

3.4.2 **Amendment to the 283/1995 Refugee Law**

New provisions to the Refugee Law were introduced by an amendment to the 283/1995 Law, Law No. 309 of 19 September 2000. It entered into force on 1 November 2000 and the substantial changes introduced by this amendment were:
- the abolition of the '24-hour-rule' for lodging an asylum claim,
- the extension of the grounds for granting refugee status by inserting a new paragraph on family reunification, and
- the addition to the list of grounds for starting an accelerated procedure in cases where the applicant came from a third safe country or a safe country of origin.

Following the abolition of the criticised '24-hour-rule' for lodging an asylum claim, asylum seekers can lodge an application either at the border at the time of

548. After this period, the stay of a refugee in the territory of the former Czechoslovakia was considered in conformance with at that time valid Law on the Stay of Aliens (Law on the Stay of Aliens in the territory of the Czech and Slovak Socialistic Republic, No. 68/1965). Taking into consideration the alien's level of integration into the society, he/she could be granted permission for a permanent stay under the condition that he/she has stayed in the territory of the CSFR continuously.

549. Cf. the 1999 Regular Report from the Commission on Slovakia's progress towards accession.

entry the territory of Slovakia or after crossing the border, at any time at a police department at the place of their stay.[550]

The complete harmonisation of the Slovak asylum law with the Community law had to progress in three stages, starting with the adoption of the amending 309/2000 Law. The next proposed stages have been the adoption of a new Asylum Law and finally the complete implementation of the EU law in the field of asylum achieved upon Slovakia's accession to the EU.[551]

3.4.3 Asylum Law 480/2002

A proposal for a new Asylum Law was submitted to the Slovak Parliament according to a negotiation position reflected in the Negotiation Chapter 24 (Cooperation in the field of JHA). In June 2002 the Slovak Parliament adopted a new Asylum Law, which entered into force on 1 January 2003. The main purpose of the Asylum Law of 20 June 2002, No. 480 has been to attain standards comparable to the standards of the EU Member States.[552] Since the EU asylum system itself has been further developing, according to the goals set in the first pillar, especially Article 63 TEC, it has been inevitable to respond to the new developments in the way of further amending the national legislation.[553]

The 480/2002 Law introduced a new terminology, including its title. Instead of 'Refugee Law', it is now named 'Asylum Law', in order to harmonise the corresponding terminology used in the national legislation with the Community legislation.[554] In Article 2 the Asylum Law newly defines the terms 'safe third country', 'safe country of origin' and 'persecution':

A safe third country shall mean a stable country with the rule of law and democratic order different from the country of alien's nationality or, in case of a stateless person, it shall mean a country different from the country of his residence,

- if the alien was there and had the opportunity to seek protection under an international treaty prior to his arrival in the territory of the Slovak Republic,
- where the alien may be returned to and may apply for protection without being exposed to persecution, torture, cruel, inhuman or humiliating treatment or punishment and,
- if it is not a country to which the ban of expulsion or *refoulement* under Article 47 applies,
- if the country ensures protection under Article 47 (prohibition of expulsion or *refoulement*).

550. In Art. 4(2)(b) the words 'within 24 hours' were omitted.

551. Explanatory memorandum of the Slovak Government to the 309/2000 Law.

552. Explanatory memorandum of the Slovak Government to the 480/2002 Law.

553. At the time of finalising this study the 480/2002 Asylum Law has been further amended by the following laws: 606/2003, 207/2004 and 1/2005.

554. *Supra* 552.

A safe country of origin shall mean a stable country with the rule of law and democratic order the alien is a national of or, in case of a stateless person, it shall mean the country of his/her residence,

- in which the state authority protects human rights and fundamental freedoms and ensures their observance,
- which is, in general, not left by its citizens or stateless persons having residence in it on grounds given in Article 8 (granting asylum),
- which ratified and complies with international treaties on human rights and fundamental freedoms, and
- which allows activities by legal entities supervising human right observance in the country.[555]

Persecution shall mean serious or repeated acts causing a threat to life or freedom; or other acts causing mental pressure on a person when performed, supported or tolerated by country authorities in the country of alien's nationality; or in the country where the alien had his/her residence, when the person concerned is a stateless person or when this country is not capable of ensuring appropriate protection from such acts.

According to the 480/2002 Asylum Law, the asylum procedure remains unrestricted (Art. 3). It shall start upon applicant's statement. The competent authority to receive such statement is a police department at the place of border check point at the moment of entry to the territory of the Slovak Republic; or after entering the territory at the police department competent for the location where the alien is staying.

The 480/2002 Law broadens the *grounds for granting asylum* (Arts. 8–10). The Ministry *shall* grant asylum to an applicant who has well-founded fear of being persecuted on grounds of race, ethnic origin or religion, for reasons of holding certain political opinions or belonging to a certain social group in the view of this fear he/she cannot or does not want to return to that country. The Ministry shall grant asylum to an applicant who is persecuted for exercising political rights and freedoms in the country of his/her nationality or, in case of a stateless person, in the country where he/she has a residence (Art. 8).

Article 9 determines that the Ministry *may* grant asylum also on humanitarian grounds, even when no reasons under Article 8 are established in the procedure. This provision undoubtedly represents the principle of subsidiary protection, when the asylum status can be granted also beyond the grounds set by the 1951 Geneva Convention (and as laid down in Article 8 of the Asylum Law).

The Ministry *shall* also grant asylum for the purpose of family reunification to:

555. In addition, new Governmental Decree No. 716/2002, effective as from 1 January 2003 on safe third countries and safe countries of origin was adopted.

- the spouse of the person granted asylum if their marriage is continuing to exist in the country, which the person granted asylum left for any reason under Article 8, and the person granted asylum gave his/her prior written consent,
- unmarried children, of the person granted asylum, younger than 18 years of age or
- parents of an unmarried person granted asylum younger than 18 years of age, if the person granted asylum agrees with this in advance (Art. 10).

The Asylum Law introduced more complex procedures for granting *temporary protection* (Arts. 29–36). Temporary protection shall be granted for the purpose of protecting aliens from war conflicts, impacts of humanitarian disasters or permanent or mass violation of human rights in the country of their nationality or, in case of a stateless person, in the country of his/her residence. The government shall determine the commencement, the conditions and the termination of temporary protection and shall earmark the funds to cover the costs related to granting of temporary protection. Since 1 January 2000, when temporary protection for displaced Yugoslav persons from Kosovo region expired, no person was granted temporary protection in Slovakia.[556]

An alien (a TCN) applying for temporary protection shall make a statement on it when entering the territory of the Slovak Republic (at the competent police department at the place of border check-point). He/she can also do so after entering the territory at the police department competent for the location where he/she is staying. The competent police department shall record the statement and send it to the Ministry without delay. This police department shall also arrange taking the alien's fingerprints. The alien has the obligation to arrive at the reception centre within 24 hours from the moment of making the statement, unless prevented from doing so by serious reasons. The police department shall then issue an identity document to this person, valid for 24 hours.

After arrival at the reception centre, the alien shall be issued a document of tolerated stay on the territory of the Slovak Republic marked 'ODÍDENEC' (meaning 'displaced person' in Slovak) in case the arrival was arranged by the UNHCR or another international organisation (Art. 31(1)). The displaced person shall also be issued a card of an alien applying for temporary protection as his/her identity document until the Ministry decides on granting temporary protection. The Ministry shall decide not later than 15 days after the lodging of an application. Identity cards are renewable in case of extension of the temporary protection.

The Ministry shall cease the procedure for granting temporary protection if the alien withdraws his /her application, voluntarily leaves the territory of the Slovak Republic, or dies during the procedure or if he/she applies for asylum or is granted temporary stay or permanent residence in the Slovak Republic. The Ministry shall

556. Based on an interview at the UNHCR BO, Bratislava, on 2 September 2004.

reject an application for temporary protection when the alien fails to comply with the requirements for granting such protection.

A remedy against the decision of the Ministry to reject or to cease an application for temporary protection can be brought before a competent Regional Court within seven days after delivery of the negative decision. This application shall have suspensive effect and the Regional Court shall decide on the appeal against such decision without delay.

Regarding the possibility of employment of displaced persons and their entitlement to social benefits during their stay in Slovakia, these are governed by the same special regulations for employment that apply to refugees. Displaced persons are obliged to remain in the reception centre during the quarantine period upon arrival in the Slovak Republic. They have to undergo medical examination, photographing and finger-printing, observe the law and other generally binding legal regulations valid in the territory of the Slovak Republic, notify the police department without delay of loss of the identification card or if such identification card had been stolen. They also have to observe the internal instructions whilst staying in the reception or humanitarian centres.

The 480/2002 Asylum Law redefines the cooperation with international organisations and NGOs (Art. 42 and following). The Ministry shall co-operate with the Office of the UNHCR in the course of the asylum procedure.[557] The authorised representative of the Office can participate in the asylum procedure at any stage, establish contact with a party to the procedure, and look into the file of a party to the procedure. The authorised representative has also the right to use facts found out when looking into the file and/or when orally communicating, in order to comply with tasks under international law. The Ministry shall give the Office of the UNHCR information concerning decisions issued in asylum procedure and statistical data on applicants (Arts. 42, 43).

The Asylum Law also formulates the guarantees for the principle of *non-refoulement* and prohibits expulsion, in line with the 1951 Geneva Convention and also Article 3 of the ECHR (Art. 47) and introduces data exchange protection provisions (Art. 49).[558]

557. Art. 35 of the 1951 Geneva Convention lays down the commitment of the Contracting States to co-operate with the office of the UNHCR or any other agency of the United Nations, which may succeed it, in the exercise of its functions, and shall in particular facilitate its duty of supervising the application of the provisions of this Convention.

558. It should be noted that besides the 480/2002 Asylum Law, the 48/2002 Aliens Law of 13 December 2001 (as amended by Law 408/2002, which entered into force on 25 July 2002) also defines certain aspects of the legal position of asylum seekers and refugees in Slovakia.

3.4.3.1 *Procedural aspects*

In the asylum procedure the Ministry[559] shall decide within 90 days from the day of commencing the procedure. The Migration Office makes its decisions mainly based on the results from the interviews and the information on the applicant's country of origin. In justified cases the decision-making time limit may be extended by the superior of the employee (the decision-maker) acting in the case. The Migration Office informs the applicant on the extension of the time limit for the decision on the application for asylum in writing.

Decisions on granting asylum are issued for an indefinite period. In case the Migration Office rejects an application as manifestly unfounded or it decides not to grant asylum or to withdraw asylum, it shall state in the terms of the decision whether the ban on expulsion or *refoulement* under Article 47 applies.

The decision in asylum procedure shall be delivered to the party in a place and at a time determined by the Ministry in a written call for acceptation of the decision. When receiving the decision the party to the procedure must be informed on the decision in a language he/she understands. The decision in asylum procedure shall also be delivered to the representative of the party to the procedure or his/her guardian.

The asylum facility in which the applicant is placed, the UNHCR, the police department competent for the location of the asylum facility in which the applicant is placed or competent for the location of the permanent residence of the person granted asylum, shall be notified of the decision (Art. 20).

The 480/2002 Asylum Law introduced different kinds of negative decisions, made by the first administrative instance, which is the Migration Office (Arts. 11–13). They can be summarised as follows:

a. Inadmissible asylum application

An asylum application is rejected as inadmissible when another country is responsible to act under an international treaty binding the Slovak Republic (Art. 11(1)(a)) or the applicant comes from a country considered by the Slovak Republic as a safe third country (Art. 11(1)(b)). The latter shall not apply when in the case of an asylum seeker this country cannot be considered such a country, or when the applicant cannot be effectively returned to a safe third country.

Pursuant to Article 11(2) the Ministry shall determine in its decision the State responsible to act in the asylum procedure. This provision apparently refers to the application of the Council Regulation establishing the criteria and mechanisms for determining the Member State responsible for examining an asylum application lodged in one of the Member States by a TCN ('Dublin II'), which came into

559. In practice these tasks are carried out by the Migration Office of the Ministry of Interior (further referred to as the Migration Office).

effect on the day when the Treaty on the Accession became valid, i.e., on 1 May 2004.

The Ministry shall decide under Article 11(1)(b) within 30 days from the commencing of the procedure; after a lapse of this time limit no application can be rejected as inadmissible.

b. Manifestly unfounded application

An application for asylum, not based on the grounds laid down in Article 8 or Article 10 of the 480/2002 Asylum Law, shall be rejected by the Ministry as manifestly unfounded (Art. 12(1)). It can occur when, for example, the application is based on grounds like seeking employment or better living conditions, where a due explanation is lacking or the application is based on false identity or forged documents, even though the applicant claimed them to be genuine; or when he/she repeatedly and without serious grounds refuses to appear for the interviews or comes from a country considered by the Slovak Republic a safe country of origin.

The Ministry shall also reject an application for asylum as manifestly unfounded when it is a repeated application and the applicant declares the same facts as in the previous procedure. This shall not apply when the asylum-determination procedure was ceased in cases specified by the Law.[560]

The Ministry shall decide within 30 days from the day of commencing the procedure. After a lapse of this time limit no application can be rejected as manifestly unfounded. The Ministry shall not reject an application as manifestly unfounded when asylum is sought by an unaccompanied minor (Art. 12(4)).

c. Other reasons for rejecting an asylum application

The Ministry shall not grant asylum when there is a proved suspicion that the applicant has committed a crime against peace, a war crime or a crime against humanity under international instruments containing provisions on these crimes, or has committed a serious non-political crime outside the territory of the Slovak Republic prior to applying for asylum, or is guilty of acts, which are in contradiction to the objectives and principles of the United Nations. The Ministry shall neither grant asylum to an applicant who is a national of several countries and who refuses the protection of the country of his nationality, while this is not a country where he would risk a persecution (Art. 13).

3.4.3.2 *Review of decisions*

The 480/2002 Asylum Law introduced a new asylum system, where appeals against negative decisions of the first administrative instance (the Migration

560. See Art. 19(1)(a)–(c), (f), (g).

Office) may proceed to an appeal court (Art. 21).[561] This Court can examine the cases in merits. Two Regional Courts were granted the competence to hear the asylum appeal cases – one in the capital Bratislava in the south-west of Slovakia and the other one in the east of the country, in Košice. The following types of decisions of the Migration Office can be reviewed by the Regional Courts:

a. Decisions not to grant asylum or to withdraw asylum:

A remedy against the decision of the Migration Office not to grant asylum or to withdraw asylum can be brought before the Court within 30 days from its delivery. The appeal shall have suspensive effect, meaning that no one can be expelled from the Slovak territory before the Court decides on his/her appeal.

b. Decisions rejecting an application for asylum as inadmissible when another country is competent to act:

A remedy against a decision, rejecting an application for asylum as inadmissible, when another country is competent to act, as laid down in Article 11(1)(a), can be brought before a Court within seven days from its delivery and it has no suspensive effect, unless otherwise decided by the Court.

The Migration Office is responsible for the application of the 'Dublin II' Regulation in Slovakia. Although this is not expressly written in the 480/2002 Asylum Law, it seems to refer to this Regulation in Article 11(1)(a).[562] Therefore the lack of a suspensive effect in the appeals falling under this decision could be well justifiable, since the asylum seeker should not be sent to a third country, but his/her case should be examined by another EU Member State. On the other hand, considering that a Regional Court may (according to Article 21(2)) overrule the decision of the Migration Office (on rejecting an application for asylum as inadmissible when another country is competent to act) in cases where the 'Dublin II' Regulation applies, a question may arise whether a national court might rule against the strict set of criteria laid down in this Council Regulation; unless Article 3(2) of 'Dublin II' (the sovereignty clause) applies.

c. Decisions rejecting an application for asylum as inadmissible when the applicant comes from a safe third country:[563]

A remedy against a decision rejecting an application for asylum as inadmissible under Article 11(1)(b) can be filed with a Court within seven days from its deliv-

561. Art. 21(2) entered into force on the day when the Treaty on the Accession of the Slovak Republic to the European Communities became valid (1 May 2004).

562. Art. 11(1)(a) entered into force on 1 May 2004, on the same day as the 'Dublin II' Regulation started to apply in Slovakia.

563. This shall not be applicable when the principle of *non-refoulement* would be violated.

ery and it shall have suspensive effect. The Court shall decide on the remedy within 30 days from the delivery of the appeal request.

d. Decisions rejecting an application for asylum as manifestly unfounded:

An appeal against a decision rejecting an application for asylum as manifestly unfounded can be lodged with a Court within seven days from its delivery and it has a suspensive effect. The Court shall decide on the appeal without a delay.

e. Decisions during the time when the applicant is placed in a reception centre in the transit area of an international airport.

A remedy against a decision of the Migration Office in an asylum procedure during the time when the applicant is placed in a reception centre in the transit area of an international airport can be filed with a Court within seven days from its delivery.[564]

3.4.4 Two examples of Court decisions

As mentioned above, the 480/2002 Asylum Law granted the competence to hear asylum appeal cases to two Regional Courts. Two examples of case-law from the Regional Court in Bratislava will be described in order to demonstrate its operation within the newly granted jurisdiction in asylum matters. One of the court decisions which follow confirms a decision of the Migration Office, which rejected to grant asylum status in Slovakia; the second court decision, on the contrary, cancels the Migration Office's decision not to grant asylum to an asylum applicant.[565]

A court decision confirming a decision of the Migration Office[566]

The asylum seeker (further referred to as plaintiff) was a national of Serbia and Montenegro. He applied for asylum in Slovakia, claiming that his house was bombed several years ago and he also lost all his close family members. Based on the investigation carried out by the Migration Office (further referred to as defendant) it was proved, that he applied for asylum in Slovakia repeatedly. He justified his action by his repeated persecution by the police in his country of origin.

Because the facts, on which the plaintiff based his appeal, were not proved reliable and his statements were often controversial, and moreover his behaviour in-

564. The 1/2005 Law, which amended the 480/2002 Asylum Law, provides that the last sentence which read: 'The lodging of such appeal shall have suspensive effect.' shall be omitted.

565. Based on an interview with an asylum judge of the Regional Court, Bratislava on 7 September 2004.

566. Judgement record No. 10 Saz 12/2004.

dicated that he did not show a real interest in asylum, since he left the reception centre, where he was placed before and made an attempt to get to Germany, the defendant decided not to grant him asylum status in Slovakia.

There was also a well-grounded suspicion that he applied for asylum in Slovakia only to avoid his extradition back to his country, since he was already twice returned to Slovakia by the Czech police and was denied admission to the territory of Slovakia for 5 years.

The defendant justified the negative decision in this case stating that it was not proved that the plaintiff would have a well-founded fear of persecution in his country of origin, based on the reasons of his race, nationality, religion, his political opinions or his belonging to a certain social group, according to the 1951 Geneva Convention. Since the beginning of the procedure before the Migration Office no evidence was found, which would prevent to return the plaintiff to his country of origin and thus violate the principle of *non-refoulement.*

The competent Regional Court examined the challenged decision, issued by the Migration Office and after considering all facts, including the hearing of the plaintiff's evidence and the facts collected and presented by a representative of the Migration Office (for example information about the situation in plaintiff's country of origin) it upheld the rejecting decision of the Migration Office. The Court did not find any objective reasons for granting asylum. Furthermore, the facts claimed by the plaintiff were considered not reliable, especially because of the controversy of the facts he was claiming. An appeal was sustained towards this Court decision within 30 days from its delivery, on the signed Court.[567]

A court decision annulling a decision of the Migration Office[568]

The asylum applicant (further referred to as plaintiff) comes from Ghana, where he was chosen to be king in the tribal kingdom of Fanti, after the previous king had died. Since a condition for his enthronement was to execute a murder of a 12-year-old girl, who was pregnant and he did not agree with this ritual (he converted to be a Christian and this act was in controversy with his conscience), he left the palace and consequently also the country and applied for asylum in Europe, in Slovakia.

The plaintiff stated that he left his country because of his serious fears to be persecuted by the authorities of the above-mentioned tribal kingdom. He pointed out that the president of the country, as well as the executive are tolerating such pagan rituals and even the police participate in looking for a victim; on the other hand the police do not help in cases when someone finds himself in danger.

---

567. Although the possible appeal in this case would be heard by the Supreme Court, the appeal has to be delivered to the Court which made the decision (in this case it is the Regional Court).

568. Judgement record No. 11 Saz 8/2004.

The plaintiff explained that Ghana is divided into several autonomous parts led by kings (owners of the land) who are at the same time counsellors to the president of the country. From the facts provided by the plaintiff, it could be concluded that he would be persecuted not only by non-state actors, but also by the representatives of the state itself. He applied for asylum in Slovakia, at a police office at a border-crossing point. Regarding his application for asylum, he was interviewed 11 days later in the reception centre where he was placed after submitting his asylum claim.

The Migration Office (further referred to as defendant) issued a negative decision in the plaintiff's case, dated 28 November 2003. The defendant decided that the application was manifestly unfounded according to Article 12 of the Asylum Law and that the *non-refoulement* provision (Art. 47) did not apply.

Nevertheless, the decision of the defendant was delivered to the plaintiff only on 4 March 2004 (i.e., 125 days following the decision). Article 21 of the Asylum Law states that a remedy against a decision, denying to grant asylum can be filed with a competent Regional Court within 30 days from its delivery. According to the Slovak Administrative Procedure Code (Art. 51) the parties have to be notified about all decisions made in their case. The day of delivery of a decision is considered to be the day of the notification. Therefore the plaintiff correctly pointed to a procedural lapse caused by the defendant, who incorrectly applied the provision of Article 12(3) of the Asylum Law, after the 30-day time limit expired.

If the date of the decision would be decisive, regardless when the decision would be delivered to the applicant for asylum, this could lead to absurd consequences, when a decision could be delivered after several months or even years, whilst the efficiency of an accelerated administrative procedure would loose its substantiation.

Considering the aforementioned facts, the Regional Court in Bratislava concluded that the defendant also incorrectly applied the provisions of Article 12(1)(c) of the Asylum Law (that the asylum seeker comes from a country considered by the Slovak Republic a safe country of origin). Taking this into account, further proceeding of the defendant in the context based on the reason regarding the safe country of origin principle, concerning the country of origin of the plaintiff, must be considered incorrect. The defendant made a serious failure in the asylum procedure (regarding the time limit), as well as the facts on which the asylum application was based were not evaluated sufficiently. There was no further appeal admissible in this case. The Migration Office had to reconsider its decision, based above all on an interview with the plaintiff (the applicant for asylum). The collected information should be considered on the account of the information on the country of origin, which should be gathered independently (besides the information provided by the applicant), and also the existence of the tribal kingdom of Fanti and the manner in which a new king is enthroned have to be re-examined.

The new decision is therefore expected to be well reasoned, based on substantial facts of the case.[569]

3.4.5 Considerations concerning the Slovak Asylum Law

To sum up, the 480/2002 Asylum Law aims at making the asylum procedure more effective, above all by preventing the still frequent cases of misusing the procedure by persons who do not qualify for such protection. This Asylum Law was adopted in order to comply with the EU *acquis* and the 1951 Geneva Convention.

According to the statistics provided by the Migration Office, there were 1556 asylum applications in total in 2000; in 2001 the number increased up to 8151; in 2002 to 9743; in 2003 to 10,358 and in 2004 up to 11,391. In 2005, on the other hand, the number of applications dropped to 3,549. The countries of origin of the asylum applicants were for example Afghanistan, Iraq, China, India, Bangladesh, and the Russian Federation.[570] Despite the increasing number of asylum seekers in the previous years, Slovakia is still predominantly a transit country. The high percentage of terminated procedures points towards this reality. The applicants leave the Slovak territory voluntarily and for the most part illegally, before the final decisions in their cases are made.[571] It is expected that in the future there will be an increase in the number of applicants entering the asylum procedure, as well as those who will stay in Slovakia after being granted the asylum status. It means Slovakia may become a country of destination, instead of being a country of transition. This is very likely to be true since the implementation of the 'Dublin II' Regulation and the Eurodac system that started to operate in Slovakia; and also after the minimum standards on the reception of asylum seekers in Member States as laid down in the Council Directive 2003/9/EC will be fully implemented in practice.

The adoption of the 480/2002 Asylum Law was the second step in the gradual implementation of the asylum *acquis* into the Slovak legal order. The completion of the harmonisation of the Slovak legislation, as laid down in the Negotiation Chapter 24, was attained to the date of the accession to the EU. A constant implementation of a new *acquis communautaire* in the field of asylum will be necessary. Therefore the 480/2002 Asylum Law has to be updated and the current *acquis* must be adopted, in order to guarantee a continuous harmonisation of the asylum practice in Slovakia with the EU measures. This need of a continuous

569. At the time of the interview at the Regional Court this case was still pending.

570. This reflects the situation in January-March 2004. Source: the Migration Office of the Ministry of Interior of the Slovak Republic.

571. For instance, 11,586 cases were terminated in 2004; 2,923 cases in 2005. Source: the Migration Office of the Ministry of Interior of the Slovak Republic.

harmonisation was shown shortly after 1 May 2004, when a proposal for an amendment to the current Asylum Law was presented.[572]

3.4.6 Amendments to the 480/2002 Asylum Law

The amendment to the 480/2002 Asylum Law, No. 1/2005 of 2 December 2004, was adopted by the Slovak Parliament in December 2004 and entered into force on 1 February 2005. The main purpose of this amendment has been to transpose into the national legislation the Reception Directive and the Temporary Protection Directive;[573] and thus to make a further step to bring the Slovak legislation on asylum in line with the primary (especially Articles 61 and 63 TEC) and the secondary (the above-mentioned Council Directives) Community law. It should be noted that all EU Member States were required to transfer the Reception Directive into their national laws before 6 February 2005.[574] The main changes introduced by the 1/2005 Law are:

- it newly regulates locations where aliens can apply for asylum;
- sets a time limit, within which the asylum applicant must be informed about his rights and duties during the procedure for the determination of the asylum status;
- newly determines, who is legitimately authorised to have access to documents and information in the asylum procedure;
- provides for the first time that asylum applicants will have access to the labour market in Slovakia, if the Ministry does not issue a decision regarding the granting of the asylum status within one year from the commencement of the asylum determination procedure;
- provides that during the asylum-determination procedure asylum seekers are granted accommodation, food or board allowance, basic hygienic articles and other necessary articles, urgent medical care (or more extensive medical care in specific cases) and pocket money, unless otherwise stated by the Asylum Law;
- to asylum seekers, who are unaccompanied minors, will be appointed a guardian by a court.[575]

In two particular points the opinion of the UNHCR differed from that of the Migration Office and the Ministry of Interior. In one draft proposal (similar to a Czech model) a two year ban for reapplying to the asylum procedure for those applicants with already rejected claims was introduced. A similar proposal could

572. Based on an interview at the Institute for the Approximation of the Law of the Slovak Government, Bratislava on 31 August 2004.

573. See Annex 5 to the amended 480/2002 Asylum Law.

574. Reception Directive, Art. 26.

575. Based on an explanatory memorandum of the Slovak Government to the amendment to the Asylum Law and on information from the UNHCR BO, Bratislava.

have been in contrast with the right to seek asylum pursuant to the 1951 Geneva Convention. The proposal was then taken out of the text before being sent to the approval to the cabinet of ministers. On a second proposal there was more discussion. The draft, introducing in the asylum system special centres for applicants who 'misbehaved', reached the plenary session of the Slovak Parliament. UNHCR and the Slovak Helsinki Committee presented a detailed report with legal and practical reasons opposing such measure. They obtained the support of the President of the Parliamentary Committee for Human Rights, who also opposed the proposal with the argument that it is more effective to prevent than to try to cure. 77 MPs finally voted against this proposal and only 12 supported the opinion of the Ministry of Interior.

The 'confrontation' at the plenary session of the Slovak Parliament shows how sensitive the issue of the transposition of EU *acquis* into the national asylum systems could be. If not carefully monitored, the action could allow the introduction of new amendments to the existing national legislation, which would be in obvious contrast with the already quite low level of the minimum standards laid down in some provisions of the EU asylum *acquis*. Divergence in the legislation and practice of neighbouring Member States could also exacerbate the debate on the fairness of the Common European Asylum System. For example the significant difference in the recognition rate between Austria (91% in 2005) and Slovak Republic (nearly 0%) on Chechen applicants is a concrete proof of the need of having a more coordinated approach on asylum.[576]

A proposal for a further amendment to the Slovak Asylum Law (further referred to as the amendment-proposal) has been introduced in order to comply with the obligation to transpose the Qualification Directive into the national legislation. Once the new amendment enters into force, the asylum-determination procedure will include not only assessment of asylum claims, but also the determination whether a third-county national qualifies for a subsidiary form of protection (the single procedure approach).

The amendment will introduce a number of substantial changes, for example, it:

- defines the terms: international protection, subsidiary protection, serious harm, actors of persecution, country of origin;
- redefines the term 'persecution' and specifies the reasons for persecution;
- broadens the grounds for rejection of an asylum application as inadmissible;
- includes new circumstances under which the asylum is not granted or is revoked;
- introduces the grounds for granting, for refusal to grant, for ending and revocation of subsidiary protection;
- enables to grant subsidiary protection for the purpose of family reunification;

576. Based on an interview at the UNHCR BO, Bratislava, 2 May 2006.

- introduces the right of the third country nationals, who have been granted a subsidiary form of protection, to be informed about their rights and duties, related to such protection;
- determines the time period for which the asylum status for the purpose of family reunification is initially granted.

I will not go into details regarding all provisions in the amendment-proposal. Instead, based on a discussion with the representative of the UNHCR in Slovakia, I would like to draw your attention to one Article, the new Article 20, paragraphs (2) and (3):

The proposal under Article 20(2) states that asylum shall be granted for an indefinite period of time, while asylum for the purpose of family reunification shall be granted initially for a period of 3 years. Subsequently, it may be extended upon the request of the applicant for an indefinite period of time, provided that the requirements under Article 10 (granting asylum for the purpose of family reunification) are met. This proposed provision puts the family members of the person granted asylum in a disadvantageous position on account of their derivative refugee status. This proposed distinction is incompatible with the legal requirement of non-discrimination contained under various international human rights treaties. It is also important to bear in mind that in its Final Act, the UN Conference of Plenipotentiaries, which adopted the 1951 Geneva Convention, unanimously approved Recommendation B on the subject of family unity in the case of refugees emphasizing that the

> 'unity of the family, the natural and fundamental group unit of society, is an essential right of the refugee, and that such unit is constantly threatened, and noting with satisfaction that according to the official commentary of the ad hoc Committee on Statelessness and Related Problems (E/1616, p.40) the rights granted to a refugee are extended to the members of his family'.

Further, the fundamental importance of the family and the need to protect it have consistently received recognition in international human rights law both at the universal and regional level and it is clear that these protective provisions apply to refugees and beneficiaries of subsidiary protection. The following international legal instruments form the foundation in support of family reunification:

- the Universal Declaration of Human Rights (Art. 16);
- the International Covenant on Civil and Political Rights (Arts. 17, 23);
- the International Covenant on Economic, Social and Cultural Rights (Art. 10);
- the Convention on the Rights of the Child (Arts. 7–10, 18, 22);
- the ECHR (Art. 8).

The proposed administrative requirement that this status shall be first granted for three years, with the possibility to apply for an indefinite status, appears to be incompatible with the body of law and practice outlined above. The Slovak authorities justified this provision by referring to Article 24(1) of the Qualification Directive on residence permits. Moreover, the approach taken in the amendment-proposal suggests a refugee status that can be terminated purely on the basis of expiration of time, a cessation provision infringing the 1951 Refugee Convention and the Qualification Directive, as well.

As regards Article 20(3) of the amendment-proposal, the beneficiaries of subsidiary protection, as well as their family members, would need to renew their status annually. Having a status that has to be renewed every year would cause major challenges to the beneficiaries of subsidiary protection. Furthermore, the Qualification Directive does not recommend that time limitations should be attached to subsidiary protection status. On the contrary, according to the Qualification Directive, subsidiary protection status is a durable status that can only be terminated on the grounds laid down in Article 19. Therefore, the time limitation proposed in the amendment seems to be below the minimum standards established by the Directive. The Slovak authorities justify the one-year time limitation of the subsidiary protection status by the minimum duration of residence permits issued to the beneficiaries of subsidiary protection according to Article 24(2) of the Qualification Directive.

According to the UNHCR representative, from a legal point of view there is a qualitative difference between a time limit on the status itself and a time limit on a residence permit for the status holder. It is stated in the Qualification Directive that as long as the person holds the status, he/she is automatically entitled to the residence permit. Thus, in order to refuse the granting of or renewal of the residence permit, the status which provides the entitlement would need to be terminated first. In order to avoid confusion, this distinction must be clearly reflected in the amendment to the Asylum Law; otherwise one can speak about an incorrect interpretation and consequently an incorrect transposition of the EU Qualification Directive.

As far as the transposition process of the Qualification Directive into the Slovak legislation is concerned, at the time of finalising this book the situation was as follows:

1. On 5 September 2006, the Legislative Council of the Slovak Government discussed the amendment-proposal in order to ensure the transposition of the Qualification Directive.
2. On 20 September 2006, the Slovak Government approved the proposal.
3. In order to become a law, the proposal needs to be adopted by the Slovak Parliament. The adoption of the proposal by the Slovak Parliament was still pending; the expected entering into force of the amendment to the Asylum Law is 1 January 2007, as stated in the final provisions to the amendment-proposal.

Slovakia thus did not meet the transposition deadline of 10 October 2006 as laid down in Article 38(1) of the Qualification Directive *to bring into force* the laws, regulations and administrative provisions necessary to comply with this Directive.

3.5 Assessment by the European Commission

The European Commission was observing the development in the acceding Member States, in order to put forward suggestions for future actions, necessary to be taken before the accession. In its Regular Reports, published annually between 1998 and 2003 the Commission made assessment on each of the Negotiation Chapters, covering the fields where legal and political transformations had to take place. Negotiation Chapter 24 dealt with the policies on JHA. We will have a closer look at it in the next paragraphs, specifically at the developments in the field of asylum.

The Regular Reports from the Commission on Slovakia's progress towards accession notified the following progress and the gaps in the Slovak legislation on asylum as well. The first 'Regular Report of 1998'[577] informed that there was no progress in alignment of asylum legislation in Slovakia,[578] but a joint EU–Slovak working group made recommendations on how the legislation should be improved. The main criticism was directed to the '24-hour-rule' for lodging an asylum claim and to the appeal procedure which did not comply with the EU requirements.

In the 'Regular Report of 1999'[579] the Commission also emphasised the attention which needed to be paid to the practical application of provisions relating to the concept of 'safe third country' under the Dublin Convention including the preparation of the respective national legislation.[580]

In the 'Regular Report of 2000'[581] the Commission evaluated the progress registered in the Slovak Republic since the 1999 Regular Report in the field of asylum as significant. Progress was reported in the alignment of asylum legislation; for example the Slovak Parliament approved an amendment to the Refugee Law in September 2000 (the 309/2000 Law), which included the abolition of the '24-hour-rule' for lodging an asylum claim, one of the 1999 Accession Partnership short-term priorities. After removing the condition to apply for asylum within 24 hours after crossing the border, analogous situations are covered by the second

---

577. Commission Report COM(1998) 703 final, not published in the Official Journal.

578. At the time of publishing the 1998 and 1999 Regular Reports the 283/1995 Refugee Law was still in force.

579. Commission Report COM(1999) 511 final, not published in the Official Journal.

580. In the Common, Interim and Final Provisions of the 283/1995 Refugee Law there is a notice that the Government of the Slovak Republic will issue a list of safe third countries and safe countries of origin (Art. 29).

581. Commission Report COM(2000) 711 final, not published in the *Official Journal*.

option, i.e., 'after crossing the border...at the Police Department at the place of his/her stay...'. That means an alien can lodge an application for asylum from the moment of crossing the border of the Slovak Republic and later at any time at the responsible authority.

Furthermore the above-mentioned Law amended the definition of manifestly unfounded cases, established the right to recognition as a refugee for purposes of family reunification and lengthened the accelerated procedure and the appeal procedure. The list of safe third countries and safe countries of origin was amended. The independent body as the second instance in the asylum procedure still was not established.

Despite the progress reported, Slovakia was not yet fully in line with the *acquis* in the field of asylum, as stated in the overall assessment on the Negotiation Chapter 24. The exclusion clause of the Refugee Law was considered too broad, its *non-refoulement* provisions were not in line with international requirements and the provisions for recognition for purposes of family unity were too narrow. Continued attention needed to be paid to the practical application of provisions relating to the concept of 'safe third countries'. The different responsibilities of the Migration Office and the Aliens and Border Police for determining the need for international protection were a constant cause for concern, since they did not guarantee a consistent, competent assessment of refugee cases. Moreover, administrative capacities needed to be strengthened; in particular the staff and equipment of the Migration Office needed to be increased and training continued.

The 'Regular Report of 2001'[582] informed that Slovakia was not yet fully in line with the *acquis* in the field of asylum. In particular, an independent body as the second instance in the asylum procedure still needed to be established. Furthermore, the exclusion clauses of the Refugee Law were too broad and its *non-refoulement* provisions remained to be brought into line with international agreements. According to the Commission, a special attention needed to be paid to the practical application of provisions relating to the concept of 'safe third country'. The different responsibilities of the Migration Office and the Aliens and Border Police in determining the need for international protection remained a cause for concern (as they still did not guarantee a consistent and competent assessment of refugee cases).

Moreover, the competence of the border police in the area of asylum policy should be further clarified. The section of immigration officers at the Migration Office needed additional reinforcement and professional training. Extra attention should be devoted to the accommodation of asylum seekers and to eliminating the backlog of pending asylum cases and to implementing the Dublin Convention. In the first seven months of 2001, a total of around 3000 asylum applications were lodged in the Slovak Republic, but only one applicant was recognised as a refu-

582. Commission Report COM(2001) 700 final – SEC(2001) 1754, not published in the *Official Journal*.

gee. In 2000, there were 1556 applications (1320 in 1999). The largest groups of asylum seekers in 2000 came from Afghanistan, India, Pakistan, Iraq, Sri Lanka, Bangladesh and Kosovo. The fact that the number of asylum seekers was increasing, while the number of persons recognised as refugees was actually decreasing, was considered as disturbing.

'Regular Report of October 2002'[583] informed about a further progress made since the last Regular Report in the area of JHA (Negotiation Chapter 24), particularly in the fields of data protection, visas, border control, migration, asylum and police cooperation.

The last of the series of the Regular Reports from the Commission on the Slovakia's progress towards accession was the 'Regular Report of November 2003' (Comprehensive monitoring report on Slovakia's preparations for membership).[584]

Significant progress was achieved by Slovakia with the adoption of the new Asylum Law in June 2002, which entered into force on 1 January 2003. The new 480/2002 Asylum Law lays down new rules on the principle of *non-refoulement*, regulates in detail the procedure for granting asylum and contains new definitions as regards the safe third country concept. In particular, the new Law covers the establishment of an independent review authority to reconsider negative decisions taken at first instance.

Regarding the implementing capacity, the number of officers at the Migration Office is still insufficient to cope with the increased number of cases. In 2001 a sharp increase (423%) in the number of applications (8151) was registered in comparison to 2000. The Migration Office issued 5395 first instance decisions, 18 of which granting and 130 denying refugee status; in 5247 cases the procedure was terminated because the applicant had left the country. A new refugee reception centre with a capacity of 140 people was opened at Rohovce in the western part of the Slovak Republic in October 2001. The Report pointed out that the administrative capacity of the Migration Office, in particular the staff in charge of processing the asylum claims, should be substantially strengthened. Professional training provided to staff both in the Migration Office and in the Border and Aliens Police should also be reinforced. Moreover, cooperation between the Migration Office and the Border and Aliens Police should continue to be improved at both local and central level. The completion of a comprehensive Migration Strategy should be ensured. Reception centres still need to be expanded and improved (in particular in the east of the country and the processing has to be conducted there instead of transferring applicants near the border with Austria).

The area of asylum was mentioned in the Report among those areas, where Slovakia partially met the commitments and requirements, and needed to make

---

583. Commission Report COM(2002) 700 final – SEC(2002) 1410, not published in the *Official Journal*.

584. Comprehensive monitoring report of the European Commission on the state of preparedness for EU membership of the Czech Republic, Estonia, Cyprus, Latvia, Lithuania, Hungary, Malta, Poland, Slovenia and Slovakia, COM(2003) 675 final.

enhanced efforts in order to complete its preparations for accession. The Report further stated that in the field of asylum, Slovakia had notably aligned its legislation with the *acquis*, by the adoption of the new Asylum Law in June 2002. However, the new Law ensured only partial alignment with the Dublin II and the Eurodac Regulations and the necessary alignment was therefore required. According to the 2003 Report, Slovakia should also accelerate its preparation for active participation in Eurodac and still needs to take the necessary measures to ensure the establishment of its National Access Points.

Concerning the external border controls, the Commission reported that although Slovakia took a number of measures to reinforce such controls, it should continue to strengthen border control management and to improve capacity to control external borders, especially by giving priority to the border with Ukraine. Slovakia was encouraged to fully implement its plans to phase out the use of conscripts at all its borders by 1 January 2003. Further training for border guards should also be ensured. In addition, cooperation with neighbouring states should be enhanced. Slovakia should intensify efforts to achieve a more effective cooperation in the control of the common borders with Poland, Hungary and Ukraine.

3.6 Implementation

'The European Council is determined to develop the Union as an area of freedom, security and justice and will place and maintain this objective at the very top of the political agenda...It would be in contradiction with Europe's traditions to deny such freedom to those whose circumstances lead them justifiably to seek access to our territory. This in turn requires the Union to develop common policies on asylum and immigration...these common policies must be based on principles which are both clear to our own citizens and also offer guarantees to those who seek protection in or access to the European Union.'[585]

In the previous paragraphs the evolution of the Slovak asylum legislation was described. Although the harmonisation of the national legislation with the EU *acquis* on asylum was one of the conditions for accession to the EU (see the Copenhagen criteria) and due to this of major importance, the following phase – the implementation of the legislation in practice, is the most crucial phase; given that by bringing into practice the EU-harmonised national laws, the Common European Asylum System is being put into action. In relation to the integration process carried out by the Ministry of Interior of the Slovak Republic and other authorities, the formulation of principles of the new migration policy of Slovakia has been one of the priorities. This policy, which is still an ongoing process, should

585. Tampere, Introduction and par. 3.

also comply with the Presidency Conclusions of Tampere and Seville. In practice it means:

- a need to draft a common policy for specific, but closely related issues of asylum and immigration;
- to make sure that migration flows are steered in accordance with the law and in collaboration with the countries of origin and transit; in this regard it is necessary to adopt a comprehensive plan for the fight against illegal migration and for safeguarding the EU's external borders;
- a balance has to be struck between, on the one hand, the policy on integration of aliens with a legal stay and the asylum policy corresponding to international conventions, especially the 1951 Geneva Convention and, on the other hand, resolute measures to fight illegal migration and trafficking on human beings, through short-term and medium-term arrangements focusing on joint steering of migration flows.[586]

The practical impact of Slovakia's membership in the EU in the field of asylum will be examined by evaluating the functioning of the asylum system within the new conditions. In order to specify the standard of the asylum system in Slovakia, a fictitious case has been made,[587] outlining the procedures in practice. This case will start from the moment of the reception of the asylum seeker and will continue through all stages foreseen by the law. The case was constructed deliberately in order to highlight the areas in need of further improvement.[588]

3.6.1 A fictitious case

A person coming from country X[589] crossed the Ukrainian-Slovak border illegally. In his country of origin he feared to be persecuted by the government for voicing

---

586. Assessment of the Asylum System in the Slovak Republic – Final Report (May 2003 – April 2004) prepared by UNHCR, The Ministry of Interior (Migration Office, Aliens and Border Police), The Ministry of Labour, Social Affairs and Family, The European Commission Delegation in the Slovak Republic, The International Organisation for Migration, The Embassy of the USA, The Embassy of the Kingdom of the Netherlands, The Slovak Helsinki Committee, The Björnson Society, The Goodwill Society (further referred to as the 'Assessment of the Asylum System in Slovakia – Final Report'), 12.

587. This fictitious case and the evaluation could be carried out thanks to the information gathered at the UNHCR BO, Bratislava, the Migration Office of the Ministry of Interior of the Slovak Republic, the Institute for the Approximation of the Law of the Slovak Government and the Bratislava Regional Court.

588. For the sake of clarity, the explanations to the fictitious case have been placed in a grey background. The numbering of Articles takes into account the situation prior to the transposition of the Qualification Directive (see chapter 3, 3.4.6).

589. The statistics show that in 2005 among the most frequent countries/regions of origin of the asylum seekers in Slovakia were: Chechnya (893), Moldavia (307), China (253), Georgia (214) and India (213). Based on a Statistical Review from the Migration Office of the Ministry of Interior of the Slovak Republic.

different opinions on the observation of human rights.[590] Caught by the police nearby Bratislava, he applied for asylum.

In case this person would not apply for asylum, he would be handed over to the Ukrainian authorities, since he came to Slovakia via Ukraine. Slovakia has signed a readmission agreement with Ukraine. Even though this agreement is not considered by the Slovak authorities as working very effectively, in reality it is more effective than during the previous years (e.g., in 2003 Ukraine rejected 1,130 persons, in 2004 it was 'only' 802). During 2002 Ukraine gradually ceased to observe the applicable readmission agreement with Slovakia, thereby putting a stop to the process of handing over and receiving persons, who crossed the state border with Ukraine illegally.[591] In 2005, 1,841 third country nationals were returned to Ukraine by the Slovak authorities.

The case would also develop in different way, if the alien (TCN) would cross the Slovak territory and enter Austria, without being checked. If he would apply for asylum in Austria, he could be returned back to Slovakia on the basis of the 'Dublin II' Regulation (Art. 10),[592] unless Austria applies Article 3(2) of the same Regulation (the 'sovereignty clause') and decides to examine his case.

Since no other Member State could be determined to be responsible to examine his asylum application, the last criterion of the 'Dublin II' Regulation applied (the Member State, where the application for asylum was first lodged, is responsible for dealing with the application),[593] and the Slovak authorities commenced the asylum determination procedure.

The competent Slovak authorities can also apply the principle of 'safe third country' or 'safe country of origin' (where this is known) and return the person on the basis of a readmission agreement; unless there is a threat to his life (principle of non-refoulement must always be observed).

590. Cf. the definition in the 1951 Geneva Convention, Art. 1A(2).

591. In 2003, there was an improvement in this adverse situation through the activity of chief border plenipotentiaries of Slovakia and Ukraine. Nevertheless, it was still not running on the desired level. For example, in the year 2002 a total of 2,391 illegal migrants (749 asylum applications) arrived in the territory of the Slovak Republic from Ukraine; the number increased in 2003 to 5468 illegal migrants (3906 asylum applications). See 'Assessment of the Slovak Asylum System – Final Report', 11.

592. Art. 10 of the 'Dublin II' Regulation deals with irregular crossings of the borders of Member States by asylum seekers.

593. *Dublin II*, Art. 13.

Within the whole asylum-determination procedure described in the 480/2002 Asylum Law, different partial procedures could be distinguished:

- the entry into the asylum procedure (declaration made at the police unit);
- registration at the reception centre;
- procedure leading to the first-instance decision made by the Migration Office;
- first-instance decision;
- (final) decision issued by the appeal court.

3.6.1.1 *Entry into the asylum procedure*

The TCNs illegally present in the territory of Slovakia, who were caught by police in the Bratislava region and expressed their intention to apply for asylum, were transferred to Jarovce border-control department – a special border-control department, where an Asylum Group was located.[594] Since in the fictitious case the person crossed the borders irregularly, but applied for asylum, he was located in this facility.

Following the reception of the applicant, the asylum procedure began. Before being transferred to a reception centre for asylum applicants, he was fingerprinted and photographed and an interview was also carried out in the border-control department.[595] A form of declaration of his intention to apply for asylum was filled out,[596] as well as a Protocol on explanation, where he explained why, how and when he entered the territory and the reasons for his application. He was then issued with a temporary ID card valid for three days and a train ticket to the place, where the reception centre is located.[597]

The described border-control department was not suitable to accommodate persons for longer than several hours. This was because of the inappropriate accommodation conditions for the asylum seekers, lack of warm meals, as well as the inadequate hygienic and sanitary conditions of the facility. In spite of the state of the facility, the registration procedure and the detention itself took too long.[598] It

594. This special border-control department covered 12 kilometres of the common border with Austria. Jarovce border-control department has been closed after the recommendation of a Task Force which have noticed treatments not in line with the respect of basic human rights. The Aliens and Border Police has opened three new centres for registration (in Opatovská Nová Ves, Liptovské Vlachy and Adamov) in order to expedite the process of transferring the asylum cases to the Migration Office.

595. The Aliens and Border Police is responsible for taking fingerprints of asylum applicants. Through its database the data enter the Eurodac database. An Institute of Criminalistics and Expert Examinations of the Police Force administers the Eurodac system in Slovakia.

596. See Annex 1 to 480/2002 Asylum Law – Alien's Statement.

597. In some cases, usually in cases of large groups of asylum applicants, these are escorted to the reception centre by the police.

598. Assessment of the Asylum System in Slovakia – Final Report, 13–14, 26–28.

should be noted that in 2004 two special border-control departments, where asylum seekers used to be located (including the above-mentioned department in Jarovce), were closed. The reason was that their standards did not meet the EU criteria. However, a new refugee centre was opened in central Slovakia, what should help to increase the capacity for receiving asylum seekers.[599]

The asylum applicant was registered with the assistance of an interpreter.

Caused by a lack of interpreters, who should be present during the registration procedure, the procedures are often prolonged. This still happens in practice, as witnessed by the working group preparing the Assessment of the Asylum System in the Slovak Republic – Final Report. At the time of their visit, for example, a police officer on duty registered one Palestinian without the presence of an interpreter.[600] However, there is a reference to the right of an asylum applicant to have an interpreter, if he/she does not have command of the Slovak language, in Article 18 of the 480/2002 Asylum Law. Article 4(2) states that prior to filling in the questionnaire the authorised employee shall instruct the applicant of his/her rights and obligations during the asylum procedure and also of the possibility of having a legal representative.

Another problem causing delays could also be that the technical equipment of the office was bellow standards. If the only computer available stopped working, no new data could be registered. All these factors could result in delaying the process beyond the prescribed 48 hours time limit.[601] Since a great deal of the whole procedure regarding the aliens applying for asylum took place in the special border control department, this did not help to speed-up the registration procedure, just on the contrary.

3.6.1.2 *Registration at the reception centre*

In the fictitious case the asylum applicant was sent further to a reception centre located nearby the border with the Czech Republic.[602]

599. Source: Notes from a press conference of the UNHCR BO, Bratislava, 25 January 2005.

600. *Supra* 598, at 27.

601. Ibid.

602. The objective of the reception centres is to receive new asylum applicants for the period of quarantine, which lasts usually 30 days. Then the asylum applicants are transferred to accommodation centres, located close to the borders with Austria and the Czech Republic. Two new centres were opened: in 2003 in Opatovská Nová Ves (with capacity 150) and in 2004 in Liptovské Vlachy (capacity 200), in the central region of Slovakia. In 2006 a new centre is expected to be opened near the border with Ukraine, what might help to decrease the problem of the 'disappearing' asylum applicants (in 2004, 90%; in 2005, 70% of cases were terminated for this reason).

Asylum applicants are sent to a reception centre or a detention centre after being detained by the police, when they express their intention to apply for asylum in Slovakia. The asylum applicant is permitted to enter the reception centre on the basis of his/her temporary ID card, issued by the police for the purpose of transfer to the centre.

At 6 A.M. the reception officers undertook the 'counting', in order to ascertain who and how many asylum applicants came to the camp since the previous day.

This information is needed for procedural purposes, but also for ordering meals. It is then recorded into the registration system called 'Utečenec'[603] (meaning 'refugee' in Slovak) by a reception officer. The system is connected on-line with the Migration Office Directorate and with the Procedural Department of the Migration Office, both located in the capital Bratislava.
Regarding the accommodation in one of the refugee-reception centres, there was a newly renovated building with 23 rooms available for the applicants. There were also metal cabins located in the reception centre, aimed for situations of emergency influx. Nevertheless, they were used for accommodating the 'regular' asylum applicants.

Being newly arrived, the asylum applicant was registered. First, he had to hand over to the reception officer his temporary ID card. The officer then filled in the registration card in the electronic version, containing personal data (name, surname, date and place of birth, nationality, etc.) and photograph (no fingerprints) of the applicant.[604] Following that, the reception officer provided the asylum applicant with the Instructions on Rights and Obligations of Asylum Applicant in the Asylum Procedure.[605] The asylum applicant kept the original of the Instructions and a copy in Slovak language signed by him was sent to the Migration

603. Registration in the system 'Utečenec' records those, who arrived to the reception centre with the temporary ID card and passed the registration procedure, conducted by a reception officer. The registration also records those, who did not arrive to the reception centre, but expressed their intention to apply for asylum at the Aliens Police Department, were registered there as asylum applicants and were sent (or transported) to the reception centre, regardless to whether they arrived to the centre or not.

604. The information gathered by the police is not handed over to the Migration Office and therefore the Migration Office has to create its own registration database. The criticism of a too much decentralised asylum procedure is grounded on the fact that the time, which the asylum seekers spend in the asylum facility, is unnecessarily long. Especially the registration-related procedures could be centralised into one place.

605. This document was developed by the Migration Office in March 2003 and is available in 13 languages.

Office and filed. He was also instructed of the possibility of having a legal representative.[606]

After this procedure, the reception officer filled out with the asylum applicant the Questionnaire containing 42 questions;[607] these relate to his personal data, country of origin, route to Slovakia, circumstances of the transportation from the country of origin to the country of destination, reasons for leaving the country of origin, persecution and reasons for preventing the asylum applicant to return to his country.

> In case of language barrier, all procedures relating to the instructions and the questionnaire wait for a decision-maker, coming from the Migration Office with an interpreter.

In this case, the asylum applicant required an interpreter; therefore the procedure was interrupted until the arrival of a decision-maker of the Migration Office, accompanied by an interpreter.

3.6.1.3 *Procedure leading to a first-instance decision*

Once the reception officer registered the asylum applicant, who signed the instructions on rights and obligations and filled in the questionnaire; the reception officer completed the file, which was then prepared for the decision-maker, who also interviewed the asylum applicant.

> In practice, an employee from the Procedural Department comes to the reception centre, receives all files and takes them back to the Migration Office in Bratislava.[608]

606. See 480/2002 Asylum Law, Art. 4(2). No free legal aid for asylum seekers and refugees is provided. Through the projects funded by UNHCR the asylum applicants who need assistance or legal representation are able to get free of charge services of a lawyer. There are also several NGOs who provide legal aid to asylum seekers free of charge.

607. See Annex 2 to 480/2002 Asylum Law – Specimen of the Questionnaire of the asylum seeker, as amended by the 1/2005 Law.

608. Regarding the communication between the Alien Police and the Migration Office, the Alien Police faxes within 24 hours the information on asylum applicants arriving to the reception centre, but the file on each individual applicant (Declaration, Record of Interview prepared by the police) arrives to the Migration Office several days later (sometimes with a delay of 2–3 weeks). In case of large groups, the police fax within 24 hours only the names of asylum applicants. The Migration Office does not start to interview asylum applicant before it receives the file. See *supra* 586, at 30–31.

Since the asylum seeker was in the quarantine period, he was not invited to the Migration Office in Bratislava for an interview.

Most of the asylum applicants (between 50% to 90%, depending on the reception centre) disappear from the asylum facility prior to the invitation for an interview and before the end of the quarantine period. Therefore it is not always possible to fill in the questionnaire.[609]

If the decision-maker comes to the conclusion that an asylum application can be processed under the accelerated procedure (where there is an indication to a manifestly unfounded case) he/she requests the Migration Office in Bratislava to send back the applicant's file. Each case rejected in the reception centre has to be sent to the Migration Office Directorate in Bratislava for signature and then back to the reception centre.[610]

At the end, a record of the interview is printed and read by the interpreter to the asylum applicant. In case the asylum applicant has additional remarks or proposals, the decision-maker is obliged to add them into the record. Then the applicant signs this record of interview in the presence of the interpreter.

3.6.1.4 *First-instance decision*

After all necessary information was gathered in the asylum applicant's file, the decision-maker began to draft the first instance decision.[611] The draft was then submitted to the Director of the Procedural Department, who forwarded it to the Director of the Migration Office for final approval and signature.[612] After the signing of the decision by the Director of the Migration Office, the file was returned to the administrative staff of the Procedural Department, who prepared a sufficient number of copies and delivered the decision to the applicant, his legal representative, the refugee centre and the UNHCR in accordance with the instructions prepared by the decision-maker at the time of the drafting of the decision. Then the file returned to the responsible decision-maker, who was waiting whether an appeal would be lodged.

609. Interestingly, most of the refugee centres in Slovakia were located less than 20 km from the Austrian, Hungarian or Czech borders. One centre is located approximately 40 km from the Ukrainian border. A new centre was opened in the central Slovakia in 2004. A new large reception centre with a capacity of 500 places is planned to be opened near the border with Ukraine in 2006.

610. In accordance with the Instruction of the Minister of Interior No. 4/2003, the Director of the Migration Office is authorised to sign all decisions made in the asylum procedure.

611. A decision-maker with a short working experience prepares together with the supervising senior decision-maker a draft of the decision and other junior decision-makers prepare the draft decisions themselves and send it for approval to the supervising senior decision-makers.

612. In practice the draft decision goes through four internal steps before the first-instance decision is issued.

If the Migration Office grants asylum to the applicant, the file is submitted to the Procedural Department and the Department of Integration and Migration of the Migration Office for further process.

As regards the fictitious case, the asylum seeker's application was rejected on the basis that it was not proven that he had been persecuted in his country of origin, although he obviously received a less favourable treatment in that country due to his public views on the lacking respect for human rights by the state authorities.

It is important to distinguish between 'discrimination' and 'persecution'. According to the UNHCR Handbook on procedures and criteria for determining refugee status, differences in the treatment of various groups do indeed exist to a greater or lesser extent in many societies. Persons who receive less favourable treatment as a result of such differences are not necessarily victims of persecution. It is only in certain circumstances that discrimination will amount to persecution. This would be so if measures of discrimination lead to consequences of a substantially prejudicial nature for the person concerned, e.g., serious restrictions on his/her right to earn his livelihood, his/her right to practise his/her religion, or his/her access to normally available educational facilities.[613]

'Nevertheless, discriminatory measures may give rise to a reasonable fear of persecution if they produce, in mind of the person concerned, a feeling of apprehension and insecurity as regards his/her future existence. Whether or not such measures of discrimination in themselves amount to persecution must be determined in the light of all the circumstances. A claim to fear of persecution will of course be stronger where a person has been the victim of a number of discriminatory measures of this type and where there is thus a cumulative element involved.

In addition, an applicant may have been subjected to various measures not in themselves amounting to persecution (e.g., discrimination in different forms), in some cases combined with other adverse factors (e.g., general atmosphere of insecurity in the country of origin). In such situations, the various elements involved may, if taken together, produce an effect on the mind of the applicant that can reasonably justify a claim to well-founded fear of persecution on 'cumulative grounds'. Needless to say, it is not possible to lay down a general rule as to what cumulative reasons can give rise to a valid claim to refugee status. This depends on all the circumstances.'[614]

613. *UNHCR Handbook,* 14–15.
614. Ibid., par. 53, 55.

The first-instance decision was based on the grounds that he was discriminated, but not persecuted, even though that the discriminatory measures against him had been on the rise since they first started two years ago.

The controversy is that despite receiving one of the highest number of asylum applications in Central Europe (and in 2004 more applications than for example the Netherlands, Norway or Spain), the number of positive decisions issued (the acceptance rate) is only something about 2 percent (1.14% in 2004; 2.9% in 2005) of the number of applicants and the number of decisions on merit of the case, which is one of the lowest in Europe. This percentage covers the cases decided on the merit; thus this remarkably low percentage does not include the high number of cases terminated before the final decision could be issued (11,586 cases in 2004; 2923 cases in 2005), brought by the fact that the asylum seekers flee before the refugee status determination procedure is finished.[615]

3.6.1.5 *Appeal against a first-instance decision*

As a result of the rejection of his case, the asylum applicant appealed against the first-instance decision directly to the Regional Court in Bratislava (the appeal court).[616] The Migration Office received the information about the case lodged after the appeal court requested the file of the rejected asylum applicant.

In practice this can take several weeks or even months after the date the first-instance decision was issued. Should the appeal be lodged, the Procedural Department of the Migration Office sends the file via the Legal Department to the appeal court. This department is then responsible for the legal representation of the Migration Office before the court.[617]

The appeal court may either confirm the first-instance negative decision or it may cancel it and return it to the Migration Office for further proceedings together with legally binding instructions. At present, the appeal court cannot change the first-instance negative decision and grant asylum.

The asylum agenda at the two Regional Courts is relatively new, introduced by the 480/2002 Asylum Law. The asylum agenda is additional to other court agenda (usually civil law agenda) of the asylum judges. The competence of the appeal court is established according to the asylum reception/accommodation centre where the

615. Assessment of the Asylum System in Slovakia – Final Report, 25; information from UNHCR BO, Bratislava and the statistics of the Migration Office.

616. Depending on the location of the asylum facility, where the asylum applicant was placed at the time of the decision, he/she can appeal to the Regional Court in Bratislava or in Košice.

617. Based on an interview with an asylum judge of the Bratislava Regional Court, on 7 September 2004.

asylum applicant (plaintiff) has been placed. The judge decides the asylum cases as a single judge, although the Regional Courts otherwise decide in senates. However, it has to be borne in mind that for asylum cases, the Regional Court is a first-instance court.

As already mentioned the asylum judge may either confirm the decision made by the Migration Office or cancel it. He/she cannot, however, grant asylum to the applicant, although in asylum cases the Court has also probative competence (it provides evidence). In cases where the Court confirms the decision of the Migration Office, there is still a further possibility to appeal. Nevertheless, it depends on the decision of the Regional Court judge whether such appeal to the higher instance (the Supreme Court) is approved.[618] The Supreme Court's composition, when deciding asylum cases, is in administrative senates, since there are no specialised asylum senates within the Supreme Court.

Regarding the appeal procedure at the Regional Court, the parties present are:

- asylum applicant;
- interpreter of the asylum applicant;
- a lawyer or an NGO, representing the asylum applicant (not obligatory);
- representative of the Migration Office;
- UNHCR representative (not obligatory; present usually in special cases).[619]

Appeal (whether at the Regional Court or at the Supreme Court) has a suspensive effect (except when an asylum application was refused as inadmissible, because other State is responsible to examine the application; or during the time when the applicant is placed in a reception centre in the transit area of an international airport). It means that the asylum applicant cannot be sent back to his country of origin or to a country of transit, before his case is finally decided.

The most common reason for the appeals, as follows from the applicants' evidence, is the insufficient investigation of their case, especially as far as the principle of the country of origin is concerned.[620] The interviewed judge also sees a problem in the approach taken by the Migration Office. For example, where the 'economic motive' appears (in some cases only a slight indication to an economic reason for migration in the applicant's part, in addition to other reasons worthy of consideration), the applicant is usually not granted asylum. At the same time, however, the international law is not always fully taken into account (e.g., Articles 3 and 8 of the ECHR). The practical problem seems to be, that the decisions made by the Migration Office are usually strictly based on the Asylum Law (especially Article 47

618. Art. 250j (4) of the Civil Procedure Code states that a provision on the basis of which a decision of an administrative authority was cancelled shall be mentioned in the court decision. Whether an appeal is admissible depends on the statement laid down in the court decision.

619. In principle, the same applies for the hearings concerning asylum cases at the Supreme Court.

620. On the basis of the Instruction of the Minister of Interior No. 40/2001 of 15 July 2001 a specialised Department of Documentation and External Cooperation was established within the Migration Office. Besides the main objective of this Department (the gathering and processing of information on countries of origin), it also facilitates translations of expert documents, agenda relating to the business trips abroad, as well as multilateral and bi-lateral cooperation and library services.

(1)),[621] but often disregard the international law instruments, binding for Slovakia, as well as Article 20(3) of the Asylum Law. Article 20(3) states, that in case the Ministry (i.e., in practice the Migration Office) rejects an application as manifestly unfounded or it decides not to grant asylum or to withdraw asylum, it shall state in the terms of the decision whether the ban on expulsion or *refoulement* under Article 47 applies.

The high expectations that the introduction of the independent second instance (Regional Appeal Courts in Bratislava and Košice since January 2003) considerably improve the system have not materialised. In total the Regional Courts in Bratislava and Košice have decided 250 appeals, 64 were confirmed, 23 were cancelled (29%), but these rejections of the first-instance decisions have not had effect on the recognition rate, due to the lack of decision on the merit by the judges. In 2005 the two Regional Courts decided 197 cases: they confirmed the first-instance decision in 87 cases, and they cancelled it in 18 cases. In 39 cases the procedure was terminated due to the disappearance of the applicant. In 37 cases the application was rejected for administrative reasons.[622]

Regarding the accession of Slovakia to the EU, the acquis communautaire shall be applied by national judges at the national courts. In asylum matters Article 68 TEC applies, which limits the jurisdiction of the ECJ.[623] In the case of Slovakia, the application of the aforementioned Article will be very interesting:

As explained above, not every appeal rejected by the Regional Court can be further appealed to the Supreme Court. Therefore, at least in theory, the Supreme Court and also the Regional Courts could be considered as courts of final instance (depending on each individual case) and thus should be entitled to refer a preliminary question to the Court of Justice in Luxembourg.

Although the system of the court appeals in asylum matters is rather new, the practice has already pointed out several shortcomings. There is an intention to draft a reform of the appeal procedure. The following concepts have been considered in this respect:

1. The complaint would be decided by a senate of three judges (instead of a single judge) at the two Regional Courts. There would also be a possibility to submit a request for cassation towards the court decision. Then the Supreme Court would decide.
2. Other possibility would be to establish a specialised tribunal dealing with asylum matters.

Part of this reform could also be the introduction of 'ex officio' appointed lawyers for the asylum applicants. At present, there is no compulsory legal representation of the asylum applicants by a lawyer. In practice the UNHCR office is always informed about each court procedure on asylum matters. An NGO may be addressed in order to represent an asylum seeker (usually the Slovak Humanitarian Council or

621. Prohibition of expulsion and *refoulement*.

622. Based on an interview with an asylum judge of the Bratislava Regional Court (7 September 2004) and on an interview at UNHCR BO, Bratislava (2 May 2006).

623. On the application of Art. 68 TEC see chapter 1, 1.10.3.

the Slovak Helsinki Committee). The NGOs also assist with searching information about the countries of origin.

The following changes have been drafted in order to simplify and accelerate the asylum procedure in Slovakia:

- Formalisation of the procedure, meaning there would be a special judicial procedure applied exclusively in asylum cases. The Court would not have to prove the motives of the asylum seeker anymore, but it would only deal with the legality of the Migration Office's decisions from the aspect of following the procedural due process, interpretation and the jurisprudence.
- In cases of the Migration Office being wrong in its decision (e.g., cases of insufficient verification of facts, insufficient reasoning of the decision, confusion when interpreting the law), the decision of the Migration Office would be cancelled and returned back for a new procedure.
- In cases when the Migration Office would establish the facts correctly, but the decision itself would not be correct (e.g., drawing an incorrect legal opinion), a possibility should exist that the court would have the right to decide on granting asylum. This approach would speed up the whole procedure and would be also more economical.
- As regards the Supreme Court, this should deal only with legal questions. The intention is that the Supreme Court would decide without any hearing; its decision would be based only on the grounds provided by the Migration Office and the Regional Court.[624]

Coming back to the fictitious case, an appointed judge from the Bratislava Regional Court heard the case; based on the evidence gathered by the Court, the judge decided that the discriminatory measures applied against the asylum applicant were cumulative in nature and due to all the circumstances the fear of persecution was well founded. Since this is one of the grounds on which asylum should be granted, the judge sent the case back to the Migration Office for reconsideration, together with a legally binding opinion (meaning that the Migration Office has to take it into consideration when revising the case, however it can once again reject to grant asylum status to the applicant).

This fictitious case was constructed on the basis of the information provided by persons directly involved in the asylum procedure in Slovakia. The main purpose of the fictitious case was to bring into focus the asylum procedure and interaction between the different institutions forming the Slovak asylum system. An evaluation of this system follows, taking the Tampere goals as the measuring criteria.

---

624. Based on an interview with an asylum judge of the Bratislava Regional Court, on 7 September 2004.

3.7 Conclusions

To be able to evaluate the asylum system in Slovakia, two areas were considered: the Slovak legislation on asylum and its implementation in practice. Regarding the legislation, the Tampere Conclusions encouraged a full and immediate implementation of the Treaty of Amsterdam on the basis of the Vienna Action Plan and also called for the development of a common EU policy that would include asylum.[625] Given that the Treaty of Amsterdam introduced asylum issues in the supranational (first) pillar, the national legislation of the Member States had to be brought in line with the EU *acquis* on asylum. In Slovakia, this happened before its accession to the EU as regards the *acquis* applicable at that time. Concerning the implementation of the Slovak asylum legislation, some drawbacks would come across if compared with the goals set in Tampere:

- Paragraph 4 of the Tampere Presidency Conclusions stipulates that 'the aim is an open and secure European Union, fully committed to the obligations of the Geneva Refugee Convention and other relevant human rights instruments'.[626]
- Paragraph 13 of the Tampere Presidency Conclusions expresses the importance 'the Union and the Member States attach to the absolute respect of the right to seek asylum. It has agreed to work towards establishing a Common European Asylum System based on the full and inclusive application of the Geneva Convention, thus ensuring that nobody is sent back to persecution, i.e., maintaining the principle of non-refoulement'.
- Paragraph 14 of the Tampere Presidency Conclusions provides that 'this System should include, in the short term, common standards for a fair and efficient asylum procedure,… and the approximation of rules on the recognition and content of the refugee status'.

Although Slovakia as a new EU Member State has been committed, pursuant to the Tampere Conclusions, to co-operate on the strengthening of the external borders of the Union (especially its common borders with Ukraine), this obligation should not go against its commitment to the absolute respect of the right to seek asylum.[627] The term 'absolute respect' used in the Tampere Presidency Conclusions logically presupposes the intention to reaffirm the importance of the right to

625. Tampere, par. 9–10.

626. For example the ECHR. Slovakia signed the ECHR on 21 February 1991 and ratified it on 18 March 1992; for Slovakia the ECHR entered into force on 1 January 1993.

627. The elimination of the illegal migration, often linked to the misusing of the asylum procedures, has been treated, for instance, in the amendment to the 48/2002 Law on Aliens (No. 606/2003), which imposed stricter criteria for the entry and stay of aliens in the territory of the Slovak Republic; on the other hand it relaxes the criteria applied to the stay of EU citizens. The amended legislation reflects also the need for protection against international terrorism and illegal migration from crisis states. Furthermore, the Slovak Parliament approved the Act on the Protection of State Border No. 477/2003.

seek asylum; therefore, it can be understood that this right should not be considered less important than strengthening the external borders. Nevertheless, the only express reference to the then candidate countries (including Slovakia) in the Tampere Conclusions was done in paragraph 25:

> 'The candidate countries must accept in full the Schengen acquis and further measures building upon it. The European Council stresses the importance of the effective control of the Union's future external borders by specialised trained professionals.'[628]

Paragraph 25 of the Tampere Conclusions should be in line with both paragraphs 4 and 13, which means that the border police should be trained to identify and deal professionally with asylum applicants. In the case of Slovakia this should mean to strengthen, stabilise and improve the quality of staffing of basic units of the border police with policemen who are involved in the first contact with aliens seeking asylum; these policemen should be remunerated correspondingly and their working conditions and working environment should also improve.[629]

The asylum-determination procedure starts upon applicant's statement to seek asylum[630] and ends with the issuing of the final decision to grant or to reject the asylum claim.[631] Tampere aims for a Common European Asylum System, which is fair and efficient in its procedure, meets at least minimum conditions for the reception of asylum seekers and also has rules on the recognition and content of the refugee status that are comparable between the Member States.

Slovakia has one of the lowest positive decision rates on granted asylum in Europe (1.14% in 2004 when only 15 applicants were granted refugee status out of 11,391 lodged asylum applications; 2.9% in 2005 when 25 applicants were granted asylum out of 3549 asylum applicants).[632] The extremely low percentage noticed in 2004 is even more surprising when compared for example to Hungary, a country that has very similar geographical conditions, but held a positive decision rate of 15%. The difference with neighbouring Austria, where in 2005 nearly 5000 cases were decided positively, should be also noted.[633] The two main causes of the low positive decision rate in Slovakia seem to be that:

---

628. Cf. Protocol integrating the Schengen *acquis* into the framework of the European Union, Art. 8.

629. See also Asylum Procedures Directive, Art. 6(5).

630. 480/2002 Asylum Law, Art. 3.

631. Id., Art. 20.

632. Statistics of the Migration Office for years 2004 and 2005.

633. UNHCR, 'Population and Geographic Data Section Geneva: Trends in Refugee Status Determination' (1 January–30 June 2004), 'Asylum Applications, Refugee Status Determination and Pending Cases in 81, mostly developing', Countries, 20 September 2004; available at: http://www.unhcr.ch/statistics. Information from the UNHCR BO, Bratislava.

1. a high percentage of asylum applicants flee the asylum reception centres before the final decision on their cases is made, what causes the high number of terminated cases;
2. many of the asylum claims are considered manifestly unfounded or inadmissible.

Regarding the high percentage of asylum applicants that run away from the asylum reception centres, one cannot exclude as probable reasons for this problem unsuitable conditions for their reception, lengthy procedures, and possible *a priori* knowledge hold by the asylum seekers of the high number of not granted refugee status in Slovakia. Taking into consideration the application of the 'Dublin II' Regulation in Slovakia, a rejection of an asylum claim lodged in Slovakia would mean a rejection of his/her application lodged in other Member States based on the same grounds. The application of the 'Dublin II' Regulation in Slovakia brought about some concerns regarding the limited reception capacity for asylum seekers and a possible collapse of the system with repercussions on the length of the procedures. However, the statistics show an evident gap between the number of requests received from other EU Member States and the number of persons actually returned to Slovakia in 2005.[634]

In reference to the number of asylum claims considered as manifestly unfounded or inadmissible, the 480/2002 Asylum Law provides three grounds for the rejection of an application for asylum (as inadmissible, as manifestly unfounded and denial of asylum). It can be presumed that most of the rejected applications by the Migration Office are classified as manifestly unfounded or inadmissible, since the denial of asylum is made only when there is a well-founded suspicion that the applicant has committed crime against peace, war crime or crime against humanity under international instruments, serious non-political crime outside Slovakia prior to applying for asylum or is guilty of acts, which are in contradiction to the objectives and principles of the United Nations.[635]

Another issue worth noting in the implementation of the Slovak asylum law regards the principle of *non-refoulement*, markedly emphasised in the Tampere Conclusions, in reference to the full and inclusive application of the 1951 Geneva Convention. Based on the interviews it transpires that the above-mentioned principle might in practice not be emphasised as it should be, even though the 480/2002 Asylum Law upholds it and requires the Ministry (the Migration Office) to state in the terms of a decision to reject an application for asylum, whether the ban on expulsion or *refoulement* applies.[636]

The previously mentioned issues seem not to comply entirely with the spirit of Tampere regarding an asylum system which is fair and efficient in its procedure,

634. Based on interviews at the UNHCR BO, Bratislava on 2 September 2004 and 2 May 2006.
635. Cf. 480/2002 Asylum Law, Art. 13(1).
636. Id., Art. 20(3).

meets the minimum conditions for reception of asylum seekers and also has rules on the recognition and content of the refugee status that are approximated between the Member States. The fact that the Slovak Republic is one of the most restrictive countries in Europe as regards the number of recognised asylum cases, casts some doubts on the fairness of the asylum system.[637]

The process of implementation of the asylum legislation in practice proved to be one of the biggest challenges for the Slovak asylum system. That is why an extensive training of the officers as well as asylum judges has been necessary. One way how to expedite the whole procedure is to employ more decision-makers, who would be able, in the shortest possible time, to assess and determine actual asylum seekers and separate them from those TCNs who are manifestly abusing the asylum system.

Without sufficiently trained staff there is just a small chance for a successful implementation of the laws. The quality and the pace of the implementation process is thus very much dependent on the level of adequately trained staff of the Border and Aliens Police, the Migration Office as well as the judges competent in the judicial review of the asylum cases. Likewise, the way how the asylum rules are applied in practice is decisive for a proper functioning of the Common European Asylum System, as laid down in the Tampere Presidency Conclusions. The UNHCR has been involved in number of trainings for judges, NGOs and civil servants in Slovakia.

In addition, regarding the 'Dublin II' mechanism and its impact on the national asylum system, it did not prove to be particularly effective. Only in 316 cases the asylum applicants were returned to the territory of the Slovak Republic out of 1900 cases accepted by the Slovak authorities on the requests of other EU countries (mainly Austria, 175; Germany, 89; and the United Kingdom, 23). Most of these applicants in fact absconded while pending the procedure in another EU country. The fact that only 1,900 out of 11,400 cases registered in Slovakia had been intercepted in other EU Member States suggests that many applicants have remained illegally and undetected in other EU countries.[638]

The previous example demonstrates the strong interrelation between the Common European Asylum System and the national asylum systems. Bearing this relation in mind, the current limitations of the Slovak asylum system should be addressed by the EU. The need to avoid a malfunction of the national asylum systems with its repercussions on the entire Common European Asylum System should help to motivate Member States to adopt an effective burden-sharing mechanism; and to find effective schemes in which the Member States with more

637. The differences between refugee recognition rates are particularly striking when Slovakia's recognition rate for Chechens was 0%, compared for example to Austria's rate of 96%, Hungary's 75%, Germany's 16%, Poland's 11%, Spain's 36%, the Czech Republic's 5%. In 2005 the acceptance rate for Chechens in Austria was 91%, while in Slovakia again 0%. Based on information gathered during interviews at the UNHCR BO, Bratislava on 2 September 2004 and on 2 May 2006.

638. Based on information from the UNHCR BO, Bratislava, May 2005.

developed asylum systems, registering a decrease in applications, could provide human and technical resources to the relatively new asylum systems in the new Member States located on the external border.

The interviews carried out in Slovakia showed how the national authorities involved in the implementation of the asylum legislation have faced the challenges brought about by Slovakia's preparation for membership and its actual membership in the EU. Despite the current shortcomings in the implementation of the EU-harmonised Slovak asylum legislation, the future of the asylum system in Slovakia ought to improve with the further integration of the Common European Asylum System. By the standardisation of the national asylum systems of the Member States, the differences in the implementation of their laws should be more noticeable and by this the shortcomings of the implementation might strike more, be criticised and should improve.

The evaluation of the current state of affairs of the Common European Asylum System as a whole is an ambitious task, going beyond the scope of this book. Nevertheless, by analysing the situation in Slovakia, one of the EU Member States and therefore part of this System, that faces the practical difficulties under specific circumstances (new Member State, geographical location, considerable number of asylum applications), it is hoped that the overview of the implementation and difficulties arisen in this respect could highlight the difficulties and produce means of achieving a proper implementation of the Common European Asylum System in practice.

Chapter 4

EU POLICY ON ASYLUM

4.1 Introduction

Besides the Common European Asylum System the partnership with countries of origin, fair treatment of TCNs, and the management of migration flows form the Common EU Asylum (and Migration) Policy.[639] Taking this into consideration the Common European Asylum Policy could be seen as bi-dimensional:

The *internal dimension* of the Common European Asylum Policy can be delimited by the actions undertaken by the Union and/or the Member States as from the moment of reaching their borders by asylum seekers. The internal dimension should comprise all initiatives directed towards the reception of the asylum applicants, managing the asylum determination procedure, as well as the integration of recognised refugees and persons granted other forms of protection (subsidiary protection). The internal dimension could be interpreted as embracing the relations and the procedures taking place between the Member States themselves and between the Member States and the persons in need of international protection.

The *external dimension* of the Common European Asylum Policy can be delimited by several aspects concerning the EU relations with non-EU countries (third countries), as: pre-frontier actions undertaken by the EU, humanitarian aid for third countries, visa policy insofar it influences the asylum seekers' entry to the EU, as well as readmission of unsuccessful asylum applicants (based on the readmission agreements concluded between the Community/Member States and third countries).[640] These two dimensions are present in most of the policy instruments related to the issue of asylum in the EU.

In the previous chapters the focus was on the legislative developments in the area of the Common European Asylum System, followed by an example of the implementation in practice in one of the new EU Member States. The legislation and its implementation were evaluated according to the Tampere Conclusions – a policy document chosen as a 'measuring instrument' in order to assess the developments and the current state of affairs of the EU asylum legislation.

The main purpose of this chapter is to describe a selection of policy instruments that followed the Presidency Conclusions of Tampere, so as to assess the continuity of the policy direction and to better understand the evolution of the policy leading to the adoption of the Hague Programme; and also to observe the future

639. Tampere, section A. A Common EU Asylum and Migration Policy.

640. On the external dimension see, e.g., Boswell, C.: 'The "external dimension" of EU immigration and asylum policy', *International Affairs* 79(3) (2003) 619–638.

perspectives. The selected general policy documents consist of Communications from the Commission to the Council and the European Parliament, JHA Council Conclusions and European Council Presidency Conclusions.

4.2 Communications of the Commission

Communications from the Commission addressed to the Council and to the European Parliament, together with the Conclusions from the (European) Council meetings are policy documents, which are not legally binding. The Communications analyse the approach that the EU should take on certain issues and express policy objectives of the Union in the given policy areas. The Communications are relatively detailed, especially as far as the future planning and the implementation of legal instruments are concerned. Selected Commission Communications on the subject of asylum were studied and observations on their content will be referred to in the following paragraphs. They have been chosen especially for being up-to-date and by this well reflecting the present direction of the Common European Asylum System. These Communications are:

- Communication from the Commission to the Council and the European Parliament 'Towards more accessible, equitable and managed asylum systems';[641]
- Communication from the Commission to the Council and the European Parliament 'Area of Freedom, Security and Justice: Assessment of the Tampere programme and future orientations';[642]
- Communication from the Commission to the Council and the European Parliament 'On the Managed Entry in the EU of Persons in Need of International Protection and the Enhancement of the Protection Capacity of the Regions of Origin – Improving Access to Durable Solutions';[643]
- Communication from the Commission to the Council and the European Parliament 'A More Efficient Common European Asylum System: The Single Procedure as the Next Step';[644]
- Communication from the Commission to the Council and the European Parliament 'On Strengthened Practical Cooperation. New Structures, New Approaches: Improving the Quality of Decision Making in the Common European Asylum System'.[645]

641. COM(2003) 315 final, 3.6.2003.
642. COM(2004) 401 final, 2.6.2004.
643. COM(2004) 410 final, 4.6.2004.
644. COM(2004) 503 final, 15.7.2004.
645. COM(2006) 67 final, 17.2.2006.

4.2.1 'Towards more accessible, equitable and managed asylum systems'

Despite the continued relevance of the 1951 Geneva Convention and the 1967 New York Protocol, the UNHCR acknowledged that the Convention and the Protocol cannot address all the pressing issues pertaining to refugee protection in today's changing world. For this reason it launched the 'Convention Plus' process in order to include durable solutions for refugees in a more effective way and for the creation of mechanism to share the responsibility for admitting and protecting refugees. The Convention Plus process is being developed through generic multilateral agreements with States to tackle three priority challenges: the strategic use of resettlement as a tool of protection, a more effective targeting of development assistance to support durable solutions and the clarification of the responsibilities of States in the event of irregular secondary movements of refugees and asylum seekers.

In response to this initiative the United Kingdom drew a Paper describing an approach to the Convention Plus. On 27 March 2003, the UK Home Office published details of its proposals for a 'new vision' of refugee protection in 'New international approaches to asylum processing and protection' (further referred to as the UK Paper or the Paper).[646] The proposals were presented to the EU informal JHA Committee on 28 March where it was agreed that the United Kingdom and its partners would 'produce a worked up set of proposals for the June European Council (in Thessaloniki), when heads of government have agreed to take this forward'.[647]

The UK Paper identified four factors which all substantially undermine the credibility, integrity, efficiency of and the public support for the asylum system; not only in the EU, but also globally:

- (financial) support for refugees is badly distributed;
- current asylum system requires those fleeing persecution to enter the EU illegally, using smugglers whereas the majority of refugees including probably the most vulnerable ones, stay in poorly resourced refugee camps in third countries;
- majority of asylum seekers in the EU do not meet the criteria for refugee or subsidiary protection status;
- those found not to be in need of international protection are not returned to their country of origin.[648]

---

646. The UK proposals on the zones of protection are available in 'Press Releases' at: www.homeoffice.gov.uk.

647. Refugee Council Briefing, 'The UK government's 'new vision' of refugee protection: a summary', May 2003.

648. *Supra* 641, at 5.

The UK proposals were presented in very broad terms, providing little detail. Nevertheless, it is clear that they have two main aspects: a development of *transit processing centres (transit zones)* along major transit routes into the EU, close to the EU borders; and the establishment of *regional protection zones* in refugee-producing regions and development of managed resettlement routes from source regions to Europe. Unsuccessful asylum applicants from transit processing centres may be returned to regional protection zones in their region of origin, if their country of origin remains unsafe.[649] Managed resettlement schemes are central to the proposals, according to which EU Member States would accept a quota of recognised refugees for resettlement. Refugees accepted for resettlement would be brought from a regional protection zone or transit processing centre into an EU Member State and would be provided with support to rebuild their lives and integrate into the local community.[650]

The proposal for 'regional protection areas (zones)' broadly involves establishing protection centres in states such as, for example, Turkey, Iran, Morocco or Somalia, for those in need of temporary protection, while the proposal concerning 'transit processing centres' involves creating processing centres on the edge of the EU where the asylum claims of those on the 'safe' white list might be rapidly dealt with.[651]

In reply to the invitation from the spring 2003 European Council[652] to explore the ideas raised in the UK Paper and the UNHCR proposals concerning new approaches to effective international protection ('Agenda for Protection', 'Convention Plus') and within the framework of its 'Communication on the common asylum policy and the Agenda for protection',[653] the Commission set out its views on the basic premises of and objectives for a possible new approach towards more accessible, equitable and managed asylum systems. The Communication 'Towards more accessible, equitable and managed asylum systems' examines in more detail the structural shortages of the current international protection system and observes that there is a clear need to explore a new approach to complement the stage-by-stage approach adopted in Tampere.

The Commission took the view that this new approach must be based on compliance with international legal obligations, in particular those arising from the 1951 Geneva Convention on Refugees, and on complementarity with the Common European Asylum System called for by the Tampere European Council.

---

649. *Supra* 647.

650. Ibid.

651. Fraser, U.: 'Not In My Back Yard: Reforming the Asylum System', available at: www.opendemocracy.net/debates/article6-28-1168jsp. See also Betts, A.: 'The political economy of extra-territorial processing: separating "purchaser" from "provider" in asylum policy' (New Issues in Refuge Research, Working Paper No. 91, UNHCR).

652. Cf. Presidency Conclusions, Brussels European Council, 20 and 21 March 2003, par. 63.

653. COM(2003) 152 final, 26.3.2003.

The Commission also believes that policy developments should be built upon the first phase of that System and be integrated into the second phase, thus paving the way for a 'Tampere II' agenda.[654] In addition, any new approach should be built upon a genuine burden-sharing system both within the EU and with host third countries, rather than shifting the burden to the third countries. Any new system should therefore be based upon full partnership with and between countries of origin, transit, first asylum and destination.

The Communication recognised a number of legal, practical and financial obstacles to the implementation of such initiative. Concerning the idea of transit processing centres, the question was raised where such centres would be located: within or outside the EU? The Communication raised concerns, for example, about the compatibility of the UK Paper with the EU legislation, national legislation of EU Member States, legislation of the envisaged countries hosting such centres or zones, and also its compatibility with the European Convention on Human Rights (ECHR). Furthermore, the Communication called for a clarification on which procedural rules (EU or national legislation) such centres or zones would be governed.[655] The Communication also raised a question on the legality of transfer of persons who 'have not transited through or otherwise stayed in' relevant zones or countries, recognising that this represents a significant departure from the 'safe third country' concept.[656] The Communication then sets out ten basic premises, which, it states, should underpin new approaches to asylum:

- full respect for international legal standards;
- addressing the root causes of forced migration;
- ensuring access to legal migration channels (in particular facilitation of legal entry of TCNs into the EU for employment and/or family reunification purposes);
- combating illegal migration, whilst respecting humanitarian obligations;
- genuine burden-sharing system both within the EU and with host third countries, as opposed to burden shifting;
- building upon existing policy objectives, including improving the quality of decisions as early as possible in national asylum systems ('frontloading'), consolidation of protection capacity in regions of origin, protected entry schemes and resettlement programmes;
- complementarity, rather than substitution, with the Common European Asylum System, called for in Tampere; its integration in the second phase of that System and paving the way for a 'Tampere-II' political agenda on asylum policies, based on the new Treaty;

---

654. Before adopting the Hague Programme in November 2004, the future agenda for the fields of justice and home affairs used to be referred to as the 'Tampere II', since it should build on the Tampere programme. On the Hague Programme further see chapter 4, 4.4.

655. *Supra* 641, at 6.

656. Ibid.; see also 'UK/EU/UNHCR: Unlawful and Unworkable, Amnesty International's views on proposals for extra-territorial processing of asylum claims'.

- no delay to present negotiations on directives for the Common European Asylum System;
- being in line with and enforcing the UNHCR's global initiatives (Agenda for Protection and Convention Plus);
- possible financial consequences for the Community budget; need to respect the current financial perspective.[657]

The Communication states that this new approach to asylum systems is based on three specific but complementary *policy objectives*:
- the orderly and managed arrival of refugees and persons in need of international protection in the EU from their regions of origin;
- burden- and responsibility-sharing within the EU as well as with regions of origin;
- the development of efficient and enforceable asylum decision making and return procedures.[658]

In addition to these three policy objectives, another important element in achieving the overall aim is referred to in the Communication: that economic migrants should as much as possible be discouraged from abusing the asylum system for non-protection related reasons.[659]

In conclusion to this Communication of June 2003, the Commission proclaimed that the EU is at a turning point in the development of the Common European Asylum System, with its first phase being nearly completed. The time has now come to decide how best to further shape the second phase of this System, in addition to what Tampere already decided. The introduction of the UK Paper was well-timed; linked well to the global momentum created by the Agenda for Protection and the Convention Plus initiatives. The Communication indicates the preparation of the 'Tampere II' agenda (the Hague Programme), the enlarged EU and the future Constitutional Treaty; and to this end it asked the Council and the European Council to approve this Communication as the basis for contributing to more accessible, equitable and managed asylum systems.[660]

4.2.2 'Area of freedom, security and justice: assessment of the Tampere programme and future orientations'

The Communication from the Commission to the Council and the European Parliament 'Area of Freedom, Security and Justice: Assessment of the Tampere programme and future orientations' recalls the developments, which led to the estab-

657. *Supra* 641, at 11–13.
658. Id., 13.
659. Ibid.
660. Id., 22.

lishment of the area of freedom security and justice, including the ambitious programme adopted in Tampere in October 1999. As the document's name indicates, besides focusing on the evaluation of the Tampere programme, which set out policy guidelines and practical objectives, it also points out the priorities for the future.

The progress achieved under the Tampere programme was regularly reviewed every six months in the 'Scoreboard to review progress on the creation of an area of freedom, security and justice in the European Union'.[661] Moreover, the Commission initiated a public consultation process, calling on interested parties and individuals to send their contributions on the new five-year programme.[662]

In this Communication the Commission emphasised especially the following achievements, attained under the first five-year programme (the Tampere programme):

- substantial progress made in most areas of JHA, compared to the situation in 1999;
- public opinion supports to the development of European action in the field of JHA;[663]
- the JHA dimension is now firmly identified as one of the Union's priority policies;
- the Union has proved it can act efficiently and rapidly when the situation demands; namely the events of 11 September 2001 in New York and 11 March 2004 in Madrid.[664]

At the same time the Commission admitted that despite the resolute line taken by the Tampere Conclusions, it was not always possible to reach agreement at European level for the adoption of certain sensitive measures relating to policies which remain at the core of national sovereignty. The Commission further acknowledged that in spite of the considerable success achieved, the original ambition was limited by institutional constraints, and sometimes by a lack of sufficient political consensus; and also that the objectives set in Tampere have not yet been all achieved (the pending Asylum Procedure Directive and the not yet completed list of safe countries of origin could be used as examples).

Most of the projects in hand flow logically from the Tampere programme, and there is consequently some overlap between them and the future priorities. Therefore regarding the priorities for the future of the area of freedom, security and justice, the ambition of this Communication is to be the starting point for studying

661. See COM(2000) 167 final, 24.3.2000; COM(2000)782 final, 30.11.2000; COM(2001)278 final, 23.05.2001; COM(2001)628 final, 30.10.2001; COM(2002)261 final, 30.5.2002; COM(2002) 738 final,16.12.2002; COM(2003)291 final, 22.5.2003; COM(2003)812 final, 30.12.2003.

662. Assessment of Tampere (see *supra* 642), 3.

663. A Eurobarometer conducted in December 2003 confirmed the results of previous Eurobarometers that the citizens of the EU are in favour of a common policy on asylum and immigration.

664. Assessment of Tampere, 3–4.

the development of a future programme of measures identifying priorities in the field of JHA for the period 2004–2009.[665]

Regarding the development of a Common European Asylum Policy, the Communication provides that a better balance between the efforts made by the Member States in the reception of refugees and displaced persons will be achieved by means of the principle of solidarity. An approach based on partnership and cooperation with third countries of origin and of transit, countries of first asylum request and of destination, will have to be established.

The Communication further states that the following main objective of the Common European Asylum System will be to determine a uniform asylum and subsidiary protection status, a common procedure for granting and withdrawing this status and a common system of temporary protection; and that at the same time there is a need for an integrated approach involving efficient administrative decision-making procedures on returns, reintegration schemes and entry procedures that deter unfounded requests and combat networks of people traffickers. This approach is all the more important as the victims of abuse of the System are often genuine refugees.[666]

The improvement of the protection of persons in the exercise of their fundamental rights is one of the priorities for the future of the area of freedom, security and justice. By incorporating the Charter of Fundamental Rights of the Union into the Constitutional Treaty and the possible accession to the ECHR will place the Union, including its Institutions, under a legal obligation to ensure that in all its areas of activity, fundamental rights are not only respected but also actively promoted. This should also have an effect on the rights of persons seeking asylum, since according to the Charter of Fundamental Rights of the Union the *right to asylum* shall be guaranteed. The same goes for the *protection in the event of removal, expulsion or extradition.*[667]

In the subsection named 'Resolute external action' the Communication provides that the assessment of the achievements since Tampere and the initial thinking on future priorities reveal that the Union's external action must take into account the JHA dimension and that general Union activities must be better coordinated. In addition, to ensure that the Union can speak with one voice without undermining common priorities, it will be necessary that Member States support Union activity and observe more solidarity and discipline in their bilateral relations.[668]

In the Conclusions to the Communication 'Area of Freedom, Security and Justice: Assessment of the Tampere programme and future orientations' the Commission

---

665. Id., 4, 5, 7.

666. Id., 10.

667. Assessment of Tampere, 8; see also Arts. II-78 and II-79 of the Treaty establishing a Constitution for Europe (OJ C 310, 16.12.2004).

668. Assessment of Tampere, 16.

expressed its opinion that considerable work has been done since the Tampere European Council, even if much still remains to be done to complete the area of freedom, security and justice. Union's action must continue and take practical form in a second European programme for the area of freedom, security and justice, with detailed priorities and a precise timetable. The Commission says that the working method followed in Tampere is good and should be preserved; and that it can already undertake to continue in the future with its follow-up work through the regular Scoreboard. No further details on the working method are provided in the Communication. In addition, the Commission intends to present an additional Communication within the context of the new financial perspective.

The Communication calls for achieving a political consensus on a new programme with the European Parliament and the Council, during the second half of 2004. The European Council is asked to preserve its essential guiding role in the definition of strategic guidelines and the planning of future action on JHA. A significant proclamation is made at the very end of this Communication, namely that the establishment of the area of freedom, security and justice is a 'major political objective' and 'one of the most important challenges that have to be taken on together with the citizens'. By making a comparison with the internal market, there is a call to continue showing the same degree of ambition and determination as the Union did for the completion of the internal market.[669]

4.2.3 'On the managed entry in the EU of persons in need of international protection and the enhancement of the protection capacity of the regions of origin – Improving access to durable solutions'

In the Communication 'Towards more accessible, equitable and managed asylum systems' the Commission discussed issues related to the orderly and managed arrival of persons in need of international protection in the EU from the regions of origin, including an EU-wide resettlement scheme, burden sharing within the EU and with the regions of origin.[670]

On 4 June 2004 the Commission published a Communication, making more detailed proposals 'On the managed entry in the EU of persons in need of international protection and the enhancement of the protection capacity of the regions of origin – Improving access to durable solutions.'[671] This Communication is a response to Conclusion 26 of the Thessaloniki European Council, in which the Commission was invited 'to explore all parameters in order to ensure more orderly and managed entry in the EU of persons in need of international protection, and to examine ways and means to enhance the protection capacity of regions of

669. Id., 16, 17.
670. *Supra* 641.
671. Improving access to durable solutions (see *supra* 643).

origin.'[672] In this Communication the Commission further suggests to establish EU Regional Protection Programmes.

Conclusion 26, First Objective: '...to explore all parameters in order to ensure orderly and managed entry in the EU of persons in need of international protection...'.

Referring to the EU policy framework, the Communication says that the repeatedly asked question of how to more effectively manage who enters the EU and under which circumstances is a primary characteristic of the EU immigration and asylum policy. In the Communication an importance is attached to expanding *resettlement opportunities* within Europe. Resettlement fulfils many important roles at the global level; three of which are fundamental and should act as the guiding principles for any expanded resettlement activities in Europe:

- a tool of international protection;
- a durable solution;
- demonstration of international solidarity and responsibility-sharing with countries of first asylum.

The Communication further refers to two studies, delivered by the Commission, on options for processing asylum claims external to the EU:

- a Study on the feasibility of processing asylum claims outside the EU against the background of the Common European Asylum System and the goal of a common asylum procedure (published in March 2003); and
- a Study on the feasibility of setting up resettlement schemes in EU Member States or at EU level against the background of the Common European Asylum System and the goal of a common asylum procedure (published in May 2004).[673]

The first of these two Studies focused on the possibilities afforded to Member States by Protected Entry Procedures (PEPs). This notion is understood to allow a non-national to approach the potential host state outside its territory with a claim for asylum or other form of international protection; and to be granted an entry permit in case of a positive response to his/her claim (be it preliminary or final).[674] In practice PEPs would thus allow refugees to submit their asylum applications at embassies or diplomatic representations in third countries. The second Study focused on the practice of *refugee resettlement* where refugees are transferred from a first host country to a second country where they enjoy guarantees

---

672. Presidency Conclusions, Thessaloniki European Council, 19 and 20 June 2003, par. 26; on the Thessaloniki European Council further see chapter 4, 4.3.5.

673. Improving access to durable solutions, par. 13.

674. Five of the EU Member States already have PEPs: Austria, France, The Netherlands, Spain and the UK; Denmark abolished its PEP scheme in 2002.

of protection, including residence, and prospects for integration and autonomy.[675] Both resettlement and PEPs are considered to be methods of ensuring more orderly and managed entry to the EU.

In this respect a rather astonishing idea was expressed by the Commission that the legal, orderly and managed entry to the EU would allow the Member States to anticipate the arrival of the persons determined to be in need of international protection. This 'advance notice', as it is referred to in the Communication, could allegedly bring a number of advantages in terms of planning (e.g., for housing and the inevitable financial impact). The Commission further states that the setting up of tailor-made integration programmes for specific categories of refugees would also be much more easily devised, if a country knew in advance who was arriving on its territory to stay. Resettling and allowing physical access to the territory of the Union of persons whose identity and history have been screened in advance would also be preferable from a security perspective.[676]

Regarding the above-mentioned 'setting up of tailor-made integration programmes for specific categories of refugees', it is not clear from the Communication which refugees belong to these categories. Although the idea of 'anticipated arrivals' of refugees to the EU appears to be the perfect solution in order to improve access to durable solutions, at the same time it does not seem very realistic. One should bear in mind that the arrivals of people in need of international protection are usually spontaneous, depending on each case. Therefore any 'planning' or 'advance notice' can hardly be pictured, unless this policy relies on the fact that the asylum seekers may be retained in third countries before their entrance to the EU is 'approved'. If this would be the case, then the more orderly and managed entry in the EU of asylum seekers and refugees might be achieved at the expense of third countries, which generally have less resources than the EU Member States.

Resettlement should not be therefore considered a potential substitute for States' obligations under international law to examine applications for asylum on their territory. Resettlement should be complementary and without prejudice to the proper treatment of individual request in the context of spontaneous arrivals in the EU.

Further in Chapter I of this Communication, under the subtitle 'Policy Measures proposed', there is a reference to the UNHCR's Agenda for Protection, where three durable solutions for refugees are laid down (resettlement, voluntary repatriation and local integration) and also to the setting up of an 'EU Resettlement Scheme'. The key elements of an EU Resettlement Scheme [677] are briefly outlined as follows:

---

675. Improving access to durable solutions, par. 14.
676. Id., par. 17.
677. Id., par. 22–34.

According to the Communication an EU Resettlement Scheme is a targeted and comprehensive approach aimed at a specific caseload, limited in number but appropriate to the specific situations in which resettlement is deemed necessary. This approach should have a significant effect. The Commission proposed the eventual setting up of an EU-wide resettlement scheme. The EU Resettlement Scheme is complementary and without prejudice to Member States' obligations to determine asylum claims and to provide protection in their territories in accordance with international law. An EU resettlement scheme would be adaptable to the differing characteristics of global refugee needs, including protracted refugee protection situations in various regions, as well as being adaptable to the ability of Member States to resettle certain caseloads in given years. The participation in such scheme would be flexible, although all Member States would participate in an EU-wide Resettlement Scheme.

The main goals of an EU Resettlement Scheme are to provide international protection and to offer a durable solution in the EU to those who genuinely need it and to facilitate their managed arrival in the EU; also to express solidarity and share the burden with countries in the regions of origin faced with protracted refugee situations.

Another element of an EU Resettlement Scheme worth mentioning is the setting of targets. The Communication provides that it is likely that in a future proposal for an EU Resettlement Scheme, the Commission will propose the setting of targets rather than of quota or ceilings. Although there is no explanation of what should exactly be understood under 'targets', the Communication says that they have most potential for success, being more flexible.

The selection of candidates for resettlement must be primarily targeted at those who qualify for international protection according to the criteria defined and codified in the Qualification Directive. How selection criteria are formulated will be a matter for negotiation in any future proposal but there may be legal implications to the application of such criteria. The question of how to deal fairly with the dissatisfaction of those not selected for resettlement and the rationale for proposing one durable solution to one particular group of people but not to another, when both groups are in similar situations, will also have to be carefully managed. Selection criteria could be set as EU collective selection criteria or as Member State specific criteria within a broad, flexible, EU-level programme.

The Communication specifies that orientation programmes taking place pre-departure in the host country should have regard to an EU scheme and assist in instilling realistic expectations and preparing refugees for the future awaiting them. It further provides that there would also be a provision for pre-departure security checks which could facilitate the exclusion from the resettlement programmes of persons who are not entitled to international protection because they fall under the exclusion clauses of the Qualification Directive.

As regards financial implications, the Communication lays down that in terms of financing such an EU resettlement scheme the explicit inclusion of resettled refugees as beneficiaries of the second phase of the ERF will reinforce the collective and cooperative notion underlying any such scheme. The goal therefore is to provide an EU-level budgetary mechanism to support those Member States which have or will have a resettlement programme.[678]

To draw a comparison between Resettlement and the PEPs, the Communication informs that it has become clear from the Member States' relevant legislative practice that with regard to the potential of PEPs, there is not the same level of common perspective and confidence among Member States as exists *vis-à-vis* resettlement. The Commission does not therefore plan to suggest the setting up at EU level of an EU Protected Entry Procedure mechanism as a self standing policy proposal. However, as the Communication further states, in certain circumstances a protected entry in the EU of persons with immediate and urgent protection needs could be procedurally facilitated (e.g., featured as an 'emergency strand' or wider resettlement action), though at the full discretion of individual Member States and if local circumstances warranted such availability. Such procedures would obviously have similar legal implications to those described in the context of the EU Resettlement Scheme with the important difference that the refugee status determination would take place in the EU (after a screening process).[679]

Conclusion 26, Second Objective: '…to examine ways and means to enhance the protection capacity of regions of origin.'

Chapter II of the Communication deals with the second objective – Conclusion 26 of the Thessaloniki European Council from two perspectives: EU policy framework[680] and global policy framework:[681]

As regards the EU policy framework, the Communication recalls the March 2003 Communication,[682] where the Commission had set the development of a common European asylum policy in the context of developments on the global stage and called for increased co-ordination between the EU's internal process and the external aspect of the governance of refugees. The March 2003 Communication had highlighted the importance of sharing responsibility for managing refugees with third countries and particularly countries of first asylum and the need for more effective cooperation to reinforce the protection capacities of countries receiving refugees. It also refers to the June 2003 Communication,[683] which

678. In this respect the Council Decision of 13 June 2002 (OJ L 161, 19.6.2002, 11), adopting an action programme for administrative cooperation in the fields of external borders, visas, asylum and immigration (ARGO programme), Art. 6(e) should also be mentioned; which calls for supporting the activities of the Member States in the area of asylum intended to develop resettlement and entry facilities, and legal means for admission into Member States on humanitarian grounds.

679. Improving access to durable solutions, par. 35.

680. Id., par. 36–39.

681. Id., par. 40–47.

682. COM(2003)152 final, 26.3.2003, 'On the Common Asylum Policy and the Agenda for Protection'.

683. *Supra* 641.

had stressed in particular that possible new approaches to asylum should focus more sharply on action that could be taken outside the EU, within a framework of genuine burden- and responsibility-sharing. The overall aim of such an approach should be to better manage asylum-related flows in their European territorial dimension and in regions of origin, resulting in more accessible, equitable and managed systems.[684]

In reference to the global policy framework, according to the UNHCR, there is a collective duty of the broader community of states to equip states receiving or likely to receive asylum seekers, with the means to live up to international standards in their treatment of refugees. From the perspective of international burden sharing, those regions that host the smallest number of refugees relative to their wealth can be expected to assist those with the highest number of refugees in relation to their economies. The UNHCR says that if protection capacities are adequately developed and enhanced in the last-mentioned states, asylum seekers and refugees will be better protected and assisted.[685]

In order to evaluate the standards for the protection of refugees and asylum seekers in all stages of a refugee protection, it is important to select indicators for ongoing work on protection in third countries which are both measurable and achievable. To do this the EU should first look at the elements it uses itself when guaranteeing protection to those who require it and which are largely contained in Article 63 TEC. These measures focus on protection from persecution and *refoulement* (minimum standards on qualification as a refugee), access to a legal procedure (minimum standards on procedures) and the possibility of adequate subsistence (minimum standards on reception conditions). The EU is aware of the fact that the levels of subsistence will differ from country to country.[686] For this reason on 10 March 2004 the European Parliament and the Council adopted the 'Regulation establishing a programme for financial and technical assistance to third countries in the areas of migration and asylum' (AENEAS).[687] This programme provides support for capacity-building in third countries in the fields of reception conditions and protection capacity for asylum seekers, of readmission and the durable reintegration of returnees and of resettlement programmes.[688]

The adoption of the AENEAS programme follows the Tampere goals underlining the need for a comprehensive approach to migration addressing political, human rights and development issues in third countries and calling for a greater coherence between the internal and external policies of the EU.[689]

The Communication provides that there is a long way to go before most of the current refugee-hosting countries in the regions of origin could be considered to

684. Improving access to durable solutions, par. 38.
685. Id., par. 40.
686. Id., par. 43.
687. Regulation (EC) No. 491/2004, OJ L 80, 18.3.2004, 1.
688. Id., Art.2(2)(k).
689. Tampere, par. 22, 26, 27.

meet such a standard. 'None of the durable solutions can be arrived at overnight; they should be products of long-term planning'. In this context it is vital that third countries are assisted in a multi-annual engagement by the EU in this transformation process.[690]

For a long time the EU has had as an aim a wider and more comprehensive approach to immigration and asylum issues. Tampere underpinned the need for such a comprehensive approach and stressed the importance of partnership with third countries in the regions of origin and transit as a key element of the success of policies on immigration and asylum. Further, a targeted approach in the EU relation with third countries was called for during the Seville European Council. Later, the Thessaloniki European Council stated the importance of an evaluation mechanism for the monitoring of relations with third countries that should include participation by these third countries in international instruments related to asylum and human rights.[691] It should be borne in mind that the EU is entering a new phase in the development of the Common European Asylum System and it needs to decide what shape it should give to the System's second phase. The year 2004 proved crucial in that the global momentum created by the Agenda for Protection and The Convention Plus initiatives had to be met by action at EU level. Policy developments should build upon the first phase of the Common European Asylum System and be integrated in the second phase, paving the way for a 'Tampere II' agenda (the Hague Programme).[692]

To conclude, through this Communication the Commission recommended three elements, needed in the short- to mid-term, for achieving more orderly and managed arrivals of asylum seekers and refugees in the EU and the enhancement of the protection capacity of regions of origin:

- EU Regional Protection Programmes as a key policy tool to address protracted refugee situations globally;
- The identification of the indicators of protection capacity as a means of reaching agreed targets of effective protection as set out in this Communication;
- An EU resettlement scheme proposal to be submitted to the Council by July 2005, including a proposal for technical assistance underpinning such scheme.[693]

4.2.4 'A more efficient Common European Asylum System: the Single Procedure as the next step'

This Communication intends to launch further discussion on the *single procedure* on qualification of TCNs and stateless persons as refugees or as persons who

690. Improving access to durable solutions, par. 46.
691. Id., par. 48.
692. Id., par. 55.
693. Id., par. 59.

otherwise need international protection (subsidiary protection), which will subsequently take place in the Council and the European Parliament. After a preparatory phase is completed, the Commission will bring forward a proposal for Community legislation.[694]

One can ask what the reason for the establishment of a single procedure is and what its advantages are. The first and most obvious advantage of such a procedure is the increase in speed and efficiency of the refugee status (or subsidiary protection) determination procedure. A procedure which focuses on assessment of the protection needs defined in the Qualification Directive and where a single authority makes a decision on the basis of either of these two sets of criteria clearly has the potential to be quicker than the scenario of consecutive applications to one or more authorities where similar facts are assessed and appeals against the decisions of different authorities run in parallel. The centralisation of resources for dealing with applications for protection can achieve clear benefits. This would be a real gain for Member States – a quicker and more efficient system that helps the integration of refugees and the removal of those without protection needs.[695]

Another benefit of a single procedure is related to the protection aspects of applications for international protection. There can be no expectation that an applicant for international protection can evaluate whether his/her claim relates to the criteria set out in the 1951 Geneva Convention or have any knowledge of the other human rights instruments, which underlie other forms of international protection. By an introduction of a single procedure, this problem could be solved. The credibility of the applicants may also be improved if they do not have to face a sequence of procedures with the risk of their statements being adjusted to take account of the differing criteria against which it will be measured by different authorities.

The Commission Communication 'On the common asylum policy and the Agenda for protection' spoke of a crisis in the asylum system and a growing malaise in public opinion.[696] Where one decision on protection follows a quick, comprehensive procedure followed by the possibility of an appeal against that decision, ambiguity and the damaging perception that there are countless possibilities to stay in a country for protection reasons could be dispelled.[697]

A single procedure will also add value to the asylum systems of the Member States in their efforts to return those who do not qualify for international protection. 'Where all possible protection obligations are included in one procedure, the chance of further protection-related obstacles being raised to delay or prevent removal is all but removed'.[698] There are several possibilities for the key goals underlying legislative action:

---

694. A more efficient Asylum System (see *supra* 644), Introduction.
695. Id., par. 3, 4.
696. COM(2003)152 final, 26.3.2003, Introduction.
697. A more efficient Asylum System, par. 5–7.
698. Id., par. 8.

- to extend to applications for subsidiary protection the guarantees for first instance examination applicable to applications for refugee status (pursuant to Chapter II of the Asylum Procedure Directive);
- to subject negative decisions on applications for subsidiary protection to the notion of an effective remedy before a court or tribunal as for decisions rejecting an application for refuge status (under Chapter V of the Asylum Procedures Directive);
- to extend the scope of the Reception Directive to applicants for subsidiary protection;
- to extend the scope of the Dublin II Regulation to cover applications for subsidiary protection;
- to introduce a common administrative approach to the examination procedures such as the introduction of a single authority for the examination of applications for both refuge status and subsidiary protection;
- to extend the scope of any of the above Community standards on procedures to other grounds, preventing removal from the EU with a view to an all inclusive single procedure.

In order to ensure that EC legislation is built on sound foundations of consensus, mutual knowledge and understanding of the challenges faced in changing the asylum systems of the Member States to adapt to a single procedure, a preparatory phase is required to lay down these foundations. The Communication states that the *Preparatory Phase* will begin in January 2005 and run in tandem with the implementation of the first stage legislation of the Common European Asylum System. It also states that the Commission will submit a paper outlining a 'One Stop Shop Action Plan' to implement this period of consultation, debate and preparation on what Member States could do to unify their procedures.[699] The aim of the Preparatory Phase would be threefold:

1. to steer and inform at a technical level the discussion on how the EU should move towards the adoption of a single procedure;
2. to identify those elements of change which need to take place; and
3. to make those changes by the adjustment of operational practices as much as possible before or in parallel with a legislative approach.

The Preparatory Phase would also serve as a platform for the consultative process which needs to take place ahead of the bringing forward of EC legislation.[700] The Commission states that it will work towards achieving the objectives identified in the Communication, in close cooperation with Member States and the European Parliament, UNHCR and other relevant stakeholders. The Commission will bring

699. Id., par. 17, 27.
700. Id., par. 28.

forward the 'One Stop Shop Action Plan' as the main implementing tool of the Preparatory Phase necessary before the application of the relevant legislation takes place.[701] The Commission asked the Council and the European Parliament to endorse the two-step approach set out in this Communication as the next step along the road to achieving the common asylum procedure leading to a uniform status valid throughout the Union for those granted asylum in view of the progress made so far on the Tampere agenda.[702]

This Communication represents the next step in the continuation of the process of the establishment of the Common European Asylum System by calling for a single procedure ('One Stop Shop'). It explicitly recognises the importance of not undermining the refugee status based on the 1951 Geneva Convention; and recommends a predetermined sequence of examination so that claims for subsidiary protection are examined only after a negative assessment of the 1951 Geneva Convention grounds, and also the provision of a properly reasoned decision for rejecting 1951 Geneva Convention status where subsidiary protection is granted.[703] There must be access to judicial review mechanism for persons who find that they were not granted the appropriate status in order to ensure the correct interpretation of the 1951 Geneva Convention and other international obligations. This would help to develop relevant jurisprudence in the field of asylum.

4.2.5 'On Strengthened Practical Cooperation. New Structures, New Approaches: Improving the Quality of Decision Making in the Common European Asylum System'

This Communication sets out how practical cooperation between Member States can support the accomplishment of the goals set at Tampere and in the Hague Programme. In a EU without internal borders, the management of asylum cannot be effectively dealt with by individual Member States. The *raison d'être* of the Common European Asylum System is to deal with the management of asylum together. A common legislative framework has been introduced in the first stage of the Common European Asylum System. However, it proved inevitable to harmonise not only the legislation, but also the practice in Member States. The Commission states that the main goal of practical cooperation is to improve convergence in decision making by Member States within the framework of the rules set by the Community asylum legislation.[704] The Commission also believes that

701. The activities launching the preparatory phase, corresponding to the 'One Stop Shop Action Plan' of the Single Procedure Communication, are set out in detail in the Communication COM (2006) 67 final, Annex B (see *supra* 645).

702. A more efficient Asylum System, par. 31–33.

703. Id., par. 22; see also Comments of the ECRE on the Communication from the Commission to the Council and the European Parliament on 'A more efficient common European asylum system – the single procedure as the next step', September 2004.

704. On Strengthened Practical Cooperation (see *supra* 645), par. 2–4.

through using the same tools and applying the same safeguards Member States will build trust and confidence in each others' systems and achieve greater consistency in practice.[705] The Commission intends to propose the establishment of a network with a clear mandate for cooperation in each of the priority fields identified in the Hague Programme (asylum cooperation network). Other forms of co-operation between Member States on specific issues (e.g., a General Directors of Immigration Services Conference) will continue to be supported through the financial programmes.[706]

The Qualification Directive obliges Member States to assess facts and circumstances relating to an application for international protection in exactly the same way for both refugee status and subsidiary protection. The Commission Communication 'A More Efficient Common European Asylum System: The Single Procedure as the Next Step' highlighted a potential protection gap for applications for international protection, not covered by the guarantees of the Asylum Procedures Directive. The Communication proposed various actions that could be taken to enable a greater convergence between Member States in ensuring that all applications for protection in the EU are covered by the same procedural guarantees.[707] The results of activities envisaged to be taken would inform the preparation of legislative action, to ensure that, at a minimum, the guarantees agreed as applicable to claims for refugee status in the Asylum Procedures Directive extend to applications for subsidiary protection.[708]

Information about the countries of origin is essential for the decision making in all asylum cases. Therefore it is important that the information is available for the asylum authorities of Member States. A Country of Origin Information (COI) should enable the asylum authorities to verify statements made by applicants concerning their need for protection and to establish whether the applicant should benefit from international protection. An objective, transparent and accurate COI system that delivers official, rapid and reliable information is therefore central to any assessment of whether a person should benefit from international protection.[709]

Other issue discussed in this Communication is how to pool resources and ensure that asylum burden is not felt disproportionately by a few Member States, which is technically difficult and politically sensitive subject. According to the Commission, the EU needs to find responses to this challenge through better management of migratory flows, improved internal coordination in addressing illegal immigration and assistance to third countries, in full partnership, using existing

705. Id., par. 5.

706. Id., par. 6–8. For each of the objectives set out in the Hague Programme a number of steps should be taken, which are described in detail in Annexes B, C and D to this Communication. Annex A includes a full policy background.

707. Id., par. 10, 11.

708. Id., 3.1. Single Procedure, summary.

709. Id., par. 12.

Community funds, where appropriate, to improve their capacity for migration management and refugee protection. In addition, the application of the first stage legislation and the onset of the practical cooperation phase, with the increases in efficiency which it brings, should go some way to enable Member States to respond better to particular pressures situations. In this respect the Commission intends to propose amendments to the ERF to enable Member States to access funds quickly and with a minimum of bureaucratic process to deal with the consequences of sudden arrivals of large numbers of people who may be in need of international protection.[710]

In the Communication the Commission underlines the importance of training of asylum service personnel, which should remain central to the implementation of the Common European Asylum System. The Commission also refers to coordination of the range of relevant activities and the need to provide the necessary support to Member States asylum authorities.[711] The support and sustainability of the programme of activities put forward in this Communication needs to be assured. The Commission intends to make proposals to amend the existing financial opportunities (ARGO Programme, ERF) to ensure that the Hague priorities will be supported.[712]

This Communication is focused on various aspects of practical cooperation between Member States. It calls for a strengthened cooperation that would be positive for the Common European Asylum System and beneficial for persons in need of international protection. In order to achieve this goal, a high quality assessment of the application of the first stage of the Common European Asylum System is essential, which would provide a good basis for the launching of the second phase instruments.

4.3 Activities of the Council and the European Council

4.3.1 Evaluation of the Conclusions of Tampere (6 December 2001)

This report on the achievements of Tampere came at a strategically ideal time (preparation of a draft Treaty establishing a Constitution for Europe, preparation for a new EU enlargement, two years after the Tampere programme was adopted, preparation for the Laeken European Council) to conduct an initial evaluation of

710. Id., par. 16–19. It should be noted that the Commission refers to the first evaluation of the Dublin II Regulation. The Commission states that the evaluation will provide a useful focal point for consideration of how the Regulation might be adjusted in certain situations to ensure that Member States were not unduly disadvantaged by their geographic location (cf. *supra* 195).

711. Id., par 20, 21.

712. Id., par. 24.

the results obtained and the difficulties encountered.[713] As stated in the Tampere Conclusions, the debate should be 'a full debate assessing progress'. The scoreboard produced by the Commission revealed a wealth of achievements in the various areas of police cooperation and judicial cooperation in civil and criminal matters but, to a lesser extent asylum and immigration.[714]

At the time of issuing this Evaluation, several Member States had recently adopted or were adopting laws on asylum and immigration. A concern was expressed regarding the adoption of national laws, which in certain cases might complicate the discussion on proposals for Community legislative acts which the Commission had referred to the Council. The European Council was asked to reflect on possible ways of ensuring greater convergence in Member State legislation on asylum and immigration.[715]

Despite the political determination to make progress in the area of asylum (besides other areas), the Evaluation acknowledged that the discussions within the Council were not progressing as rapidly as might have been hoped (e.g., regarding asylum procedures). Therefore ways of overcoming these obstacles were needed with a view to formulating common policies. For this purpose, the following guidelines and principles were set out:

- The framework defined by the Amsterdam Treaty, the Vienna Action Plan and the Tampere Conclusions, as summarised in the Commission's scoreboard, must continue to serve as a guide for action by the Union, its institutions and its Member States in the years to come;
- It is vital that the Laeken European Council injects lasting dynamism into the process; certain specific matters must be given an impetus so as to unblock them and to enable formal adoption to take place as soon as possible (this was the case with the three proposals concerning asylum procedures, minimum standards for the reception of applicants for asylum and bringing the Dublin Convention and the proposal for a Directive on the status of long-term residents into the Community sphere);
- In view of the significant responsibilities retained by Member States for the implementation of immigration and asylum policies, the convergence process in these areas could be made easier by the establishment of an open coordination policy as proposed by the Commission: the adoption of guidelines could provide an opportunity to define the common terms of reference for agreement by Member States on immigration and asylum matters; this flexible method of convergence could ensure that the prerogatives which Member States consider they must retain, at least during a transitional phase, are respected while ensuring progress towards common objectives; in no circum-

713. See Belgian Presidency of the Union, 6 December 2001, Evaluation of the Conclusions of the Tampere European Council, 14926/01 LIMITE JAI 166.

714. Id., Section I. (Introduction), 1.

715. Id., 3.

stances could it replace the legislative work essential to fulfilling the Treaty aims.[716]

The above-mentioned circumstances show that the changeover to the Community pillar has not been enough to give a decisive impetus to work in the area of asylum (and immigration). Maintaining the unanimity rule at the time was clearly a serious hindrance to progress. The move to the QMV, as provided for in the Treaties, would allow speeding up the proceedings.[717]

4.3.2 Laeken European Council (14–15 December 2001)

Two years after the Tampere European Council took place, the Laeken European Council described the progress achieved in the areas of asylum and immigration as 'slower and less substantial than expected'[718] and therefore a call for a new approach appeared in the European Council conclusions. The European Council undertook to adopt, on the basis of the Tampere Conclusions and as soon as possible, a common policy on asylum (and immigration), which would maintain the necessary balance between protection of refugees, in accordance with the principles of the 1951 Geneva Convention, the legitimate aspiration to a better life and the reception capacities of the Union and its Member States. The following instruments were deemed necessary for the establishment of a true common asylum and immigration policy:

- the integration of the policy on migratory flows into the EU's foreign policy; in particular, European readmission agreements must be concluded with the countries concerned on the basis of a new list of priorities and a clear action plan; the European Council called for an action plan to be developed on the basis of the Commission Communication on illegal immigration and the smuggling of human beings;[719]
- the development of a European system for exchanging information on asylum, migration and countries of origin; the implementation of Eurodac and a Regulation for the more efficient application of the Dublin Convention, with rapid and efficient procedures;
- the establishment of common standards on procedures for asylum, reception and family reunification, including accelerated procedures where justified;

716. Id., Section II. (Immigration, asylum, controls at external borders), 4–5.

717. It should be noted that meanwhile the decision-making procedure concerning asylum has changed; see chapter 1, 1.10.1.

718. Presidency Conclusions, Laeken European Council, 14 and 15 December 2001, par. 38.

719. On the basis of the Commission's Communication on a common policy on illegal immigration of 15 November 2001, COM(2001) 672, on 28 February 2002 the EU Council of Ministers adopted a comprehensive plan to combat illegal immigration and trafficking in human beings in the European Union.

these standards should take account of the need to offer help to asylum applicants;
- the establishment of specific programmes to combat discrimination and racism.[720]

The Laeken Presidency Conclusions contain both the internal and the external dimension of the Common European Asylum Policy. The *internal dimension* is reflected in the elements regarding the development of a European system for exchanging information on asylum, migration and countries of origin, the implementation of Eurodac, the establishment of common standards on procedures for asylum, reception and family reunification.[721] The *external dimension* is clearly present in the requirement to integrate the policy on migratory flows into the EU's foreign policy. In this respect especially the European readmission agreements[722] are emphasised. The Conclusions also underline a 'more effective control of external borders' and focus on a need for a better management of the Union's external border controls in the fight against terrorism, illegal immigration networks and the trafficking in human beings. Regrettably, the passage mentioning a more effective control of the external borders and the fight against illegal immigration lacks the consideration of a possible hindrance that these measures may cause to the absolute respect of the right to seek asylum.[723]

4.3.2.1 *Laeken Declaration on the future of the European Union*

Annex I to the Presidency Conclusions – 'the Laeken Declaration on the future of the European Union', refers to the issue regarding asylum as one of the policies on which in the last ten years a political union in Europe was built. In reference to 'the democratic challenge facing Europe', the Laeken Declaration considers it a twin challenge indeed – finding its expression within and beyond the EU borders. Regarding asylum, within the Union the actions regarding the reception of the asylum seekers, the asylum procedures, as well as the integration of the persons holding a refugee status present a challenge. On the other hand, beyond its borders the EU is confronted with a fast-changing, globalised world, however not free from conflicts and violation of basic human rights.

---

720. Laeken Presidency Conclusions, par. 40. The European Council asked the Commission to submit (by 30 April 2002 at the latest) amended proposals concerning asylum procedures, family reunification and the 'Dublin II' Regulation. In addition, the Council was asked to expedite its proceedings on other drafts concerning reception standards, the definition of the term 'refugee' and forms of subsidiary protection.

721. Id., par. 40.

722. The main objective of the readmission agreements is to facilitate the readmission to their own country of persons residing without authorisation in a Member State.

723. Cf. Laeken Presidency Conclusions, par. 42 and Tampere, par. 13.

The Laeken Declaration also refers to the events of 11 September 2001, which made the people realise that forces like religious fanaticism, ethnic nationalism, racism and terrorism are still on increase; and regional conflicts, poverty and underdevelopment still provide a constant seedbed for these. Such conditions give raise to violence of different kinds, which could be a cause of fleeing one's country and seeking protection abroad. This brings our attention to the external dimension of the asylum policy, from the EU point of view, and brings about a question of Europe's role in this changing world.

The Declaration points out the position Europe is supposed to play, above all a role of 'a power able to play a stabilising role worldwide and to point the way ahead for many countries and peoples'.[724] The above-quoted statements of the Laeken Declaration on the future of the EU are very ambitious, setting a clear road map for the future development of the EU. The Presidency Conclusions adopted in Laeken identified the slow progress reached in the fields of asylum and immigration at the time and attempted to improve this by setting a clear plan expediting the adoption of the European legislation on asylum.

4.3.3 Seville European Council (21–22 June 2002)

The following European Council meeting to be reviewed took place in Seville on 21 and 22 June 2002. This European Council was determined to speed up the implementation of all aspects of the programme adopted in Tampere for the creation of an area of freedom, security and justice in the EU. The European Council stressed the need to develop a EU common policy on the separate, but closely related issues of asylum and immigration.[725]

The main achievement in the area of asylum over the six months of the Spanish Presidency was the adoption of the Reception Directive.[726] The European Council called on forthcoming Presidencies to continue giving migration issues a special place in their work schedules.[727] It was emphasised that the measures taken in the short and medium term for the joint management of migration flows must strike a fair balance between, on the one hand, a policy for the integration of lawfully resident immigrants and an asylum policy complying with international conventions, principally the 1951 Geneva Convention and, on the other hand, resolute action to combat illegal immigration and trafficking in human beings.[728] The acknowledgement in a single paragraph that a resolute action to combat illegal immigration and trafficking in human beings must be balanced fairly with an asylum

---

724. Laeken Presidency Conclusions, Annex I (Section: Europe's new role in a globalised world).

725. Cf. Presidency Conclusions, Seville European Council, 21 and 22 June 2002, par. 26 and Tampere, par. 10.

726. On the Reception Directive see chapter 2, 2.3.

727. Seville Presidency Conclusions (see *supra* 725), par. 27.

728. Id., par. 28.

policy complying with international obligations is a positive and most welcomed signal made during this European Council meeting.

Pursuant to the Seville Presidency Conclusions, the Union's action in the area of asylum and immigration must be based on the following principles:

- the legitimate aspiration to a better life must be reconcilable with the reception capacity of the Union and its Member States and immigration must pass through the legal channels provided for it; the integration of immigrants lawfully present in the Union entails both rights and obligations in relation to the fundamental rights recognised within the Union; combating racism and xenophobia is of essential importance here;
- in accordance with the 1951 Geneva Convention, it is important to afford refugees swift, effective protection, while making arrangements to prevent abuse of the system and ensuring that those whose asylum applications have been rejected are returned to their countries of origin more quickly.[729]

The integration of immigrants lawfully present in the territory of the EU Member States should be understood to include recognised refugees and also persons enjoying subsidiary forms of protection.

The second indent of paragraph 29 refers to the external-dimension aspect when referring to the readmission of refused asylum seekers. The European Council requested to speed up the conclusion of readmission agreements with transit countries.[730] It should be noted that readmission agreements, however, should not be used as mechanisms of responsibility-shifting to third countries and must comply with international obligations.

The European Council asked the Council and the Commission, within their respective spheres of responsibility, to review the list of third countries whose nationals require visas or are exempt from that requirement.[731] Unfortunately this request was not used as an opportunity to introduce exemptions from visa requirements for persons in need of international protection in order to enable them to gain access to Europe legally and by this decrease the operations of the smuggling and trafficking networks. The necessity to speed up legislative work on the framing of a common policy on asylum and immigration was also a point on the Seville European Council meeting agenda.[732]

The Conclusions of the Seville European Council meeting did not propose many concrete steps in the field of asylum, except for a work schedule for approving the asylum legislation under discussion (par. 37). The slow progress in adopting the relevant legal instruments in the area of asylum (and immigration) since Tampere was not openly acknowledged. The Conclusions were focused more on

729. Id., par. 29.
730. Id., par. 30, the 3rd subpar.
731. Id., par. 30, the 1st subpar.
732. Id., par. 37–39.

the enforcement measures concerning the border control (par. 31 and 32) and on the assessment of relations with host and transit countries (par. 34 and 35).

As mentioned before, the acknowledgement in a single paragraph that a resolute action to combat illegal immigration and trafficking in human beings must be balanced fairly with an asylum policy complying with international obligations is a positive contribution made during this European Council meeting. Nevertheless, regarding the relations with host and transit countries, the Union indirectly conditions economic cooperation, trade expansion and development assistance to the signing of readmission agreements that would include the readmission of both TCNs unlawfully present in the EU territory and also any other countries' nationals who can be shown to have passed through the country in question. Even though the above-mentioned condition is written under the heading 'Integration of immigration policy into the Union's relation with third countries' there is a question if this would not apply in practice also to asylum seekers who justifiably seek access to the EU territory. There could be a risk of an asylum seeker that is illegally present (by crossing the EU border irregularly or by overstaying) in a Member State territory that could be automatically returned on the basis of a readmission agreement even before being able to utilise his right to seek asylum or having his case examined.[733]

In order to start a concrete work based on the Seville Presidency Conclusions (especially paragraphs 26–39), the Presidency, after consultations with the Commission and the Council General Secretariat, drew up a Road Map with deadlines for the immediate action to be taken and delegating the various tasks precisely.[734] Regrettably, the annex to the Road Map did not focus to a great extent on an action to be taken in the field of asylum. The only reference to asylum is to be found in the part concerning the legislative framework to be adopted. It appears that the priority was given to the measures in the areas of visa policy, combating illegal immigration, management of external borders, and measures on relations with third countries.

4.3.4 **Council (5–6 June 2003)**

The Luxembourg European Council, which took place shortly before the Thessaloniki European Council (20 June 2003), intended to agree on a number of key instruments for the development of the Common European Asylum System. In the context of the preparation of the Thessaloniki European Council, this JHA Council examined three proposals for directives: for the Qualification Directive, the Asylum Procedures Directive and the Long-Term Residence Directive. It is worth recalling that at its meeting of 8 May 2003, the Council welcomed the commit-

733. Cf. Seville Presidency Conclusions, par. 33–36 and Tampere, par. 3, 13.

734. See the Road Map for the follow-up to the Conclusions of the European Council in Seville – Asylum, Immigration and border control (Brussels, 11 July 2002).

ment of the Commission to table within one year and possibly by the end of 2003 a proposal for a Directive on the extension of the long-term resident status directive to refugees and persons enjoying subsidiary protection.[735]

The Council also held a first exchange of views on a number of Presidency and Commission reports on the follow-up to Seville, among others, the Commission Communication on immigration, integration and employment[736] and the Commission Communication 'Towards more accessible, equitable and managed asylum systems'.[737] The first mentioned policy paper (communication) gives an impetus to Member States to expedite their efforts to integrate immigrants, including refugees. The other Communication was a response to the invitation extended to the European Commission by the March 2003 European Council to explore further the United Kingdom's approaches to international protection (Conclusion 61).[738]

Following a presentation of the Communications by the Commission, the Council held a first exchange of views and asked the Permanent Representatives Committee to pursue their examination, in view of the European Council of Thessaloniki. The Council took a note of the biannual update of the scoreboard to review progress on the creation of an area of freedom, security and justice in the EU.[739] It should be recalled that the scoreboard was launched by the Commission at regular intervals to monitor progress in the adoption and implementation of the set of measures needed to attain the objectives set by the Treaty of Amsterdam and the Tampere European Council Conclusions.

4.3.5 Thessaloniki European Council (19–20 June 2003)

The European Council, which met in Thessaloniki, welcomed the draft Constitutional Treaty, presented by the President of the Convention. This presentation marked a historic step in the direction of furthering the objectives of European integration.[740]

The European Council of Seville emphasised the need to speed up the implementation of all aspects of the programme approved in Tampere, especially on matters relating to the development of a common European policy on asylum and immigration.[741] The European Council in Thessaloniki reiterated its determination to establish a Common European Asylum System, as called for in Tampere (Octo-

---

735. Cf. COM(2005) 184 final (the draft Action Plan to the Hague Programme), 15, referring to a Proposal on long-term resident status for refugees to be adopted in 2005; and the Action Plan to the Hague Programme, 5, referring to a Proposal on long-term resident status for beneficiaries of international protection to be adopted in 2005.

736. COM(2003) 336 final, 3.6.2003.

737. *Supra* 641.

738. On the 'UK Paper' see the Commission Communication 'Towards more accessible, equitable and managed asylum systems', *supra* 641, at 5–7.

739. Doc. 9817/03.

740. Presidency Conclusions, Thessaloniki European Council, 19 and 20 June 2003, par. 2–7.

741. Id., par. 8.

ber 1999) and clarified in Seville (June 2002). In this context, the Council found vital the ensuring of the adoption (before the end of 2003) of the outstanding basic legislation, that is the proposal for a Qualification Directive and the proposal for an Asylum Procedures Directive.[742]

This European Council reaffirmed the importance of establishing a more efficient asylum system within the EU, in order to identify quickly all persons in need of protection, in the context of broader migration movements, and developing appropriate EU programmes. The European Council took note of the Communication from the Commission, focussing on more accessible, equitable and managed asylum systems,[743] and invited the Commission to explore all parameters in order to ensure more orderly and managed entry in the EU of persons in need of international protection, and to examine ways and means to enhance the protection capacity of regions of origin with a view to presenting to the Council (before June 2004) a comprehensive report suggesting measures to be taken, including legal implications. As part of this process, the European Council noted that a number of Member States planned to explore ways of providing better protection for refugees in their regions of origin, in conjunction with the UNHCR. This work shall be carried out in full partnership with the countries concerned, on the basis of recommendations from the UNHCR.[744]

The Thessaloniki European Council invited the Council and the Commission to examine, before the end of 2003, the possibilities of further reinforcing asylum procedures in order to make them more efficient with a view to accelerating, as much as possible, the processing of non-international protection-related applications.[745] The issue of asylum (together with immigration and frontiers) was placed high on the Thessaloniki European Council agenda,[746] what indicates its importance and also the urgency to speed up the implementation of all aspects of the programme approved in 1999 in Tampere; above all on matters relating to the development of a common European policy on asylum and immigration, as emphasised in Seville.

4.3.6 Brussels European Council (12–13 December 2003)

The Brussels European Council of December 2003 took place at the end of the Italian Presidency of the EU. This was a significant time for European Asylum Policy: according to the deadlines set by the Seville and the Thessaloniki European Councils, by the end of the Italian Presidency, instruments setting minimum

742. Id., par. 24.

743. *Supra* 641; see chapter 4, 4.2.1.

744. Thessaloniki Presidency Conclusions (see *supra* 740), par. 25–26.

745. Id., par. 27.

746. It was the second item on the agenda of this European Council meeting, immediately after the item regarding the Convention/IGC.

standards should have been adopted in all areas identified by the Amsterdam Treaty.[747]

In the conclusions of the Brussels European Council, the issue of asylum was not dealt with under a separate heading, instead, it was discussed under the heading 'Controlling migration flows'. This whole section seems to emphasise more the 'control aspect' of migration and treats asylum secondarily. The topics concerning the EU enlargement and the IGC current at the time, were also on the agenda of this European Council meeting and are both linked to asylum: the EU enlargement by extending the Common European Asylum System and by setting it up in the ten new Member States; the IGC is linked to asylum by bringing about a Constitutional Treaty for the EU which determines a new phase in the development of the whole Common European Asylum System.

The European Council welcomed the progress achieved in the negotiations regarding the adoption of the two Council Directives on asylum qualification and procedures. It also took note of persisting political obstacles that had been delaying the conclusions of these negotiations. It reaffirmed the importance of developing a Common European Policy on Asylum and invited the JHA Council to complete its work as soon as possible to ensure that the first phase of the establishment of a Common European Asylum System is fully implemented within the deadline set in Tampere.[748]

As regards the external dimension of the asylum policy, the European Council reaffirmed the importance of the dialogue with third countries of origin and transit of migratory flows and underlined the importance of continuing to assist those countries in their own efforts to stem such migratory flows. The European Council also welcomed the inter-institutional agreement reached by the European Parliament and the Council on the Regulation establishing the new financial instrument relating to cooperation with third countries in the area of asylum and migration.[749]

4.3.7 **Council (29–30 April 2004)**

The JHA Council of 29 and 30 April 2004 has already been mentioned in connection with the approval of the Directive on minimum standards for the qualification and status of TCNs and stateless persons as refugees or as persons who otherwise need international protection and the content of the protection granted (the Qualification Directive), and in connection with the Proposal for a Council Directive on minimum standards on procedures in Member States for granting and withdraw-

747. See, e.g., Memorandum, UNHCR's Recommendations for the Italian Presidency of the European Union (July-December 2003).

748. Presidency Conclusions, Brussels European Council, 12 and 13 December 2003, par. 23.

749. Id., par. 24.

ing refugee status (the Asylum Procedures Directive). The latter instrument was not formally adopted, nevertheless, the Council agreed on a general approach.[750]

4.3.8 **Council (19 July 2004)**

At the beginning of the Dutch Presidency (July–December 2004), the Council held a first, orientation debate on a new Multi-Annual Programme for JHA, following the Tampere programme. It should be noted that the European Council, at its meeting on 17 and 18 June, invited the Council and the Commission to draw up proposals for this new programme for the coming years, with a view to resolutely pursuing the objective of further developing a common area of freedom, security and justice.[751]

The JHA Council of 19 July debated on asylum and immigration issues, besides other elements on the agenda. Regarding asylum and immigration in particular, the Presidency noted a broad consensus for a Common European Asylum System even if modalities to define it need to be further examined. There was a great support for the promotion of a genuine common policy for the management of migratory flows.[752]

4.3.9 **Brussels European Council (4–5 November 2004)**

The Tampere European Council of 1999 introduced a number of principles in order to direct the creation of the area of freedom, security and justice, as well as a Common European Asylum Policy.[753] This five-year programme placed the objective of a progressive establishment of the area of freedom, security and justice at the head of the Union's political agenda.

On the Brussels European Council of 4 and 5 November 2004 the area of freedom, security and justice was the main discussed topic. The Presidency Conclusions provided that five years after the European Council meeting in Tampere, it was time for a new programme to enable the Union to build on the achievements in the area of freedom, security and justice and effectively meet the new challenges it will face. To this end the European Council approved a new multiannual programme for the next five years, to be known as 'the Hague Programme'.[754]

---

750. See 2579th Council meeting – JHA – Luxembourg, 29 April 2004, Doc. 8694/04 (Presse 123).

751. Presidency Conclusions, Brussels European Council, 17 and 18 June 2004, par. 8.

752. See 2600th Council meeting – JHA – Brussels, 19 July 2004, Doc. 11161/04 (Presse 219); the Press Release states that the Multi-Annual Programme will be discussed again at the informal meeting of JHA ministers on 30 September and 1 October, as well as at the Council of 25 and 26 October 2004.

753. Tampere, par. 3, 4, 13–17.

754. Presidency Conclusions, Brussels European Council, 4 and 5 November 2004, par. 15.

4.4 THE HAGUE PROGRAMME

The Hague Programme deals with all aspects of policies related to the area of freedom, security and justice, including their external dimension: fundamental rights and citizenship, asylum and immigration, border management, integration, fight against terrorism and organised crime, justice and police cooperation, and civil law; while a drugs strategy was said to be added in December 2004.[755]

In order to consider the future course of the Common European Asylum System, as proposed at the Brussels European Council meeting in November 2004, an overview of the provisions of Hague Programme follows:

The Hague Programme reflects the ambitions as expressed in the Treaty establishing a Constitution for Europe;[756] it takes full account of the evaluation by the Commission,[757] as well as the Recommendation adopted by the European Parliament on 14 October 2004 (in particular in respect of the passage to the JHA and the codecision as foreseen by Article 67(2) TEC).[758]

The objective of the Hague Programme is

> 'to improve the common capability of the Union and its Member States to guarantee fundamental rights, minimum procedural safeguards and access to justice, to provide protection in accordance with the Geneva Convention on Refugees and other international treaties to persons in need, to regulate migration flows and to control the external borders of the Union, to fight organised cross-border crime and repress the threat of terrorism, to realise the potential of Europol and Eurojust, to carry further the mutual recognition of judicial decisions and certificates both in civil and in criminal matters, and to eliminate legal and judicial obstacles in litigation in civil and family matters with cross-border implications. This is an objective that has to be achieved in the interests of EU citizens by the development of a Common European Asylum System and by improving access to the courts, practical police and judicial cooperation, the approximation of laws and the development of common policies'.[759]

In the light of this Programme, the European Council invited the Commission to present an Action Plan in 2005 with proposals for concrete actions and a timetable for their adoption and implementation.[760] Furthermore it invited the Commission to present to the Council an annual report on implementation of Union measures

---

755. Id., par. 16; the EU Action Plan on Drugs, COM(2005) 45, 14.2.2005, following the new European Strategy on Drugs 2005–2012.

756. OJ C 310, 16.12. 2004.

757. Communication from the Commission to the Council and the European Parliament, 'Area of Freedom, Security and Justice: Assessment of the Tampere programme and future orientations', COM(2004) 401 final, 2.6.2004 (see *supra* 642).

758. P6_TA-PROV (2004) 0022 A6-0010/2004.

759. Presidency Conclusions, Brussels European Council, 4 and 5 November 2004, Annex I: The Hague Programme, Introduction.

760. See chapter 4, 4.4.3.

('scoreboard'). The European Council will review progress on the Hague Programme in the second half of 2006.[761]

The Programme acknowledged the fact that international migration will continue. A comprehensive approach, involving all stages of migration, with respect to the root causes of migration, entry and admission policies and integration and return policies is needed. To ensure such an approach, the European Council urged the Council, the Member States and the Commission to pursue 'coordinated, strong and effective working relations between those responsible for migration and asylum policies and those responsible for other policy fields relevant to these areas'.[762]

The Hague Programme further states that the second phase of development of a common policy in the field of asylum (migration and borders) started on 1 May 2004 and it should be based on solidarity and fair sharing of responsibility including its financial implications and closer practical cooperation between Member States: technical assistance, training, and exchange of information, monitoring of the adequate and timely implementation and application of instruments as well as further harmonisation of legislation.[763] The European Council, taking into account the assessment by the Commission and the strong views expressed by the European Parliament, asked the Council to adopt a decision based on Article 67(2) TEC immediately after formal consultation of the European Parliament and no later than 1 April 2005 to apply the procedure provided in Article 251 TEC (codecision procedure) to all Title IV measures to strengthen freedom, subject to the Nice Treaty, except for legal migration.[764]

4.4.1 Common European Asylum System

The Hague Programme focuses on the Common European Asylum System in its second phase. According to the Programme the aims of this System in the second phase will be the establishment of a common asylum procedure and a uniform status for those who are granted asylum or subsidiary protection. It will be based on the full and inclusive application of the 1951 Geneva Convention and other relevant Treaties; and be built on a thorough and complete evaluation of the legal instruments that have been adopted in the first phase.[765]

It should be noted that the Hague Programme reiterates the goal to establish a Common European Asylum System. The Programme aims for the establishment of a uniform status not only to those who are granted asylum, but also to those granted subsidiary protection, what should be assessed positively. Nevertheless, in comparison with the Tampere Conclusions, there is no reference in the Hague

761. The Hague Programme (see *supra* 759), par. 17, 20.
762. The Hague Programme, 1.2. Asylum, migration and border policy.
763. Ibid.
764. Ibid; see Council Decision 2004/927/EC of 22 December 2004, OJ L 396, 31.12.2004, 45.
765. The Hague Programme, 1.3. A Common European Asylum System.

Programme to the 'validity throughout the Union of a uniform status for those who are granted asylum'.[766]

Other matter worth mentioning regards the determination that the Common European Asylum System is to be based on a full and inclusive application of the 1951 Geneva Convention on Refugees and other relevant Treaties. This determination is almost identical to the one laid down in Tampere with the exception of an explicit obligation of the Member States to comply with the principle of *non-refoulement,* which is not specifically mentioned in the Hague Programme.[767]

The European Council urged the Member States to implement fully the first phase of the Common European Asylum System without delay. In this regard the Council should adopt unanimously, in conformity with Article 67(5) TEC, the Asylum Procedures Directive as soon as possible.[768] The Commission is invited to conclude the evaluation of the first-phase legal instruments in 2007 and to submit the second-phase instruments and measures to the Council and the European Parliament with a view to their adoption before the end of 2010.[769] The end of 2010 seems to be a sufficient time to evaluate the operation of the first-phase measures with a view to the adoption of the second-phase legislation. The question, however, remains whether the second phase will be the final phase of establishing the Common European Asylum System. Since there is no clear indication, one can presume that further stages might be needed in order to complete the System.

In the framework of the adoption of the second-phase measures the European Council invited the Commission to present a study on the appropriateness, the possibilities and the difficulties, as well as the legal and practical implications of joint processing of asylum applications *within the Union*; and furthermore a separate study, to be conducted in close consultation with the UNHCR, should look into the merits, appropriateness and feasibility of joint processing of asylum applications *outside the EU territory.* This should be carried out in complementarity with the Common European Asylum System and in compliance with the relevant international standards.[770] There are no further details given in the Hague Programme concerning the above-mentioned joint processing (within or outside the EU) as part of the Common European Asylum System, for example: what would this cause, who would take decisions or whether it would be subject to appeal to

766. Cf. Tampere, par. 15 and the Hague Programme, 1.3.

767. Cf. Tampere, par. 13 and the Hague Programme, 1.3.

768. It should be noted that the Asylum Procedures Directive was adopted on 1 December 2005 by unanimity and after consulting the European Parliament, in order to follow the same procedure which was applied when the political agreement on this Directive was reached on 29 April 2004. Apart from that, all asylum measures under Art. 63(1) and (2) TEC now come under the QMV-rule and the co-decision with the European Parliament. Based on information from the General Secretariat of the Council, Brussels.

769. The Hague Programme, 1.3.

770. Ibid.

an EU Court. Moreover, regarding joint processing of asylum applications outside the EU territory, it obviously presupposes involvement of non-EU states and without their full cooperation the processing of asylum applications outside the EU territory will remain only a theoretical option.

Other provisions of the Hague Programme concern structures involving the national asylum services of the Member States with a view to facilitating practical and collaborative cooperation. Thus Member States will be assisted, *inter alia*, in achieving *a single procedure* for the assessment of applications for international protection, and in jointly compiling, assessing and applying information on countries of origin, as well as in addressing particular pressures on the asylum systems and reception capacities resulting above all from their geographical location. After a common asylum procedure is established, these structures should be transformed, on the basis of an evaluation, into a European support office for all forms of cooperation between Member States relating to the Common European Asylum System. [771]

It is not clear what 'assisting cooperation' would entail and by not specifying a clear structure, there would be obviously questions of accountability at both stages of this cooperation. The above-mentioned provisions are new, although there is presently limited coordination between national services through a body established by the Commission (the European Union Network for Asylum Practitioners (Eurasil)) and there are also obligations in EC asylum legislation to establish contact points for coordinating the implementation.[772]

The European Council welcomed the establishment of a new ERF for the period 2005–2010 and stressed the urgent need for Member States to maintain adequate asylum systems and reception facilities in the run-up to the establishment of a common asylum procedure. The European Council invited the Commission to earmark existing Community funds to assist Member States in the processing of asylum applications and in the reception of categories of TCNs. It invited the Council to designate these categories on the basis of a proposal to be submitted by the Commission in 2005.[773] However there is no deadline set by the Hague Programme for the Council to act. In addition, regarding the aforementioned funds, it is not clear whether, and to what extent, they would be connected with the ERF.

4.4.2 External dimension of asylum and migration

The external dimension of asylum and migration was strongly focused on during the Dutch Presidency, with the purpose of developing asylum and migration poli-

---

771. Ibid.; see also COM(2006) 67 final, 17.2.2006 (*supra* 645).

772. See the Hague Programme: Strengthening freedom, security and justice in the EU, Statewatch annotation (annotated by Professor Steve Peers, University of Essex), 11.

773. The Hague Programme, 1.3.

cies outside the Union. The external dimension, as laid down in the Hague Programme, is divided into three categories:
- partnership with third countries;
- partnership with countries and regions of origin;
- partnership with countries and regions of transit.

The Hague Programme stipulates that countries in regions of origin and transit will be encouraged in their efforts to strengthen the capacity for the protection of refugees. In this regard the European Council called upon all third countries to accede and adhere to the 1951 Geneva Convention on Refugees.

> 'Calling upon non-EU states to ratify and adhere to the 1951 Geneva Convention is certainly not enough to strengthen their national protection capacities in third countries and should not become a justification for making expulsions of asylum seekers to the states concerned easier. The external dimension of asylum opens up a highly complex area in which it will be extremely important:
> - to ensure strict adherence to standards of international human rights and refugee law in particular to the principle of *non-refoulement;*
> - to safeguard the possibility for those in need of protection to access safety and have their claims properly processed; and
> - to prevent solutions in the sphere of reception in regions of origin and more generally migration management which prejudice the right to seek asylum spontaneously and have the effect of undermining the international protection system.'[774]

Regarding the 'safe access to asylum procedures', besides finding protection and durable solutions in regions of origin, access to the EU Member States' asylum systems must be ensured. Otherwise a 'burden shifting' from the EU to third countries might take place, which could mean deterrence to the right to seek asylum in the EU.

The European Council welcomed the Commission Communication on improving access to durable solutions and invited the Commission to develop EU-Regional Protection Programmes in partnership with the third countries concerned and in close consultation and cooperation with the UNHCR. These programmes should focus primarily on capacity building and will include a joint resettlement programme for Member States willing to participate in such programme.[775]

The Hague Programme also stipulates that the policies which link migration, development cooperation and humanitarian assistance should be coherent and develop in partnership and dialogue with countries and regions of origin. It emphasises that these policies should be developed taking into account the root causes,

---

774. See ILPA's (Immigration Law Practitioners' Association) Response to the Hague Programme: EU Immigration and Asylum Law and Policy; available at: www.ilpa.org.uk/submissions/HagueProg.htm.

775. *The Hague Programme*, 1.6.2. Partnership with countries and regions of origin.

push factors and poverty alleviation and the European Council urges the Commission to present concrete and carefully worked out proposals by the spring of 2005.[776]

Return and readmission policy forms a significant part of the external dimension of asylum and migration. The Hague Programme provides that migrants who do no longer have the right to stay legally in the EU must return on a voluntary or, if necessary, compulsory basis. The European Council called for the establishment of an effective removal and repatriation policy based on common standards for persons to be returned in a humane manner and with full respect for their human rights and dignity. The development of a strong common policy on return is notable in the Hague Programme. A call for a prompt appointment by the Commission of a Special Representative for a common readmission policy is new. The European Council further called for timely conclusion of Community readmission agreements.[777]

Five years after the European Council meeting in Tampere took place, where a programme which laid down the foundation for important achievements in the area of freedom, security and justice was agreed, the Hague Programme is the first to clearly acknowledge that the asylum issue is an international issue and by this involves third countries. It proposes that the cooperation with third countries should be on the basis of a partnership that addresses beside other matters the root causes of migration, poverty alleviation, etc. A possible danger of an emphasis on the return and readmission policies could be that it might degenerate in a simple burden shifting of the asylum issue to third countries and obviously not solving the problem.

The future direction of the Common European Asylum System (both internal and external dimension), as well as the priorities given to certain areas within this System became more evident once the Action Plan for concrete actions and a timetable for their adoption and implementation has been launched. The Commission was invited to present an Action Plan under the Luxembourg Presidency (January–June 2005).

4.4.3 **Action Plan**

The Communication from the Commission to the Council and the European Parliament – The Hague Programme: Ten Priorities for the Next Five Years[778] (further referred to as the draft Action Plan) was adopted on 10 May 2005. It is composed of two parts:

776. Ibid.

777. The Hague Programme, 1.6.4. Return and re-admission policy.

778. Communication from the Commission to the Council and the European Parliament – The Hague Programme: Ten Priorities for the Next Five Years, The Partnership for European renewal in the field of Freedom, Security and Justice, COM(2005) 184 final, 10.5.2005.

- the first part (Chapter 2) gives an overview of the issues in question and of some of the most important aspects of the Hague Programme; it also identifies ten specific priorities upon which the Commission believes efforts for the next five years should be concentrated;
- the second part (Chapter 3) consists of an annex listing the concrete measures and actions to be taken over the next five years; this list closely adheres to the structure of the Hague Programme.[779]

The ten priorities, identified by the Commission are as follows:

1. fundamental rights and citizenship: creating fully-fledged policies;
2. the fight against terrorism: working toward a global response;
3. a common asylum area: establish an effective harmonised procedure in accordance with the Union values and humanitarian tradition;[780]
4. migration management: defining a balanced approach;
5. integration: maximising the positive impact of migration on our society and economy;
6. internal borders, external borders and visas: developing an integrated management of external borders for a safer Union;
7. privacy and security in sharing information: striking the right balance;
8. organised crime: developing a strategic concept;
9. civil and criminal justice: guaranteeing an effective European area of justice for all;[781]
10. freedom, security and justice: sharing responsibility and solidarity.[782]

For the purpose of this study the priority No. 3 ('a common asylum area') will be briefly focused on. The main goal to be achieved in the common asylum area is 'to establish an effective harmonised procedure in accordance with the Union's values and humanitarian tradition'. Moreover, respect for international obligations of the Union and the effectiveness of a harmonised procedure must be taken into consideration. According to the Commission, the work will focus on concluding the evaluation of the first-phase instruments in the next few years by 2007; and on submitting the second-phase instruments and measures in developing a common asylum policy. The Commission also emphasised the importance of reinforcing administrative cooperation between the national services of Member States, as

---

779. Id., Introduction, 3.

780. The term 'common asylum area' is not defined in this document, and one could presume that the Common European Asylum System is part of this area. See *supra* 778, at 8.

781. Approximation will be pursued, in particular through the adoption of rules ensuring a high degree of protection of persons, with a view to building mutual trust and strengthening mutual recognition, which remains the cornerstone of judicial cooperation.

782. See also 'Strategic objectives 2005–2009, Europe 2010: a partnership for European renewal', COM(2005) 12, 26.1.2005.

well as funds to assist Member States in processing applications and the reception of TCNs.[783]

In order to establish a workable Common European Asylum System, the implementation of the instruments and measures adopted will be inevitable. Furthermore, the Union needs to establish a mechanism which can adequately evaluate and assess the implementation of the area of freedom, security and justice by the Member States.[784]

As regards the second part of the draft Action Plan, it lists the main actions and measures to be taken over the next five years, including a specific set of deadlines for their presentation to the Council and the European Parliament, as required by the Hague Programme. It is also important to remember the role which the European Council has played in the defining of strategic guidelines and the planning of future action in the area of freedom, security and justice. The draft Action Plan calls for the European Council to preserve its guiding role in this process. Concerning specifically the issue of asylum, the following subjects from the list of measures and timetable for adoption (the ANNEX) should be noted: there is a plan to establish an Integration Fund (2007), which will be complementary to the European Social Fund, a Return Fund (2007) and to adjust the ERF (2007).

Regarding the Common European Asylum System, the last legal instrument still waiting for its adoption at that time was the Asylum Procedures Directive. During the second-phase developments of a common policy on asylum a 'Proposal for long-term resident status for refugees' (2005) should be launched; and the second-phase instruments and measures should be presented to the Council and the European Parliament and adopted before the end of 2005. The instruments are, however, not further specified. Establishment of structures involving the national asylum services of the Member States for promoting cooperation is planned to be adopted in the form of a Communication in 2005. A European Support Office will be established for all forms of cooperation between Member States, relating to the Common European Asylum System (after the establishment of a common asylum procedure and on the basis of an evaluation).

Two studies on the implementation of joint processing of asylum applications are to be adopted in 2006: one regarding the joint processing of asylum applications within the Union, the other one regarding the joint processing of asylum applications outside the EU territory. The latter study is to be conducted in a close consultation with the UNHCR.

As far as the external dimension of asylum and migration is concerned, main focus seems to be on the cooperation with third countries in managing migration and asylum. In this respect a Communication on migration and development, a revised version for 2006 of the reference document of the AENEAS Programme

783. *Supra* 769, at 6, 8.

784. Cf. *supra* 769, 2.4. (Implementation, evaluation and flexibility), 11–12; the Hague Programme, 3 (Implementation and evaluation), 14–15 and Constitution for Europe, Art. III-260.

2004–2006; and a completion of the integration of migration into the Country and Regional Strategy Papers for all relevant third countries are to be adopted in 2005. In addition, a Plan of action for EU-Regional Protection, including EU resettlement scheme and the launching of a pilot protection programme are also scheduled for 2005. A Report on progress and achievements in asylum and migration, within the context of the European Neighbourhood Policy[785] will be part of the intended intensified cooperation with countries of transit (to enable these countries better to manage migration and to provide adequate protection for refugees).

A partial application of the Schengen *acquis* by Ireland and the United Kingdom is referred to in the draft Action Plan, to be materialised in 2005 in the form of Council Decisions.[786]

It should be remembered that asylum policy is closely related to other areas like migration and integration, for example the integration of TCNs when the TCNs were granted asylum (or other form of international protection) in a Member State. Therefore the (draft) Action Plan should be read whilst bearing this in mind.

When examining the draft Action Plan to the Hague Programme, it becomes obvious that the emphasis is mainly on the external dimension of the Common European Asylum System (or 'the common asylum area', a new term introduced in the draft Action Plan). For that reason a Strategy on all external aspects of the Union policy on Freedom, Security and Justice, based on the measures developed in the Hague Programme should be adopted.[787]

The draft Action Plan endeavours to translate into concrete actions, including a timetable for the adoption and implementation of all actions, the aims and priorities of the Hague Programme. To meet the targets set in the draft Action Plan will require a determined action by all Community Institutions and the Member States, and their effective cooperation. Furthermore there is a reference in the draft Action Plan to the accession of the EU to the ECHR, what would be beneficial to persons seeking asylum in the EU.

At its meeting of 16 and 17 June 2005 the European Council welcomed the adoption by the Council and the Commission of the 'Action Plan implementing the Hague Programme on strengthening freedom, security and justice in the European Union'.[788] The Council and the Commission intend this Action Plan to be the

785. On the European Neighbourhood Policy see, e.g., 'Communication from the Commission to the Council, European Neighbourhood Policy, Recommendations for Armenia, Azerbaijan, Georgia and for Egypt and Lebanon', COM(2005) 72 final, 2.3.2005; European Neighbourhood Policy: the next steps (IP/05/236), Brussels, 2 March 2005; European Neighbourhood Policy – Council Conclusions, General Affairs and External Relations, 25.4.2005, Press Release (2655th Council meeting), 11.

786. *Supra* 769, at 18.

787. Id., External Relations, 30.

788. See Presidency Conclusions, Brussels European Council, 16 and 17 June 2005, par. 12–16. Text of the Action Plan is available at: http://ue.eu.int/uedocs/cmsUpload/web097781.en.pdf.

frame of reference for their work over the next five years. It sets out a list of legislative and non-legislative measures which the Council and the Commission consider necessary to put into practice, according to the guidelines set in the Hague Programme. As far as the Common European Asylum System is concerned, the main policy guidelines shall be transposed into the following measures:

- the evaluation of the first-phase legal instruments;
- second-phase development of the Common European Asylum System, establishment of common asylum procedure and a uniform status for those who are granted asylum or subsidiary protection;
- studies on the implications, appropriateness and feasibility of joint processing of asylum applications;
- cooperation between Member States relating to the Common European Asylum System, after the establishment of a common asylum procedure;
- establishment of the ERF 2005–2013.

As far as the external dimension of asylum and migration is concerned, the three main goals referred to in the Action Plan, are:

- the cooperation with third countries in managing migration and asylum;
- the development of EU-Regional Protection Programmes; and
- an intensified cooperation with countries of transit to enable these countries to better manage migration and to provide adequate protection for refugees.

In the general part of the Action Plan the Council and the Commission state that this Action Plan must retain a degree of flexibility, in order to take the greatest possible account of the demands of current events. Furthermore, it will be updated at the end of 2006, so that the European Council can establish the Union's legislative and operational priorities in the field of JHA. The most important goal is to implement the Hague Programme effectively and within the envisaged deadlines as laid down by the Action Plan.

4.5 Conclusions

The Tampere Presidency Conclusions not only set up the principles of a Common European Asylum System, they also linked this System to a comprehensive approach to migration, addressing political, human rights and development issues in countries and regions of origin and transit. The Presidency Conclusions further stated that 'clear priorities, policy objectives and measures for the Union's external action in JHA should be defined'.[789] After the completion of the first phase of the System (minimum standards for reception, qualification, procedures and

789. Tampere, par. 61.

temporary protection of persons in need of international protection) the next step forward in asylum policy was to develop its external dimension; knowing that a comprehensive approach to asylum and migration could not be taken without a working partnership with third countries (of origin, transit and first asylum).

Most of the policy instruments following Tampere are clearly focused on the external dimension (e.g., the Communications 'Towards more accessible, equitable and managed asylum systems' and 'On the Managed Entry in the EU of Persons in Need of International Protection and the Enhancement of the Protection Capacity of the Regions of Origin – Improving Access to Durable Solutions' or the Laeken Presidency Conclusions). The same trend is obvious also in the Hague Programme.

The Communication 'Towards more accessible, equitable and managed asylum systems', for example, examined in more details the structural shortages of the international protection system and observed that there is a clear need to explore a new approach to complement the stage-by-stage approach adopted in Tampere. The idea of transit processing centres was also launched. The new approach to asylum is based on three specific, but complementary policy objectives: orderly and managed arrival of refugees and persons in need of international protection in the EU from their regions of origin; burden- and responsibility-sharing within the EU and with the regions of origin; development of efficient and enforceable asylum decision making and return procedures.

The Communication 'On the Managed Entry in the EU of Persons in Need of International Protection and the Enhancement of the Protection Capacity of the Regions of Origin – Improving Access to Durable Solutions' touched upon the issues of the EU Resettlement Scheme and the Protected Entry Procedures; and it also called for the selection of indicators for ongoing work on protection of asylum seekers and refugees in third countries.

The 'Laeken Declaration on the future of the European Union' referred to the issue regarding asylum as one of the policies on which in the last ten years a political union in Europe was built upon.

Focusing on the Common European Asylum System in its second phase, especially in the framework of the adoption of the second-phase measures, the reference made in the Hague Programme to the joint processing of asylum applications within and outside the EU is in particular worth noting.

The question that now awaits to be answered is whether the actions that will be directed to tackle the root causes of asylum claims, including durable solutions, namely poverty alleviation, the strengthening of national protection capacities in third countries, etc., will be balanced with the actions directed towards a managed entry into the EU territory (e.g., the admission policies of the Member States) and the return of asylum seekers to third countries. This balance is necessary in order to guarantee the cooperation of third countries with the EU Member States and by this to contribute to the workability of the whole System.

CONCLUDING REMARKS

1. Common European Asylum System

The main purpose of this book is to analyse and evaluate the current state of affairs of the Common European Asylum System, as called for in the Tampere Presidency Conclusions of 1999. In these Conclusions an ambitious and comprehensive policy programme for the field of asylum was given for the first time, a programme fully committed to the obligations of the 1951 Geneva Refugee Convention. For these reasons the Tampere Presidency Conclusions were chosen as the 'measuring instrument' for the evaluation of the Common European Asylum System.

The idea of this study was to evaluate the continuity of the goals set in Tampere insofar they could be identified in the EU legislation on asylum, in its implementation in one of the new Member States and also in later EU policy documents related to asylum. It should be noted that since the Tampere programme is a policy document that provides the concept and main principles of the Common European Asylum System, the evaluation of the asylum legislation and its implementation was not carried out based strictly on the diction of the Tampere Conclusions but rather on its spirit.

Along with the primary purpose, the secondary goal is not less important to remember: to present the background of the Common European Asylum System (the notion of the internal market, free movement of persons, Schengen *acquis*, Dublin Convention, Treaty of Maastricht, etc.) and also to give a thorough overview of the current EU legislation on asylum.

2. Implementation in Slovakia

To be able to assess the implementation in practice of the Common European Asylum System, it proved inevitable to carry out a study in at least one of the EU Member States on its national EU-harmonised asylum legislation and its implementation. It is true that the implementation of the System in each Member State is important since it influences the functioning of the whole System; nevertheless, the influence of Slovakia is noteworthy. Slovakia is located on two major migratory routes from East to West (Russian route) and from South to North (Balkans route). Taking into account that in 2004 the number of asylum applications was the highest ever since the beginning of the asylum system in Slovakia,[790] whilst there was an opposite trend in the rest of the EU, this new Member State deserves

790. See chapter 3, 3.4.5.

special attention regarding its role in the Common European Asylum System. Moreover, the fact that about 70% of asylum cases were closed before reaching the first-instance decision due to the 'disappearance' of the applicants, as well as the extremely low recognition rate (1.14% in 2004; 2.9% in 2005) cast doubts on the effectiveness of the asylum system to reach adequate standards for the protection of refugees.[791]

The phenomenon of 'disappearance' has been justified by the Slovak authorities with the consideration that Slovakia is unable to compete with richer Member States' economies. This brings about a question whether when adopting the minimum standards required in the Reception Directive,[792] this very different economic situation in the Member States was appropriately considered for the achievement of the goals of reducing the secondary movements of asylum seekers and the comparable reception conditions.

The case of Slovakia shows that the secondary movements of asylum applicants still continue. On the other hand, what should also be mentioned in this context is that the reception centres in Slovakia were mostly located near the border with Austria and the Czech Republic. This only contributes to the 'disappearance' trends and perhaps 'save' the national asylum system by shifting the problem to other Member States, however not solving it. At the same time, it would be unfair to expect from this relatively inexperienced country to deal effectively with such large number of asylum applications, a burden that was not effectively dealt with in the past even by the 'old' EU Member States with much longer experience and with greater financial and human resources in this field.

Although the compliance with the EU *acquis* was one of the conditions for EU membership and this compliance was met by Slovakia; the expected changes in the management and administration of the asylum/migration matters were not adequately adjusted to the new system. It should be taken into account that the harmonisation process was done in a relatively short period of time despite the magnitude of the changes that were required.

The process of harmonisation evolved mainly through different projects run by the EU (e.g., PHARE), yet it seems that these projects have not handled the deep managerial and structural problems rooted in the system, by dealing mainly with technical equipment and training. The Slovak asylum system was not prepared to process a large number of applications having a limited reception capacity, lack of officers, decision-makers and interpreters.

The introduction of the Dublin II Regulation[793] has not caused, so far, the feared scenario of an increased pressure on the Slovak asylum system. In 2004, the Slovak authorities accepted on the basis of the Dublin II mechanism 1900 cases on request of other EU Member States. Only in 316 cases were the asylum appli-

791. See chapter 3, 3.6.1.4 and 3.7.
792. On the Reception Directive see chapter 2, 2.3; chapter 3, 3.4.6.
793. On the 'Dublin II' Regulation see chapter 2, 2.2.2 and 2.2.3; chapter 3, 3.7.

cants actually returned to the Slovak territory. The statistics show that in 2005 an evident gap between the number of requests received from other Member States and the number of persons physically returned to Slovakia has been registered again. This situation raises the question, why the Member States in the end decided to return only a sixth of the asylum applicants (in 2004) although the Dublin II criteria pointed to Slovakia as the responsible Member State. A possible reason could be that the Member States involved voluntarily decided to share the burden with Slovakia or it could also be due to the lower standards of reception conditions offered by Slovakia at the time.[794]

Taking the case of a new Member State located on the external border, the study has shown the structural difficulties this asylum system has to face. In addition, a more coordinated approach on asylum in the EU is needed, giving as an example the very different recognition rate of Chechen asylum applicants (e.g., in 2004 in Austria 96%, in Slovakia almost 0%; in 2005 in Austria 91%, in Slovakia 0%). Despite the existing problems portrayed, these could also be seen as a great opportunity to revise the burden-sharing mechanism and to adjust it with the current asylum situation in the EU.

3. More effective solutions?

Nowadays, the issue of asylum cannot be looked at in the same manner as it was seen at the time of the signing of the 1951 Geneva Convention. Although the 1951 Geneva Convention and the 1967 New York Protocol are still the cornerstones of the international refugee protection, they do not always cover the pressing situations occurring today. There have been some efforts to provide more effective solutions for refugees and also efforts regarding the sharing of the responsibility for admitting and protecting refugees; for example the United Nation High Commissioner for Refugees has launched the 'Convention Plus' process and the EU's subsidiary protection common notion also comes to mind.

The introduction of the subsidiary protection status in the EU asylum legislation is a very positive step, going beyond the framework of protection provided by the 1951 Geneva Convention status. Nevertheless, the fact that persons granted international protection in the form of subsidiary protection status for the moment are offered lower benefits and fewer rights than persons granted refugee status (e.g., as regards maintaining family unity, access to employment or social welfare) points to inequality between these two statuses. This could prevent integration of persons granted subsidiary forms of protection and also throw doubts on an equitable Common European Asylum System called for in Tampere.

794. Based on information from the UNHCR BO, Bratislava, June 2005.

4. A complex problem

The main problem, complicating the full establishment of a fairly functioning Common European Asylum System, seems to be that many migrants who do not qualify for international protection (e.g., economic migrants) use the institution of asylum as a channel to enter the EU. In this way they abuse this institution and by doing so the whole asylum procedure becomes less accessible especially for genuine, bona fide refugees. The Common European Asylum System attempts to:

- strictly distinguish between the genuine asylum seekers/refugees (including the persons seeking subsidiary forms of protection) and other migrants; and
- provide at least the minimum standards agreed to those who qualify for international protection;

These two aspects must be carried out simultaneously to make sure that those who deserve protection are not deprived of it or do not need to wait for it for too long. Moreover, the frequent cases of abusing the asylum system should not justify measures that would harm genuine refugees. Some instruments, used by Member States to safeguard their territory against the illegal immigration, may make it increasingly difficult for refugees to secure access to international protection (e.g., visa policy, pre-frontier measures and border management, readmission and return policies). To give at least one example, the EU common visa policy does not differentiate between persons in need of international protection and other TCNs, what could in practice jeopardise the right to seek asylum. The current leading countries of origin of asylum applicants in Europe (Serbia and Montenegro, Russian Federation, Turkey, Iraq, China and Iran)[795] are all mentioned in Annex I of the Council Regulation 539/2001, listing the third countries whose nationals must be in possession of a visa when entering the EU.[796]

5. A balanced approach

To define and put into practice a well-balanced approach that would guarantee the right to seek asylum in the EU territory, and the protection of the Member States against illegal migration is extremely difficult but essential for a just Common European Asylum System. Possible solutions in order to prevent the abusing of the asylum system could be:

---

795. See 'Asylum Levels and Trends in Industrialized Countries' (2005), 'Overview of Asylum Applications Lodged in Europe and Non-European Industrialized Countries', UNHCR (Geneva, 17 March 2006); available at: www.unhcr.org.

796. Council Regulation (EC) No. 539/2001 of 15 March 2001 listing the third countries whose nationals must be in possession of visas when crossing the external borders and those whose nationals are exempt from that requirement, OJ L 81, 21.3.2001, 1, amended by Council Regulations (EC) 2414/2001 of 7 December 2001, OJ L 327, 12.12.2001, 1 and 453/2003 of 6 March 2003, OJ L 69, 13.3.2003, 10.

- to tackle poverty in regions that generate asylum seekers;
- to develop a clearer immigration policy that would allow other legal ways for entering the EU, thus decreasing the need to abuse the asylum system.

Poverty is often perceived only as a cause for economic migration and as such it does not entitle a person to receive asylum or subsidiary forms of international protection. However, poverty could also be a cause for instability in a country or region of origin of an asylum seeker to such extent that a group of people is marginalised. This could further lead to violations of their human rights and even to persecution. The fight against poverty in third countries not only reduces the flow of economic migrants, it could also decrease situations that generate refugees.

As regards legal migration, on 11 January 2005, for example, the Commission presented a Green Paper on an 'EU approach to managing economic migration',[797] aiming to launch a process of in-depth discussion involving the EU, Member States and civil society on the most appropriate form of Community rules for admitting economic migrants and on the added value of adopting such a common framework.

6. External dimension

The EU Member States when developing the Common European Asylum System focused primarily on its internal dimension, even though a logical approach to the creation of this System should have been to concentrate first on its external dimension. By focusing first on the external dimension the main causes of the asylum problem could have been tackled sooner. The actual approach of the EU was chosen most probably due to the magnitude of the asylum problem already existing in Europe and its political implications.

The external dimension was mentioned already in the Tampere programme ('partnership with countries of origin', 'management of migratory flows'), and it is also included in the first-stage European asylum legislation (e.g., concept of safe third countries and safe countries of origin). Nonetheless, a stronger emphasis on cooperation with third countries is evident from the Hague Programme.

The Programme's addressing of a comprehensive approach ('involving all stages of migration with respect to the root causes of migration, entry and admission policies and integration and return policies'),[798] in order to better manage international migration is very positive, although the idea of joint processing of asylum applications outside EU territory provokes the question whether this would be the right way of sharing the responsibility with third countries. Moreover it is not obvious from the Hague Programme what the legal and practical implications of the potential joint processing would entail. All possible efforts

797. COM(2004) 811 final, 11.1.2005.
798. The Hague Programme, 1.2 Asylum, migration and border policy.

should be made in order to avoid that the responsibility for asylum applications is shifted to a great degree to these countries, which are, as a matter of fact, much poorer than the EU Member States. Moreover a successful burden sharing will never take place unless the third countries are actively involved in such projects and initiatives and are treated as equal partners.

The Tampere Conclusions called for a greater coherence between the internal and the external policies of the EU, and the Seville European Council highlighted the integration of immigration matters into the Union's relations with third countries. The external dimension of the Common European Asylum System should be well-balanced between the initiatives to establish the potential transit processing centres and regional protection zones, and the development cooperation, humanitarian aid and poverty alleviation for the third countries.

7. Internal dimension

The internal dimension encompasses the approach of Title IV TEC, which concentrates on the EU side of the problem (crossing of external borders, reception of refugees). The internal dimension approach at the first stage of the Common European Asylum System is marked by its 'minimum character' (minimum standards on reception, minimum standards with respect to the qualification, minimum standards on procedures, minimum standards for giving temporary protection). The Commission's proposals for the asylum legislation were good in principle, but in reality the political negotiations in the Council often resulted in a deterioration of the standards suggested initially and also in granting too much discretionary power to the Member States. This can in practice result in a lowering of the minimum standards during the transposition process and implementation of the law. Therefore whilst setting the 'minimum standards', the EU should have stated a clearer requirement not to lower more favourable standards if these already existed in any of the Member States.[799]

8. Constitutional Treaty

If the order of the Union's objectives laid down in the EU Constitutional Treaty corresponds with their significance for the EU, then one can conclude that the goal to maintain and develop the Union as an area of freedom, security and justice gained more importance. At present it is listed as the fourth objective of the Union in the TEU; in comparison with the Constitutional Treaty, where it is listed as the second objective.[800]

---

799. Cf. Reception Directive, Preamble, par. 15; Qualification Directive, Preamble, par. 8; Temporary Protection Directive, Preamble, par. 12.

800. Cf. Art. 2 TEU and the EU Constitutional Treaty, Art. I-3. Provisions referring specifically to the area of freedom, security and justice are to be found in Art. I-42 of the Constitutional Treaty.

The further development of the second phase of the Common European Asylum System with the establishment of a common asylum procedure and a uniform status for those granted asylum or subsidiary protection might be slowed down to a certain extent by the uncertainty regarding the ratification of the EU Constitutional Treaty.[801]

The Constitutional Treaty guarantees the 'right to asylum' (Charter of Fundamental Rights of the Union, Article II-78) with due respect for the rules of the 1951 Geneva Convention and the 1967 New York Protocol relating to the status of refugees. In comparison to the Tampere Conclusions, the slight difference in the wording 'right to asylum' instead of 'right to seek asylum' might be seen to go beyond the sole guarantee to enter the asylum procedure and by this perhaps follow closer the spirit of the Geneva Convention.

The explicit reference to the principle of *non-refoulement* (Charter of Fundamental Right of the Union, Article II-79(2) and Article III-266) is for the first time laid down in a European Treaty; currently it is only indirectly incorporated in the TEC by the calling for adoption of measures on asylum in accordance with the 1951 Geneva Convention and the 1967 New York Protocol.

The Constitutional Treaty further removes the concept of 'minimum standards' and incorporates a Common European Asylum System comprising:

- a uniform status of asylum for nationals of third countries, valid throughout the Union;
- a uniform status of subsidiary protection for nationals of third countries who, without obtaining European asylum, are in need of international protection;
- a common system of temporary protection for displaced persons in the event of a massive inflow;
- common procedures for the granting and withdrawing of uniform asylum or subsidiary protection status;
- criteria and mechanisms for determining which Member State is responsible for considering an application for asylum or subsidiary protection;
- standards concerning the conditions for the reception of applicants for asylum or subsidiary protection;
- partnership and cooperation with third countries for the purpose of managing inflows of people applying for asylum or subsidiary or temporary protection.[802]

The Constitutional Treaty is not built upon the pillar structure present in the Treaty of Maastricht as amended by the Treaties of Amsterdam and Nice. Chapter IV of the Constitutional Treaty thus includes the subject matters of Title IV TEC (visas, asylum, immigration and other policies related to free movement of persons) as well as of Title VI TEU (Provisions on police and judicial cooperation in criminal

801. See *supra* 19.
802. Cf. chapter 2, 2.1.

matters). The previous fragmentation is therefore eliminated and thus the notion of the area of freedom, security and justice becomes more coherent.

The elimination of the restriction laid down in Article 68 TEC, regarding the limited jurisdiction of the ECJ, should be also received positively since it would allow national courts at all levels to request the ECJ to give preliminary rulings on asylum matters. This and the other above-mentioned changes provided by the Constitutional Treaty would be beneficial for the development of the Common European Asylum System and therefore it would be regrettable if the Constitutional Treaty will not enter into force.

9. The immediate future

Despite a possible non-entry-into-force of the Constitutional Treaty, this should not be an obstacle for the development of a Common European Asylum System reflecting the spirit of the Tampere Conclusions. Although not optimal, the existing Treaty framework provides for such a System to function since it does not prevent the current minimum standards to be set at a higher level in the future. In addition, the JHA in the Council and the codecision with the European Parliament are already in force for asylum matters.[803] The determination of the Union and the Member States is vital for the ambitious aim of a Common European Asylum System to be materialised, and taking into consideration that the Member States have already built good bases; one can be hopeful that such a System will be accomplished.

803. See *supra* 768.

SELECTED BIBLIOGRAPHY

Achermann, A., Gattiker, M.: 'Safe Third Countries: European Developments', *International Journal of Refugee Law* 7 (1995), 19–38.

Albors-Llorens, A.: 'Changes in the Jurisdiction of the European Court of Justice under the Treaty of Amsterdam', *Common Market Law Review* 35 (1999), 1273–1294.

Alexander, W.: 'Free Movement of Non-EC Nationals: A Review of the Case-Law of the Court of Justice', *European Journal of International Law* 3 (1992), 53–64.

Angenendt, S. (ed.): *Asylum and Migration Policies in the European Union* (Bonn 1999).

Arboleda, E., Hoy, I.: 'The Convention Refugee Definition in the West: Disharmony of Interpretation and Application', *International Journal of Refugee Law* 5 (1993), 66–90.

Bank, R.: 'The Emergent EU Policy on Asylum and Refugees – The New Framework Set by the Treaty of Amsterdam: Landmark or Standstill?', *Nordic Journal of International Law* 68 (1999), 1–29.

Barnard, C.: *The Substantive Law of the EU* (Oxford 2004).

Barnard, C., Scott, J.: *The Law of the Single European Market: Unpacking the Premises* (Oxford 2002).

Battjes, H.: 'A Balance between Fairness and Efficiency? The Directive on International Protection and the Dublin Convention', *European Journal of Migration and Law* 4 (2002), 159–192.

Bell, M.: 'Mainstreaming equality norms into European Union asylum law', *European Law Review* 20 (2001), 20–34.

Bieber, R., Monar, J. (eds.): *Justice and Home Affairs in the European Union: The Development of the Third Pillar* (Brussels 1995).

Blake, N.: 'The Dublin Convention and Rights of Asylum Seekers in the European Union', in Guild, E., Harlow, C. (eds.): *Implementing Amsterdam: Immigration and Asylum Rights in EC Law* (Oxford 2001), 95–120.

Boeles, P.: 'Introduction: Freedom, Security and Justice for all', in Guild, E., Harlow, C. (eds.): *Implementing Amsterdam: Immigration and Asylum Rights in EC Law* (Oxford 2001), 4–9.

Boer, M. den: *Schengen Still Going Strong: Evaluation and Update* (Maastricht 2000).

Boer, M. den: *Schengen's Final Days?: The Incorporation of Schengen into the New TEU, External Borders and Information Systems* (Maastricht 1998).

Boer, M. den: *The Implementation of Schengen: First the Widening, Now the Deepening* (Maastricht 1997).

Bouteillet-Paquet, D.: 'Passing the Buck: a critical analysis of the readmission policy implemented by the European Union and its Member States', *European Journal of Migration and Law* 3 (2003), 359–377.

Bradley, K.St.C.: 'Institutional design in the Treaty of Nice', *Common Market Law Review* 38, (2001), 1095–1124.

Breuss, F.: 'Costs and Benefits of EU's Eastern European Enlargement' (WIFO Working Paper No. 78) (Vienna 1995).

Brink, A. van den: *Regelgeving in Nederland ter implementatie van EU-recht* (Deventer 2004).

Brouwer, E: *Eurodac:* 'Its Temptations and Limitations', *European Journal of Migration and Law* 4 (2002), 231–247.

Brownlie, I.: *Principles of Public International Law,* 4th ed. (Oxford 1990).

Bruycker, P. de, Sousa, C. de (eds.): *Immigration and Asylum in the European Union* (Brussels 2003).

Byrne, R.: 'Harmonization and Burden Redistribution in the Two Europes', *Journal of Refugee Studies* 16 (2003), 336–358.

Byrne, R., Shacknove, A.: 'The Safe Country Notion in European Asylum Law', *Harvard Human Rights Journal* 9 (1996), 193–194.

Byrne, R., Noll, G., Vedsted-Hansen, J.: 'Understanding Refugee Law in an Enlarged European Union', *European Journal of International Law* 15 (2004), 355–379.

Carlier, J.-Y., Vanheule, D. (eds.): *Europe and Refugees: A Challenge* (The Hague, London, Boston 1997).

Carlier, J.-Y., Vanheule, D., Hullmann, K., Pena Galiano, C. (eds.): *Who is a Refugee? A Comparative Case Law Study* (The Hague, London, Boston 1997).

Cholewinski, R.: 'The Protection of the Right of Economic Migrants to Family Reunion in Europe', *International and Comparative Law Quarterly* 43 (1994), 568–598.

Cholewinski, R.: *No Right of Entry: The Legal Regime on Crossing the EU Border,* in Groenendijk, K., Guild, E., Minderhoud, P. (eds.): *In Search of Europe's Borders* (The Hague, 2003).

Cholewinski, R.: 'European Union Policy on Irregular Migration: Human Rights Lost?', in Bogusz, B., Cholewinski, R., Cygan, A., Szyszczak, E.: *Irregular Migration and Human Rights: Theoretical, European and International Perspectives* (Leiden 2004), part III, 9.

Clayton, G.: *Immigration and Asylum Law* (Oxford 2004).

Collinson, S.: *Beyond Borders: West European Migration Policy Towards the 21st Century* (London 1993).

Craig, S.: 'The European Commission's proposals for directives to establish a common European asylum system: the challenges of accession and the dangers of negative integration', *European Law Review* 27 (2002), 497–502.

Craig, P., Búrca, G. de: *EU law: Text, Cases, and Materials,* 3rd ed. (Oxford 2003).

Czaplinski, W.: 'Emerging Regional Refugee Law in Europe', *AWR-Bulletin* 35 (1997), 79 et seq.

Dacyl, J.W.: 'Europe needs a new protection system for "Non-Convention" Refuges', *International Journal of Refugee Law* 7 (1995), 579–595.

Deards, E., Hargreaves, S.: *European Union Law* (Oxford 2004).

Dias Urbano de Sousa, C., Bruycker, P. de: *The Emergence of a European Asylum Policy* (Brussels 2004).

Donner, J.P.H.: 'Abolition of Border Controls', in Schermers, H.G. et al.: *Free Movement of Persons in Europe: Legal Problems and Experiences* (Dordrecht, Boston, London 1993), 5–26.

Drüke, L.: 'Refugee protection in the Post Cold War Europe', in Institut Européen d' Administration Publique (Edité par Alexis Pauly): *Les Accords de Schengen: Abolition des frontières intérieures ou menace pour les libertés publiques?* (Maastricht 1993), 105 et seq.

Drüke, L.: 'Harmonisation of Asylum Law and Judicial Control under the Third Pillar', in Bieber, R., Monar, J. (eds.): *Justice and Home Affairs in the European Union: The Development of the Third Pillar* (Brussels 1995), 167 et seq.

Edminster, S.: 'Recklessly Risking Lives: Restrictive Interpretations of "Agents of Persecution" in Germany and France', US Committee for Refugees Worldwide Refugee Survey (Washington 1999).

Eijsbouts, W.T.: 'Borders and Democracy: The Schengen Treaties', *Yearbook of European Studies* (1993), 57–70.

Einarsen, T.: 'The European Convention on Human Rights and the Notion of an Implied Right to de facto Asylum', *International Journal of Refugee Law* 2 (1990), 361–374.

Evans, A.: 'Third-Country Nationals and the Treaty on European Union', *European Journal of International Law* 5 (1994), 199–220.

Faria, C. (ed.): *The Dublin Convention on Asylum: Between Reality and Aspirations* (Maastricht 2001).

Fennelly, N.: 'The area of 'freedom, security and justice' and the European Court of Justice – a personal view', in *International and Comparative Law Quarterly*, 49 (2000), 1–14.

Fitzpatrick, J., Bonoan, R.: 'Cessation of Refugee Protection', in Feller, E., Türk, V., Nicholson, F. (eds.): *Refugee Protection in International Law, UNHCR's Global Consultations on International Protection* (Cambridge 2003), 491–544.

Gaudissait, M.-A., Sinnaeve, A.: 'The Role of the White Paper in the Preparation of the Eastern Enlargement', in Maresceau, M. (ed.): *Enlarging the European Union: Relations between the EU and Central and Eastern Europe* (London, New York 1997), 41 et seq.

Gilbert, G.: 'Right of Asylum: A Change of Direction', *The International and Comparative Law Quarterly* 32 (1983), 633–650.

Gilbert, G.: 'The Best Early Warning is Prevention: Refugee Flows and European Responses', *International Journal of Refugee Law* 9 (1997), 207–228.

Gless, S. (ed.): *Auslieferungsrecht der Schengen – Vertragsstaaten: neuere Entwicklungen* (Freiburg im Breisgau 2002).

Goodwin-Gill, G.: *The Refugee in International Law*, 2nd ed. (Oxford 1996).

Goodwin-Gill, G.: 'The Individual Refugee, the 1951 Convention and the Treaty of Amsterdam', in Guild, E. and Harlow, C. (eds.): *Implementing Amsterdam: Immigration and Asylum Rights in EC Law* (Oxford 2001), 141–159.

Goudsmit, C. A.: Het *Schengenrecht voor vreemdelingen en vluchtelingen: overeenkomsten tussen Schengen-Staten en Besluiten van het Uitvoerend Comité* (Utrecht 1995).

Grahl-Madsen, A.: *The Status of Refugees in International Law* (Leiden 1966).

Grief, N.: 'The Accession of the European Community to the European Convention on Human Rights', in Evans, M.D.: *Aspects of Statehood and Institutionalism in Contemporary Europe* (Dartmouth 1997), 253–276.

Groenendijk, C.A.: 'Verdrag van Amsterdam en de migratie binnen en naar de Europese Unie', *Migrantenrecht* 7 (1997), 156–161.

Groenendijk, K.: 'Reinstatement of Controls at the Internal Borders of Europe: Why and Against Whom?', *European Law Journal* 10(2) (2004), 150–170.

Guild, E.: 'Between Persecution and Protection: Refugees and the New European Asylum Policy', in Dashwood, A., Spencer, J., Ward, A., Hillion, C., *The Cambridge Yearbook of European Legal Studies* 3 (2000, 2001), 169–199.

Guild, E.: *European Community Law from a Migrant's Perspective* (Nijmegen 2000).

Guild, E.: 'Reaching into the European State: Border Pressures and International Asylum Obligations', in *Moving the Borders of Europe* (Nijmegen 2001), 52–61.

Guild, E.: 'Seeking asylum: storm clouds between international commitments and EU legislative measures', *European Law Review* 29 (2004), 198–218.

Guild, E.: 'Jurisprudence of the ECHR: Lessons for the EU Asylum Policy', in Dias Urbano de Sousa, C., Bruycker, P. de: *The Emergence of a European Asylum Policy*, (Brussels 2004), 329–342.

Guild, E., Harlow, C.: *Implementing Amsterdam: Immigration and Asylum Rights in EC Law* (Oxford 2001).

Guild, E., Niessen, J.: *The Developing Immigration and Asylum Policies of the European Union* (The Hague, London, Boston 1996).

Hailbronner, K.: 'European Immigration and Asylum Law under the Amsterdam Treaty', *Common Market Law Review* 35 (1998), 1047–1067.

Hailbronner, K.: *Immigration and Asylum Law and Policy of the European Union* (The Hague, 2000).

Hailbronner, K.: 'Asylum Law in the Context of a European Migration Policy', in Walker, N. (ed.): *Europe's Area of Freedom, Security and Justice* (Oxford 2004), 41–88.

Hailbronner, K.; Weil, P. (eds.): *Von Schengen nach Amsterdam: auf dem Weg zu einem europäischen Einwanderungs- und Asylrecht* (From Schengen to Amsterdam: towards a European immigration and asylum legislation), (Köln 1999).

Hathaway, J.: *The Law of Refugee Status* (Toronto 1991).

Hathaway, J., Foster, M.: 'Internal Protection/Relocation/Flight Alternative as an Aspect of Refugee Status Determination', in Feller, E., Türk, V., Nicholson, F. (eds.): *Refugee Protection in International Law, UNHCR's Global Consultations on International Protection* (Cambridge 2003), 357–417.

Higgins, I. (ed.), Hailbronner, K.: *Migration and Asylum Law and Policy in the European Union* (FIDE 2004 National Reports) (Cambridge 2004).

Hurwitz, A.: 'The "Schengen" Practice and Case-Law in Belgium', *European Journal of Migration and Law* 2 (2000), 37–48.

Jans, J.H., Lange, R. de, Prechal, S., Widdershoven, R.J.G.M.: *Inleiding tot het Europees Bestuursrecht*, 2nd ed. (Nijmegen 2002).

Kapteyn, P.J.G., VerLoren van Themaat, P.: *Introduction to the Law of the European Communities*, 3rd ed. (London, The Hague, Boston 1998).

Kerber, K.: 'The Temporary Protection Directive', *European Journal of Migration and Law* 4 (2002), 193–214.

Klaauw, J. van der: 'Irregular Migration and Asylum-Seeking: Forced Marriage or Reason for Divorce?', in Bogusz, B., Cholewinski, R., Cygan, A., Szyszczak, E.: *Irregular*

Migration and Human Rights: Theoretical, European and International Perspectives (Leiden 2004), II.6.

Klaauw, J. van der: 'Towards a Common Asylum Procedure', in Guild, E., Harlow, C. (eds.): *Implementing Amsterdam: Immigration and Asylum Rights in EC Law* (Oxford 2001), 165–194.

Kloth, K.: 'The Dublin Convention on Asylum – An Introduction', in Marinho, C. (ed.): *The Dublin Convention on Asylum: Its essence, Implementation and Prospects* (Maastricht 2000), 8–10.

Krieken, P.J. van: *The Consolidated Asylum and Migration Acquis* (The Hague 2004).

Kumin, J.: 'Asylum in Europe: Sharing or Shifting the Burden', World Refugee Survey (1995).

Lavenex, S.: 'EU Enlargement and the Challenge of Policy Transfer: The Case of Refugee Policy', *Journal of Ethnic and Migration Studies* 28 (2002), 701–721.

Legomsky, S.: 'Secondary Refugee Movements and the Return of Asylum Seekers to Third Countries: The Meaning of Effective Protection', *International Journal of Refugee Law* 15 (2003), 567–667.

Marinho, C. (ed.): *The Dublin Convention on Asylum: Its Essence, Implementation and Prospects* (Maastricht 2000).

Marinho, C.: *Asylum, Immigration and Schengen Post-Amsterdam: A First Assessment*, (Maastricht 2001).

Marx, R.: 'Adjusting the Dublin Convention: New Approaches to Member State Responsibility for Asylum Applications', *European Journal of Migration and Law* 3 (2001), 7–22.

Marx, R.: 'Notions of Persecution by Non-State Agents in German Jurisprudence', *Georgetown Immigration Law Journal* 15 (2001), 447.

Meijers, H.: Schengen: *Internationalization of central chapters of the law on aliens, refugees, privacy, security and the police* (Leiden 1992).

Monar, J.: 'Enlargement – related diversity in EU justice and home affairs: challenges, dimensions and management instruments', WWR working document (The Hague December 2000).

Moore, J.: 'Whither the Accountability Theory: Second-Class Status for Third-Party Refugees as a Threat to International Refugee Protection', *International Journal of Refugee Law* 13 (2001), 32 et seq.

Mullally, S.: 'Manifestly Unjust: A Report on the Fairness and Sustainability of Accelerated Procedures for Asylum Determination' (September 2001), Ch. 2, 4 (59–65).

Nagy, B.: 'Is there a need for subsidiary protection in Europe? A view from a candidate country', in D. Bouteillet-Paquet (ed.): *Subsidiary protection of Refugees in the European Union: Complementing the Geneva Convention?* (Brussels 2002).

Nicol QC, A., Harrison, S.: 'The Law and Practice in the Application of the Dublin Convention in the United Kingdom', *European Journal of Migration and Law* 1 (1999), 465–481.

Noll, G.: *Negotiating Asylum: The EU Acqius, Extraterritorial Protection and the Common Market of Deflection* (The Hague 2000).

Noll, G.: 'Fixed definitions or framework legislation? The delimitation of subsidiary protection ratione personae', Working Paper No. 55 New Issues in Refugee Research (UNHCR, 2002).

Noll, G.: 'Visions of the Exceptional: Legal and Theoretical Issues Raised by Transit Processing Centres and Protection Zones', *European Journal of Migration and Law* 5 (2003), 303–341.

Peers, S.: *EU Justice and Home Affairs Law* (London 2000).

Phuong, C.: 'Persecution by Non-state Agents: Comparative Judicial Interpretations of the 1951 Refugee Convention', *European Journal of Migration and Law* 4 (2002), 521–532.

Piotrowicz, R., Eck, C. van: 'Subsidiary Protection and Primary Rights', *International and Comparative Law Quarterly* 53 (2004), 107–138.

Plender, R., Mole, N.: 'Beyond the Geneva Convention: constructing a de facto right of asylum from international human rights instruments', in Nicholson, F., Twomey, P. (eds.): *Refugee Rights and Realities. Evolving International Concepts and Regimes* (Cambridge 1999), 81–105.

Rogers, N.: 'Minimum Standards for Reception', *European Journal of Migration and Law* 4 (2002), 215–230.

Schieffer, M.: 'Community readmission agreements with third countries – objectives, substance and current state of negotiations', *European Journal of Migration and Law* 3 (2003), 343–357.

Sinha, S. Prakas: *Asylum and International Law* (The Hague 1971).

Spijkerboer, T.: 'Subsidiarity in Asylum Law. The Personal Scope of International Protection', in Bouteillet-Paquet, D. (ed.): *Subsidiary Protection of Refugees in the European Union: Complementing the Geneva Convention?* (Brussels 2002), 19–42.

Staples, H.: 'Adjudicating Schengen', in Groenendijk, K., Guild, E., Minderhoud, P. (eds.): *In Search of Europe's Borders* (The Hague 2003).

Steenbergen, J.D.M.: 'All the King's Horses...: Probabilities and Possibilities for the Implementation of the New Title IV EC Treaty', *European Journal of Migration and Law* 1 (1999), 29–60.

Steiner, J., Woods, L., Twigg-Flesner, Ch.: *Textbook on EC Law* (Oxford 2003).

Thielemann, E.R.: 'Between Interests and Norms: Explaining Burden-Sharing in the European Union', *Journal of Refugee Studies* 16 (2003), 253–273.

Thun-Hohenstein, C.: *Der Vertrag von Amsterdam: Die neue Verfassung der EU* (Vienna 1997).

Türk, V.: 'Non-State Agents of Persecution', in Chetail, V., Gowlland-Debbas, V. (eds.): *Switzerland and the International Protection of Refugees* (The Hague 2002), 95–109.

Vedsted-Hansen, J.: 'Assessment of the Proposal for an EC Directive on the Notion of Refugee and Subsidiary Protection from the perspective of International Law', in Bouteillet-Paquet, D. (ed.): *Subsidiary Protection of Refugees in the European Union: Complementing the Geneva Convention?* (Brussels 2002), 57–78.

Weiss, F., Wooldridge, F.: *Free Movement of Persons Within the European Community* (The Hague 2000).

Wiener, A.: 'Forging Flexibility – The British 'No' to Schengen', *European Journal of Migration and Law* 1 (1999), 441–463.

Wyatt, D. (ed.): *Rudden and Wyatt's EU Treaties and Legislation* (Oxford 2004).

Zwaan, J.W. de, Bultena, A.J.: *Ruimte van vrijheid en rechtvaardigheid. De samenwerking op het gebied van Justitie en Binnenlandse Zaken in de Europese Unie* (Den Haag 2002).

SELECTED DOCUMENTS

Act concerning the conditions of accession of the Czech Republic, the Republic of Estonia, the Republic of Cyprus, the Republic of Latvia, the Republic of Lithuania, the Republic of Hungary, the Republic of Malta, the Republic of Poland, the Republic of Slovenia and the Slovak Republic and the adjustments to the Treaties on which the European Union is founded (Treaty of Accession to the European Union), OJ L 236, 23.9.2003.

Action Plan of the Council and the Commission on how best to implement the provisions of the Treaty of Amsterdam on an area of freedom, security and justice ('Vienna Action Plan'), OJ C 19, 23.01.1999, 1.

Agreement of 14 June 1985 between the Governments of the States of the Benelux Economic Union, the Federal Republic of Germany and the French Republic on the gradual abolition of checks at their common borders, OJ L 239, 22.9.2000, 13.

Agreement between the European Community and the Republic of Iceland and the Kingdom of Norway concerning the criteria and mechanisms for establishing the State responsible for examining a request for asylum lodged in a Member State or in Iceland or Norway, OJ L 93, 3.4.2001, 40.

Agreement between the European Community and the Kingdom of Denmark on the criteria and mechanisms for establishing the State responsible for examining a request for asylum lodged in Denmark or any other Member State of the European Union and Eurodac for the comparison of fingerprints for the effective application of Dublin Convention, OJ L 66, 8.3.2006, 38.

Amended Proposal for a Council Directive on minimum standards on procedures in Member States for granting and withdrawing refugee status, COM(2002) 326 final/2, 03.07.2002.

Assessment of the Asylum System in the Slovak Republic – Final Report (May 2003 – April 2004) prepared by UNHCR, The Ministry of Interior (Migration Office, Aliens and Border Police), The Ministry of Labour, Social Affairs and Family, The European Commission Delegation in the Slovak Republic, The International Organisation for Migration, The Embassy of the USA, The Embassy of the Kingdom of the Netherlands, The Slovak Helsinki Committee, The Björnson Society and The Goodwill Society.

Comments by the European Council on Refugee and Exiles (ECRE) on the Commission Proposal for a Council Decision establishing the European Refugee Fund for the period 2005–2010, CO1/03/2004/Ext/HM.

Comments from the ECRE on the Proposal for a Council Directive on minimum standards for the qualification and status of third country nationals and stateless persons as refugees or as persons who otherwise need international protection.

Comments from ECRE on the Amended proposal for a Council Directive on minimum standards on procedures in Member States for granting and withdrawing refuge status.

Commission staff working paper – Evaluation of the Dublin Convention, SEC (2001), 756.

Commission staff working paper – First annual report to the Council and the European Parliament on the activities of the Eurodac Central Unit, SEC(2004) 557, 5.5.2004.

Commission staff working paper – Revisiting the Dublin Convention: developing Community legislation for determining which Member State is responsible for considering an application for asylum submitted in one of the Member States, SEC(2000) 522.

Commission Regulation (EC) No. 1560/2003 of 2 September 2003 laying down detailed rules for the application of Council Regulation (EC) No. 343/2003 establishing the criteria and mechanisms for determining the Member State responsible for examining an asylum application lodged in one of the Member States by a third-country national OJ L 222, 5.9.2003, 3.

Communication from the Commission to the Council and the European Parliament 'Towards more accessible, equitable and managed asylum systems', COM (2003) 315 final, 3.6.2003.

Communication from the Commission to the Council and the European Parliament 'Area of Freedom, Security and Justice: Assessment of the Tampere programme and future orientations', COM(2004) 401 final, 2.6.2004.

Communication from the Commission to the Council and the European Parliament 'On the managed entry in the EU of persons in need of international protection and the enhancement of the protection capacity of the regions of origin – Improving access to durable solutions', COM(2004) 410 final, 4.6.2004.

Communication from the Commission to the Council and the European Parliament 'A more efficient Common European Asylum System: the Single Procedure as the next step', COM(2004) 503 final, 15.7.2004.

Communication from the Commission to the Council and the European Parliament 'On Strengthened Practical Cooperation. New Structures, New Approaches: Improving the Quality of Decision Making in the Common European Asylum System', COM(2006) 67 final, 17.2.2006.

Conclusions of 30 November and 1 December 1992 of the Ministers of the Member States of the European Communities responsible for immigration on countries in which there is generally no serious risk of persecution, SN 4821/92 WGI 1281 AS 145.

Convention determining the State responsible for examining applications for asylum lodged in one of the Member States of the European Communities (Dublin Convention), OJ C 254, 19.8.1997, 1.

Convention Implementing the Schengen Agreement of 14 June 1985 between the Governments of the States of the Benelux Economic Union, the Federal Republic of Germany and the French Republic on the gradual abolition of checks at their common borders, OJ L 239, 22.9.2000, 19.

Convention relating to the Status of Refugees (1951 Geneva Convention), adopted on 28 July 1951, United Nations, *Treaty Series*, vol. 189, 137.

Council Decision 2000/596/EC of 28 September 2000 establishing a European Refugee Fund, OJ L 252, 6.10.2000, 12.

Council Decision 2001/258/EC of 15 March 2001 concerning the conclusion of an Agreement between the European Community and the Republic of Iceland and the Kingdom of Norway concerning the criteria and mechanisms for establishing the State responsible for examining a request for asylum lodged in a Member State or Iceland or Norway, OJ L 93, 3.4.2001, 38.

Council Decision 2002/463/EC of 13 June 2002 adopting an action programme for administrative cooperation in the fields of external borders, visas, asylum and immigration (ARGO programme), OJ L 161, 19.6.2002, 11.

Council Decision 2004/904/EC of 2 December 2004 establishing the European Refugee Fund for the period 2005 to 2010, OJ L 381, 28.12.2004, 52.

Council Decision 2004/867/EC of 13 December 2004 amending Decision 2002/463/EC adopting an action programme for administrative cooperation in the fields of external borders, visas, asylum and immigration (ARGO programme), OJ L 371, 18.12.2004, 48.

Council Decision 2004/927/EC of 22 December 2004 providing for certain areas covered by Title IV of Part Three of the Treaty establishing the European Community to be governed by the procedure laid down in Article 251 of that Treaty, OJ L 396, 31.12.2004, 45.

Council Decision 2006/167/EC of 21 February 2006 on the conclusion of a Protocol to the Agreement between the European Community and the Republic of Iceland and the Kingdom of Norway concerning the criteria and mechanisms for establishing the State responsible for examining a request for asylum lodged in a Member State or in Iceland or Norway, OJ L 57, 28.2.2006, 15.

Council Decision 2006/188/EC of 21 February 2006 on the conclusion of the Agreement between the European Community and the Kingdom of Denmark extending to Denmark the provisions of Council Regulation (EC) No. 343/2003 establishing the criteria and mechanisms for determining the Member State responsible for examining an asylum application lodged in one of the Member States by a third-country national and Council Regulation (EC) No. 2725/2000 concerning the establishment of Eurodac for the comparison of fingerprints for the effective application of the Dublin Convention, OJ L 66, 8.3.2006, 37.

Council Directive 2001/55/EC of 20 July 2001 on minimum standards for giving temporary protection in the event of a mass influx of displaced persons and on measures promoting a balance of efforts between Member States in receiving such persons and bearing the consequences thereof, OJ L 212, 7.8.2001, 12.

Council Directive 2003/9/EC of 27 January 2003 laying down minimum standards for the reception of asylum seekers, OJ L 31, 6.2.2003, 18.

Council Directive 2003/86/EC of 22 September 2003 on the right to family reunification, OJ L 251, 3.10.2003, 12.

Council Directive 2003/109/EC of 25 November 2003 concerning the status of third-country nationals who are long-term residents, OJ L 16, 23.1.2004, 44.

Council Directive 2004/83/EC of 29 April 2004 on minimum standards for the qualification of third country nationals and stateless persons as refugees or as persons who otherwise need international protection and the content of the protection granted, OJ L 304, 30.9.2004, 12.

Council Directive 2005/85/EC of 1 December 2005 on minimum standards on procedures in Member States for granting and withdrawing refugee status, OJ L 326, 13.12.2005, 13.

Council Regulation (EC) No. 2725/2000 of 11 December 2000 concerning the establishment of 'Eurodac' for the comparison of fingerprints for the effective application of the Dublin Convention, OJ L 316, 15.12.2000, 1.

Council Regulation (EC) No. 539/2001 of 15 March 2001 listing the third countries whose nationals must be in possession of visas when crossing the external borders and those whose nationals are exempt from that requirement OJ L 81, 21.3.2001, 1.

Council Regulation (EC) No. 407/2002 of 28 February 2002 laying down certain rules to implement Regulation (EC) No. 2725/2000 concerning the establishment of 'Eurodac' for the comparison of fingerprints for the effective application of the Dublin Convention, OJ L 62, 5.3.2002, 1.

Council Regulation (EC) No. 343/2003 of 18 February 2003 establishing the criteria and mechanisms for determining the Member State responsible for examining an asylum application lodged in one of the Member States by a third-country national (Dublin II), OJ L 50, 25.2.2003, 1.

Decision No. 1/97 of 9 September 1997 of the Committee set up by Article 18 of the Dublin Convention of 15 June 1990, concerning provisions for the implementation of the Convention, OJ L 281, 14.10.1997, 1.

Decision No. 2/97 of 9 September 1997 of the Committee set up by Article 18 of the Dublin Convention of 15 June 1990, establishing the Committee's Rules of Procedure, OJ L 281, 14.10.1997, 26.

Decision 1/98 of the Article 18 Committee of the Dublin Convention, concerning provisions for the implementation of the Convention, OJ L 196, 14.7.1998, 49.

Decision No. 1/2000 of 31 October 2000 of the Committee set up by Article 18 of the Dublin Convention concerning the transfer of responsibility for family members in accordance with Article 3(4) and Article 9 of that Convention, OJ L 281, 7.11.2000, 1.

Information concerning the entry into force of the Agreement between the European Community and the Kingdom of Denmark extending to Denmark the provisions of Council Regulation (EC) No. 343/2003 establishing the criteria and mechanisms for determining the Member State responsible for examining an asylum application lodged in one of the Member States by a third-country national and Council Regulation (EC) No. 2725/2000 concerning the establishment of Eurodac for the comparison of fingerprints for the effective application of the Dublin Convention, OJ L 96, 5.4.2006, 9.

Presidency Conclusions, Tampere European Council (15 -16 October 1999), SN 200/99.

Presidency Conclusions, Laeken European Council (14–15 December 2001).

Presidency Conclusions, Seville European Council (21–22 June 2002).

Presidency Conclusions, Thessaloniki European Council (19–20 June 2003).

Presidency Conclusions, Brussels European Council (12–13 December 2003).

Presidency Conclusions, Brussels European Council (4–5 November 2004), the Hague Programme.

Presidency Conclusions, Brussels European Council (16–17 June 2005), Action Plan implementing the Hague Programme on strengthening freedom, security and justice in the European Union.

Proposal for a Council Directive on minimum standards for giving temporary protection in the event of a mass influx of displaced persons and on measures promoting a balance of efforts between Member States in receiving such persons and bearing the consequences thereof, COM(2000) 303 final, 24.5.2000.

Proposal for a Council Directive on minimum standards on procedures in Member States for granting and withdrawing refugee status COM(2000) 578 final, OJ C62 E, 27.02.2001, 231.

Proposal for a Council Directive on minimum standards on the reception of applicants for asylum in the Member States, COM(2001) 181 final, 3.4.2001.

Proposal for a Council Directive on minimum standards for the qualification and status of third country nationals and stateless persons as refugees or as persons who otherwise need international protection, COM(2001) 510, 12.9.2001.

Proposal for a Council Decision establishing the European Refugee Fund for the period 2005–2010, COM (2004)102 Final, 12.2.2004.

Protocol relating to the Status of Refugees (1967 New York Protocol), adopted on 31 January 1967, United Nations, Treaty Series, vol. 606, 267.

Regular Reports from the Commission on Slovakia's progress towards accession (1998–2003): COM(1998) 703 final; COM(1999) 511 final; COM(2000) 711 final; COM(2001) 700 final – SEC(2001) 1754; COM(2002) 700 final – SEC (2002) 1410; COM(2003) 675 final.

Regulation (EC) No. 491/2004 of the European Parliament and of the Council of 10 March 2004 establishing a programme for financial and technical assistance to third countries in the areas of migration and asylum (AENEAS), OJ L 80, 18.3.2004, 1.

Resolution of 30 November and 1 December 1992 of the ministers of the Member States of the European Communities responsible for immigration on a harmonised approach to questions concerning host third countries, SN 4823/92 WGI 1283 AS 147.

Resolution on Manifestly Unfounded Applications for Asylum, The Council, Conclusions of the meeting of the ministers responsible for immigration Doc. 10579/92 IMMIG (London, 30 Nov.-1 Dec. 1992).

Treaty on European Union (1992), OJ C 191, 29.7. 1992.

Treaty establishing the European Community (consolidated text), OJ C 325, 24.12.2002.

Treaty on European Union (consolidated text), OJ C 325, 24.12.2002.

Treaty of Nice, OJ C 80, 10.3.2001.

Treaty establishing a Constitution for Europe, OJ C 310, 16.12.2004.

UNHCR annotations for Articles 1 to 19 of the draft Council Directive on minimum standards for the qualification of third country nationals and stateless persons as refugees or as persons who otherwise need international protection and the content of the protection granted, December 2002.

UNHCR Executive Committee Conclusions, The Problem of Manifestly Unfounded or Abusive Applications for Refugee Status or Asylum (No. 30 (XXXIV)-1983).

UNHCR Handbook on procedures and criteria for determining refugee status under the 1951 Convention and the 1967 Protocol relating to the Status of Refugees (Geneva, January 1992).

UNHCR, 'UNHCR Comments on the European Commission Proposal for a Council Directive laying down minimum standards on the reception of applicants for asylum in Member States'.

Zákon o utečencoch, 16.11.1990, 498/1990 Zb. (Refugee Law of 16 November 1990, No. 498).

Zákon NR SR o utečencoch, 14.11.1995, 283/1995 Z.z. (Refugee Law of 14 November 1995, No. 283).

Zákon NR SR, ktorým sa mení a dopĺňa zákon NR SR č. 283/1995 Z.z. o utečencoch, 19.9.2000, 309/2000 Z.z. (amendment to the 283/1995 Refugee Law, Law No. 309 of 19 September 2000).

Zákon NR SR o azyle a o zmene a doplnení niektorých zákonov, 20.6.2002, 480/2002 Z.z. (Asylum Law of 20 June 2002, No. 480).

Zákon NR SR, ktorým sa mení a dopĺňa zákon č. 480/2002 Z.z. o azyle a o zmene a doplnení niektorých zákonov v znení neskorších predpisov a o zmene a doplnení niektorých zákonov, 2.12.2004, 1/2005 Z.z. (amendment to the 480/2002 Asylum Law, Law No.1/2005 of 2 December 2004).

INDEX

(References are to chapters and subchapters)

A

accelerated procedure, 2.5.3, 3.4.1, 3.4.2, 3.5, 3.6.1.3, 4.3.2
Accession Treaty (Treaty of Accession), 3.2, 3.4
Agenda for Protection, 4.2.1, 4.2.3, 4.2.4
Aliens and Border Police, 3.5, 3.6.1.2
amendment
  to the 283/1995 Refugee Law, 3.4.2
  to the 480/2002 Asylum Law, 3.4.6
appeal procedure, 2.5, 2.5.5, 3.4.1, 3.5, 3.6.1.5
area of freedom, security and justice, 1.1, 1.7., 1.7.1, 1.7.2, 1.8, 2.6, 4.2.2, 4.3.3, 4.3.4, 4.3.8, 4.3.9, 4.4
Association Agreement, 3.2
asylum claim, 1.5, 2.2.3, 2.3, 2.4.1, 2.5, 2.5.2, 2.5.5, 3.4.1, 3.4.2, 3.4.4, 3.5
  24-hour-rule, 3.4.1, 3.4.2, 3.5
asylum judge, 3.6.1.5, 3.7
asylum-determination procedure, 2.5.4, 2.5.5, 3.4.6, 3.6.1
(proposal) Asylum Procedures Directive, 1.7.1, 2.1, 2.2.3, 2.5, 2.5.3, 2.5.5, 2.8, 4.2.4, 4.3.4, 4.3.5, 4.3.7, 4.4.1, 4.4.3
asylum reception centre, 3.6.1.5, 3.7

B

borders
  external, 1.4, 1.6, 1.7.1, 1.7.2, 1.8, 1.11, 2.2.1, 2.2.3, 2.5.3, 3.1, 3.6, 3.7, 4.4.3
  internal, 1.3, 1.4, 1.7.2, 1.10.3, 1.11, 4.3.4
border procedures, 2.5.3, 2.5.5
burden of proof, 2.4.1
burden sharing, 1.10.1.1, 2.2.1, 2.6, 2.6.2, 2.6.2.1, 2.8, 3.7, 4.2.1, 4.2.3

C

cessation clause, 1.2, 2.4.2, 2.5.4
codecision procedure, 1.10.1.1, 1.10.1.3, 1.11, 4.4
Constitution
  for Europe, 1.7.1, 2.4.2, 4.3.1, 4.4
  Slovak, 3.4.1
Convention Plus, 4.2.1, 4.2.3
Council of Europe, 1.7.1, 2.5, 2.5.3
Council of the European Union (Council), 1.10.1.1
crime
  against humanity, 1.2, 3.4.1, 3.4.3.1, 3.7
  against peace, 1.2, 2.6.1, 3.4.1, 3.4.3.1, 3.7
  non-political, 1.2, 2.4.3, 3.4.3.1, 3.7
  serious, 2.4.2-2.4.4, 2.5.3
  war, 1.2, 2.4.2, 2.6.1, 3.4.3.1, 3.7

D

decision-making procedure, 1.7.2, 1.10, 1.10.1.1, 1.10.2, 2.6.1
discrimination, 1.7.1, 2.4, 3.6.1.4, 4.3.2
doubt, benefit of the, 2.4.1
Dublin Convention, 1.4, 1.5, 2.2, 2.2.1, 3.5, 4.3.1, 4.3.2
Dublin II. Regulation, 2.2, 2.2.1, 2.2.3, 2.5.3, 2.8, 3.1, 3.4.3.1, 3.4.3.2, 3.4.5, 3.5, 3.6.1, 3.7, 4.2.4

E

employment, 1.2, 2.3, 2.4, 2.4.4, 2.6.2.1, 2.7.1, 2.7.2, 2.8, 3.4.3, 3.4.3.1, 4.2.1, 4.3.4
enlargement, of the EU, 1.9, 3.2, 3.3, 4.3.1, 4.3.6
European Commission (Commission), 1.7.2, 1.9, 1.10, 1.10.1.1, 1.10.1.2, 4.2
European Convention on Human Rights and Fundamental Freedoms (ECHR), 1.6, 1.7.1, 1.7.3.1, 2.4.3, 2.5.3, 2.7.1, 3.4.3, 3.6.1.5, 4.2.1, 4.2.2, 4.4.3
European Council, 1.10.2
European Court of Human Rights, 2.4.3

European Court of Justice (ECJ), 1.10.3, 2.2.1, 2.4.3, 2.5.5, 2.7.1, 3.6.1.5
European Parliament (Parliament), 1.9, 1.10, 1.10.1.1, 1.10.1.3, 2.2.3, 2.4, 2.5, 2.6, 2.8, 3.2, 4.1, 4.2, 4.3, 4.4
EU Resettlement Scheme, 4.2.3, 4.4.3, 4.5
Eurodac, 1.5, 1.8, 2.2.1, 2.2.4, 3.1, 3.4.5, 3.5, 4.3.2
European Neighbourhood Policy, 4.4.3
European Refugee Fund (ERF), 2.2.1, 2.6.2.1, 2.8, 4.2.3, 4.4.1, 4.4.3
European Return Fund, 4.4.2
exclusion clause, 1.2, 2.4.2, 2.4.3, 3.5, 4.2.3
expulsion, 1.7.1, 2.4.2, 2.6.1, 3.4.3, 3.4.3.1, 3.6.1.5, 3.7, 4.2.2, 4.4.2
external dimension, of asylum, 4.1, 4.3.2, 4.3.6, 4.4, 4.4.2, 4.4.3, 4.5

F

family reunification, 1.3, 2.1, 2.2.1, 2.2.3, 2.4, 2.6.1, 2.7.1, 3.4.2, 3.4.3, 3.5, 4.2.1, 4.3.2
fear, well-founded, of persecution, 1.2, 2.4.1, 2.4.2, 2.5.4, 2.7.1, 3.4.1, 3.4.3, 3.4.4, 3.6.1, 3.6.1.4, 3.6.1.5
first country of asylum, 2.5.3
first-instance decision, 3.5, 3.6.1.4, 3.1
first pillar (supranational), 1.6, 1.7, 1.7.2, 3.4.3
free movement of persons, 1.1, 1.3, 1.4, 1.6, 1.7.1, 1.8, 1.11, 2.2.2

G

Geneva Convention on Refugees, 1.1, 1.2, 1.4, 1.5, 1.6, 1.7.1, 1.7.3.1, 1.8, 1.11, 2.2.1, 2.2.3, 2.4, 2.4.1, 2.4.2, 2.4.3, 2.4.4, 2.5, 2.5.1, 2.5.2, 2.5.3, 2.5.4, 2.6, 2.6.1, 2.7.1, 2.8, 3.4.3, 3.4.4, 3.4.6, 3.6, 3.6.1.5, 4.2.1, 4.2.4, 4.3.2, 4.4, 4.4.1, 4.4.2

H

Hague Programme, the, 1.10.1.1, 2.7.2, 4.1, 4.2.1, 4.2.3, 4.3.9, 4.4, 4.4.1-4.4.3, 4.5
host third country, 2.2.1, 2.5.3
human rights, 1.7.3.1, 1.8, 2.2.4, 2.4, 2.4.1, 2.4.3, 2.5.3, 2.6.1, 2.7.1, 3.2, 3.4, 3.4.1, 3.6.1, 3.6.1.4, 4.2.3, 4.3.2, 4.3.4, 4.4.2, 4.5

I

illegal entry, 1.5, 2.2.1, 2.5.3
illegal migration, 3.6, 4.2.1
inadmissible, asylum application, 2.5.3, 2.5.5, 3.4.3.1, 3.4.3.2, 3.6.1.5, 3.7
internal dimension, of asylum, 4.1, 4.3.2
internal market, 1.1, 1.3, 1.4, 1.7.1, 1.7.3.2, 1.11, 3.2., 4.2.2
international protection, content of, 2.4.4
Intergovernmental Conference (IGC), 1.7, 1.9, 4.3.6

J

joint action(s), 1.10.1.1, 1.10.3, 2.6
joint processing of asylum applications,
  within EU, 4.4.1, 4.4.3, 4.5
  outside EU, 4.4.1, 4.4.3, 4.5

K

Kosovo, 2.4.1, 2.6, 3.4.3, 3.5

L

long-term residents, 2.1, 2.7.2, 4.3.1, 4.4.3

M

manifestly unfounded, asylum applications, 2.5.3, 2.5.5, 3.4.1, 3.4.3.1, 3.4.3.2, 3.4.4, 3.5, 3.6.1.3, 3.6.1.5, 3.7
Migration Office, 3.4.3.1, 3.4.3.2, 3.4.4, 3.4.5, 3.4.6, 3.5, 3.6.1, 3.6.1.2-3.6.1.5, 3.7
Ministry of the Interior, Slovakia, 3.4, 3.4.6, 3.6

N

national asylum system, 2.5.5, 2.6, 3.4, 3.4.6, 3.7, 4.2.1
New York Protocol on Refugees, 1.1, 1.4, 1.5, 1.8, 2.2.1, 2.7.2, 4.2.1, 4.2.2
non-refoulement, 1.2, 1.7.1, 1.8, 2.4.2, 2.4.4, 2.5.2, 2.5.3-2.5.5, 2.6.1, 3.4.1, 3.4.3, 3.4.4, 3.5, 3.6.1, 3.7, 4.4.1, 4.4.2

P

Parliament, Slovakia, 3.2, 3.4.3, 3.4.6, 3.7
persecution, 1.2, 1.8, 2.4, 2.4.1-2.4.3, 2.5.2-2.5.5, 2.7.1, 3.4.1, 3.4.3, 3.4.3.1, 3.4.4, 3.6.1.2, 3.6.1.4, 3.6.1.5, 4.2.1, 4.2.3
procedure
  accelerated, 2.5.3, 3.4.1, 3.4.2, 3.5, 3.6.1.3, 4.3.2
  appeal, 2.5, 2.5.5, 3.4.1, 3.5, 3.6.1.5

examination, 2.5.3, 4.2.4
proof, burden of, 2.4.1
protected entry procedures (PEPs), 4.2.3

Q

Qualification Directive, 2.1, 2.4, 2.4.1-2.4.4, 2.5.1-2.5.5, 2.6.2.1, 2.8, 4.2.3, 4.2.4, 4.3.4, 4.3.5, 4.3.7
qualified majority voting (QMV), 1.1, 1.9, 1.10.1.1, 4.4.1

R

readmission agreements, 1.8, 2.2.3, 3.6.1, 4.1, 4.3.2, 4.3.3, 4.4.2
reception
  centre, 3.4.3, 3.4.4, 3.5, 3.6.1, 3.6.1.1-3.6.1.3, 3.6.1.5, 3.7
  conditions, 2.3, 2.6.2.1, 4.2.3
Reception Directive, 2.1, 2.3, 2.8, 3.4, 3.4.6, 4.2.4, 4.3.3
refugee,
  definition of, 1.2, 2.4, 2.4.3, 2.5
  sur place, 2.4.1
Regional Court, 3.4.3, 3.4.3.2, 3.4.4, 3.6.1.5
Regional protection programmes, 4.2.3, 4.4.2, 4.4.3
Regional protection zones, 4.2.1
resettlement schemes, 4.2.1, 4.2.3
return procedures, 4.2.1, 4.4.2, 4.5

S

safe country of origin, 2.5.3, 2.5.5, 2.8, 3.4.1-3.4.3, 3.4.3.1, 3.4.4, 3.6.1
safe third country, 2.2.1, 2.2.3, 2.5.3, 2.5.5, 2.8, 3.4.1, 3.4.3, 3.4.3.1, 3.5, 3.6.1, 4.2.1
  European (safe third country), 2.5.3
Schengen
  Agreement, 1.4
  Implementation Convention, 1.1, 1.4, 1.5
Single European Act (SEA), 1.3, 1.4, 1.10.2
single procedure, 3.4.6, 4.2.4, 4.4.1, 4.2.5
stateless person, 2.3, 2.4, 2.4.2, 2.4.3, 2.5.3, 2.5.4, 2.6.2.1, 2.8, 3.4.1, 3.4.3, 4.2.4, 4.3.7
subsidiary protection status, 2.4.3, 2.4.4, 4.2.1
super safe country, 2.5.3

T

Tampere, European Council, 1.2, 1.8, 1.11, 4.2.1, 4.2.2, 4.3.2, 4.3.4, 4.3.9
temporary protection, 1.8, 2.1, 2.2.3, 2.3, 2.6, 2.6.1, 2.6.2, 2.6.2.1, 2.7.1, 2.7.2, 3.4.1, 3.4.3, 4.2.1, 4.2.2, 4.5
Temporary Protection Directive, 2.1, 2.3, 2.6, 2.6.1, 2.6.2.1, 2.8, 3.4.6
third-country nationals, 1.3, 1.7.1, 1.8, 2.2.2, 2.3, 2.4, 2.4.2, 2.4.3, 2.5.3, 2.6.1, 2.6.2.1, 2.7.1, 2.7.2, 2.8, 4.1, 4.2.1, 4.2.4, 4.3.3, 4.3.7, 4.4.1, 4.4.3
third pillar (intergovernmental), 1.1, 1.6, 1.7, 1.7.1, 1.7.2, 1.7.3.2, 1.10.1.2, 1.10.3
transit processing centres (transit zones), 4.2.1, 4.5

U

unaccompanied minors, 2.2.3, 2.4.1, 2.4.4, 2.6.1, 3.4.6
unanimity voting, 1.10.1.1, 1.11
UNHCR, 1.2, 1.8, 2.4.1, 2.4.2, 2.5, 2.5.2-2.5.4, 2.6, 2.6.1, 3.4.1, 3.4.3, 3.4.3.1, 3.4.6, 3.6.1.4, 3.6.1.5, 4.2.1, 4.2.3, 4.2.4, 4.3.5, 4.4.1-4.4.3
UK Paper, 4.2.1

V

Vienna Action Plan, 1.1, 1.7.1, 1.7.3.2, 1.8, 1.11, 2.6, 3.7, 4.3.1
visa policy, 4.1, 4.3.3

W

working programme, 1.7.2, 1.11

X

xenophobia, 4.3.3

FSC
www.fsc.org
MIX
Papier | Fördert gute Waldnutzung
FSC® C083411

Kolibri 360 GmbH
Ferdinand-Jühlke-Straße 7
99095 Erfurt, Deutschland
produktsicherheit@kolibri360.de